SOFTWARE TESTING

SOFTWARE TESTING

Harish Gupta

ANMOL PUBLICATIONS PVT. LTD.
NEW DELHI-110 002 (INDIA)

ANMOL PUBLICATIONS PVT. LTD.

Regd. Office: 4360/4, Ansari Road, Daryaganj,
New Delhi-110002 (India)
Tel.: 23278000, 23261597, 23286875, 23255577
Fax: 91-11-23280289
Email: anmolpub@gmail.com
Visit us at: www.anmolpublications.com

Branch Office: No. 1015, Ist Main Road, BSK IIIrd Stage
IIIrd Phase, IIIrd Block, Bangalore-560 085 (India)
Tel.: 080-41723429 • Fax: 080-26723604
Email: anmolpublicationsbangalore@gmail.com

Software Testing

First Edition, 2010

ISBN 978-81-261-4388-7

PRINTED IN INDIA

Printed at Mehra Offset Press, Delhi.

Contents

Contents

Preface

Focusing on software testing in practice, this book has been planned to suit the needs of both the practitioner and the academician. Concepts of software testing have been modeled as a phase-embedded activity rather than treating them as separate and post development activity.

Each chapter starts with a set of objectives, with the prospective of targeting to achieve rather than leaving the student directionless and ends with a list of key terms, referring to certain abstract concepts for better and crisp communication along with a list of references to enable the user to find in-depth information.

Author

Chapter 1

Introduction

BACKGROUND OF TESTING

Testing is not considered to be part of the Project Management approach. More often, it is defined within the methodology being used or in a specific testing methodology. However, most Project Managers have to deal with technology development and all should wish to test their solutions before moving into live operations.

There are many approaches to software testing that attempt to control the quality of the testing process to yield useful information about the quality of the software being tested.Although most testing research is concentrated on finding effective testing techniques, it is also important to make software that can be effectively tested.

It is suggested in that software is testable if faults are likely to cause failure, since then those faults are most likely to be detected by failure during testing. Several programming techniques are suggested to raise testability, such as minimizing variable reuse and maximizing output parameters.

In it is noted that although having faults cause failure is good during testing, it is bad after delivery. For a more intuitive testability property, it is best to maximize the probability of faults being detected during testing while minimizing the probability of faults causing failure after delivery. Several programming techniques are suggested to raise testability, including assertions that observe the internal state of the software during testing but do not affect the specified output, and multiple version development in which any disagreement between versions can be reported during testing but a majority voting mechanism helps reduce the likelihood of incorrect output after delivery. Since both of those techniques are frequently used to help construct reliable systems in practice, this version of testability may capture a significant factor in software development.

For large systems, many errors are often found at the beginning of the testing process, with the observed error rate decreasing as errors are fixed in the software. When the observed error rate during testing approaches zero, statistical techniques are often used to determine a reasonable point to stop testing.

This approach has two significant weaknesses. First, the testing effort cannot be predicted in advance, since it is a function of the intermediate results of the testing effort itself. A related problem is that the testing schedule can expire long before the error rate drops to an acceptable level.

Second, and perhaps more importantly, the statistical model only predicts the estimated error rate for the underlying test case distribution being used during the testing process. It may have little or no connection to the likelihood of errors manifesting once the system is delivered or to the total number of errors present in the software.

Another common approach to testing is based on requirements analysis. A requirements specification is converted into test cases, which are then executed so that testing verifies system behaviour for at least one test case within the scope of each requirement. Although this approach is an important part of a comprehensive testing effort, it is certainly not a complete solution.

Even setting aside the fact that requirements documents are notoriously error-prone, requirements are written at a much higher level of abstraction than code. This means that there is much more detail in the code than the requirement, so a test case developed from a requirement tends to exercise only a small fraction of the software that implements that requirement. Testing only at the requirements level may miss many sources of error in the software itself.

The structured testing methodology falls into another category, the white box (or code-based, or glass box) testing approach. In white box testing, the software implementation itself is used to guide testing. A common white box testing criterion is to execute every executable statement during testing, and verify that the output is correct for all tests.

In the more rigorous branch coverage approach, every decision outcome must be executed during testing. Structured testing is still more rigorous, requiring that each decision outcome be tested independently. A fundamental strength that all white box testing strategies share is that the entire software implementation is taken into account during testing, which facilitates error detection even when the software specification is vague or incomplete.

A corresponding weakness is that if the software does not implement one or more requirements, white box testing may not detect the resultant errors of omission. Therefore, both white box and requirements-based testing are important to an effective testing process. The rest of this document deals exclusively with white box testing, concentrating on the structured testing methodology.

OBJECTIVES

It is common to think of testing as a technical issue - something that is done for technology developments. It is good practice, however, to test all elements of all solutions, whether or not technology is involved. Maybe "test" is not a good word to use. We need to be confident that every element of the solution is ready for operational use.

Here are some examples, starting with some common technical issues but moving onto critical business issues:

- Does the computer application work acceptably?
- Can the network cope with the volumes of transactions and data?
- Do we have adequate provisions for backup, recovery, and disaster recovery of the systems?
- Will the disaster recovery process work, eg staff awareness, instructions, facilities, re-routing telephone

numbers, availability of office equipment, stationery, downtime, loss of transactions in progress, etc?

- Can the workforce cope with additional workloads during cutover and early live operation?
- Do the staff have sufficient knowledge and capability to operate the new processes?
- Are the new processes documented accurately in a usable manner and accessible to the staff?
- Have our customers understood the changes that will affect them?
- Will the new product and service offerings be a commercial success?

All these aspects can, and probably should, be tested. In some cases it is possible to test multiple aspects in a single process.

Faults are Inevitable

There is a naive view that if you do the right amount of testing the end-product will be correct. There is a scientific/ mathematical view that you can logically define a test process which will cover every designed aspect of a solution and thus create a complete proof of the solution. It is a good theory but it is hard to find practical examples.

There is a practical view that the more testing you do, the closer you get to finding all the errors - but to reach a perfect result would require infinite effort. You would choose, therefore, how much effort was justified to achieve an acceptable compromise between effort and quality.

There is a realistic view, as demonstrated by Myers, that you will not approach zero errors, but, instead, approach the limit of faults that would ever be uncovered by a formalized testing process. There is a chaos-theory view that once you reach the limit, the disruption caused by further dabbling with the solution will generate more problems than are solved.

What is certain is that there is a balance between testing effort and the degree of quality. The choice should be a business decision, based on optimising benefit. There is no right answer. The manufacturers of a quality product will want to invest more time in testing than the suppliers of a cheap commodity product. A life-critical system, such as an aircraft, will warrant greater confidence levels than a non-critical application such as a typing tutor programme.

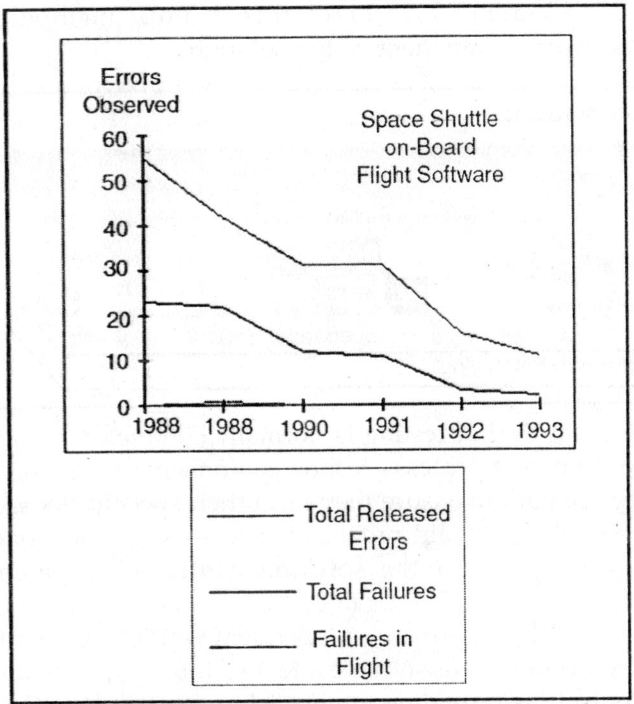

It is interesting to compare theory with reality. The onboard flight software for the Space Shuttle is a mission-critical, life-critical, national-pride-critical software application. It is hard to imagine any system that would merit greater degrees of testing and quality.

This chart shows the errors found in the code:

- Errors that got into released versions
- Failures that occurred
- Failures that occurred during flight

The pattern of reducing errors does bear an interesting resemblance to the theoretical norms. At first there is a relatively high number of faults, steadily reducing but never reaching zero.

BUILDING A SOLID

The main goal of formal testing is to produce a sound, logically valid proof that the results meet desired levels of confidence. Testing must be conducted in a carefully controlled manner to achieve this. It must methodically address every component of the solution.

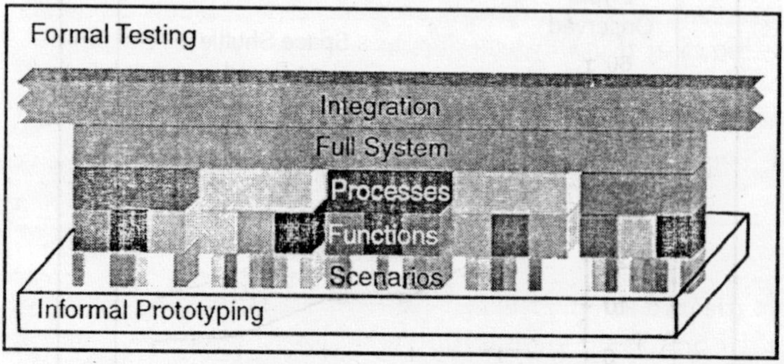

A great deal of testing is normally conducted as part of the development process - testing components of the solution as they are built to ensure they meet their specifications. This is a valuable and valid process, but it does not form part of the formal proof of the solution. Until development is completed there is no guarantee that components have been stabilised. There is also no independent verification that they met the overall needs in the context of the overall solution.

As well as providing a reasonable degree of confidence prior to formal testing, the informal tests can provide useful material and preparation for the subsequent formal tests. They lay a foundation that is the staring point for formal testing.

Testing a complex solution cannot usually be achieved in a single step. Normally the work is broken down into manageable pieces. For example, you might:

- Start by testing the various functions of the solution in isolation. Validate in full detail everything they are supposed to do. Check plausible alternative scenarios as well as the normal situations, for example, a sale might be cancelled, a payment might be rejected, an item might be out of stock. Do not check the implausible, for example, a negative quantity if it is impossible to enter it as a negative value (that is more a job for the developers to consider during their unit testing).

- When all the functions in a particular process have been validated in detail, test them together. This time you are looking for the correct passage of information and transactions throughout the entire end to end process. You do not need to repeat the detailed tests you did before. You are only looking at issues that involve the combinations of separate functions.
- When all the processes have been validated you can test the full system. Again, you do not repeat earlier tests. Only focus on issues that involve the overall operation of the system.
- Finally, when you have confidence in the new system, test how it behaves when connected to other systems and external parties.

TYPES OF TESTING

At the end of this chapter we list many specific types of testing and some variants in the terminology people use. For now, we will simply recognise the three main uses...

UNIT TESTING

Unit testing validates in detail each component that was developed. It is typically the developer's point of view - does it conform to the specification. It ignores whether that component works in the context of the completed system.

USER TESTING

User testing, or business testing, looks at the results from a business/user perspective. Does the final product do the things we want it to do? Do all the individual features work properly?

TECHNICAL TESTING AND TUNING

Technical testing and tuning examines the capability of

the solution to be operated safely, efficiently and dependably at normal and peak levels of usage.

It is concerned with the inner operational workings and procedures. It does not concern itself with whether it meets the users' functional needs, but it is concerned about the demands they will place upon it.

Testing Data

There is an art to creating good test data. Having a complete, fictitious world in which to follow realistic storylines is a good way to test out the various business scenarios.

Remember that all the sub-plots of the story have to co-exist. You will need to follow normal transactions alongside all the abnormal situations - amendments, cancellations, failures, mis-matches.

You will also want to simulate the passage of time. Follow the scenarios throughout their natural lifecycle and beyond into consequences such as management reporting and accounting. Good test data requires good preparation. The scenarios should be planned in advance.

They should be constructed to explore every aspect of the business solution in a logical manner. Expected results should be predicted alongside the test scenarios so that you are not dependent on the judgement of the tester.

- Paint the backdrops
- Tell a story
- Divide the story into acts and scenes
- Any good story has twists and turns
- Many misadventures will befall our hero
- But the hero will always find a way to escape and recover

BASELINE

The test data is intended to validate the correct functionality of the solution. But where is that correct baseline defined. Consider these possibilities as shown:

Baseline	Comments
Original Project Description	Shows the original intentions but is unlikely to contain enough detail and will probably not have been kept up to date as ideas changed.
Requirements Definition or Functional Specification	In theory these are definitive statements of what the business needs. Again, they may not contain sufficient detail and may not have been kept up to date. In some contractual procurement scenarios, these may have been defined to be the sole definition of the requirements that the developers must meet.
Systems or Technical Specification	Typically these have been developed to high degree of detail and have been maintained. One drawback is that they may be the developer's interpretation of the business needs. Testing against these will not detect errors in that interpretation.
Business users' current interpretation of their needs	Sometimes tests are defined independently of the original specifications to represent the current business needs. This may be a good test of the suitability of the end-result, but it is unlikely to match the precise details of the developed solution.
Maintained and agreed definition of requirements	Ideally, there will be a definitive statement of currently agreed requirements. As understanding of the business needs evolved and detailed designs were produced, this source will have been updated to show precisely what the solution should do. Disadvantages may be that it has been a moving target and there may be no comparison to what was originally requested.

TEST TOOLS

Many test tools are available these days. They offer control, speed, and repeatability of tests.

They are particularly useful for testing scenarios that require high volumes of transactions such as peak-volume network loading.

Repeatability is useful for running re-tests after problems have been solved and regression testing where a component of the solution has been changed and it is necessary to validate that other functionality has not been affected.

The disadvantages of test tools are the time and cost. Preparation of test data has to be exhaustive and correct. The tools themselves can represent a significant cost.

REGRESSION TESTING

Regression means going back. With testing processes we mean that you need to repeat previously successful tests any time there is a chance that subsequent changes could have affected an aspect of the solution. The testing process involved building a sequence of tests, many of which stood upon the successful results of earlier tests. If a component of the solution has been changed, all other components which relied upon it might have been affected. Similarly, all tests that relied on an earlier test might no long be valid. Consider carefully which solution and testing components need to be re-validated.

One consequence of this issue is that changes during the testing process are bad news. There will always be errors and changes during the testing, but it might be better to defer the correction of some minor problems to make better overall progress.

A seemingly innocuous example with a big hidden catch is when a software supplier suggests that a problem you are experiencing would be solved by moving to their next software release in which the problem has been fixed. Moving to a new release probably means that every test you did to date is now invalidated and will have to be repeated.

USER ACCEPTANCE TESTING

User Acceptance Testing (UAT) is a common name for the type of testing that forms the basis for the business accepting the solution from its developers (whether internal or external). It is a common requirement in many organisations and in many contracts. There are two drawbacks - it might not be very reliable and it might be a waste of effort. In fact, you might get a better solution, faster and cheaper if you do not do it.

The developers will need to conduct exhaustive methodical tests regardless of the need for independent User Acceptance Tests. Best quality will be achieved if they include the business and users in these tests to make sure they have not misunderstood the business needs.

If, therefore, the developers' formal testing is done with full participation of the business and with the responsible user managers having prime authority over the content, review and sign-off of the tests, the requirement for user acceptance can be met in a single phase of testing instead of two different phases.

Conversely, where the business is left to define and conduct its own independent testing, it is common to find that they do not have the methodical, comprehensive approach of the developers.

The reliability of the tests is often questionable. A single, combined phase of systems testing and User Acceptance Tests can produce the best results in the shortest time. Consider whether it is appropriate and permissible in your circumstances.

SOFTWARE COMPLEXITY MEASUREMENT

Software complexity is one branch of software metrics that is focused on direct measurement of software attributes, as opposed to indirect software measures such as project milestone status and reported system failures. There are hundreds of software complexity measures, ranging from the simple, such as source lines of code, to the esoteric, such as the number of variable definition/usage associations.

An important criterion for metrics selection is uniformity of application, also known as "open reengineering." The reason "open systems" are so popular for commercial software applications is that the user is guaranteed a certain level of interoperability-the applications work together in a common framework, and applications can be ported across hardware platforms with minimal impact.

The open reengineering concept is similar in that the abstract models used to represent software systems should be as independent as possible of implementation characteristics such as source code formatting and programming language. The objective is to be able to set complexity standards and interpret the resultant numbers uniformly across projects and languages.

A particular complexity value should mean the same thing whether it was calculated from source code written in Ada, C, FORTRAN, or some other language. The most basic complexity measure, the number of lines of code, does not meet the open reengineering criterion, since it is extremely sensitive to programming language, coding style, and textual formatting of the source code.

The cyclomatic complexity measure, which measures the amount of decision logic in a source code function, does meet the open reengineering criterion. It is completely independent of text formatting and is nearly independent of programming language since the same fundamental decision structures are available and uniformly used in all procedural programming languages.

Ideally, complexity measures should have both descriptive and prescriptive components. Descriptive measures identify software that is error-prone, hard to understand, hard to modify, hard to test, and so on. Prescriptive measures identify operational steps to help control software, for example splitting complex modules into several simpler ones, or indicating the amount of testing that should be performed on given modules.

COMPLEXITY AND TESTING

There is a strong connection between complexity and testing, and the structured testing methodology makes this connection explicit. First, complexity is a common source of error in software. This is true in both an abstract and a concrete sense. In the abstract sense, complexity beyond a certain point defeats the human mind's ability to perform accurate symbolic manipulations, and errors result.

The same psychological factors that limit people's ability to do mental manipulations of more than the infamous "7 +/ - 2" objects simultaneously apply to software. Structured programming techniques can push this barrier further away, but not eliminate it entirely. In the concrete sense, numerous studies and general industry experience have shown that the cyclomatic complexity measure correlates with errors in software modules.

Other factors being equal, the more complex a module is, the more likely it is to contain errors. Also, beyond a certain threshold of complexity, the likelihood that a module contains errors increases sharply.

Second, complexity can be used directly to allocate testing effort by leveraging the connection between complexity and error to concentrate testing effort on the most error-prone software. In the structured testing methodology, this allocation is precise-the number of test paths required for each software module is exactly the cyclomatic complexity.

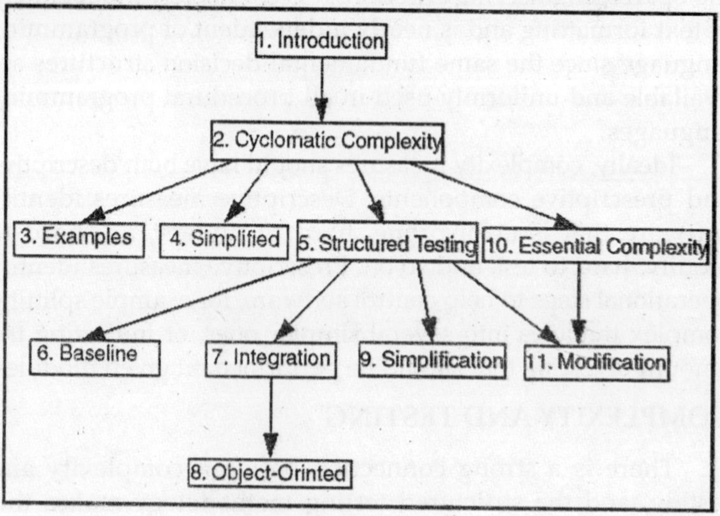

Fig. Dependencies.

Chapter 2

Testing Objectives

INTRODUCTION

First, define a comprehensive set of tests to build the solid testing "wall". Every requirement and plausible scenario should be covered - with no gaps and, preferably, with no overlaps or duplication.

Test Objectives

Ref	Test Objectives	Test Leader	Responsible User Manager & Other Interested Parties
Ref	Test Objectives	Test Leader	Responsible User Manager & Other Interested Parties

Each test may be described initially in terms of its objective, for example, an objective might be "to test that a cancelled order reverses all transaction data, works orders, stock positions and financial postings". Identify who is responsible for conducting this test and name the relevant user manager who is to approve the definition, review and sign-off of the test. At a later stage, you might add scheduling and sequencing information.

TEST

When the list of test objectives has been reviewed and agreed, detail the test scenario and steps, for example:

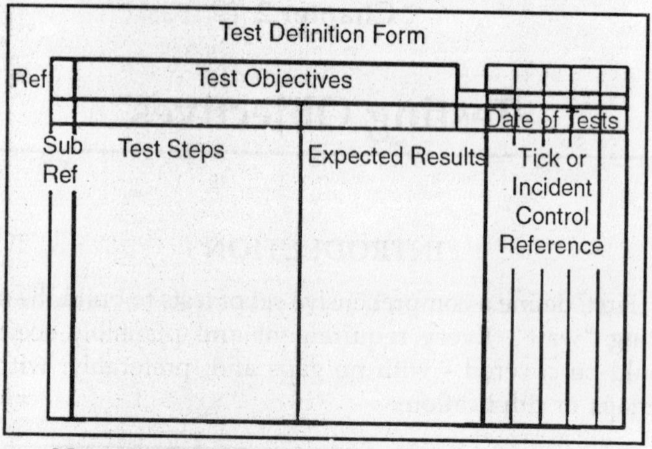

- Note stock level for item XYZ
- Note credit available for customer CUS01
- Create order #1234 for quantity 1 of item XYZ at price £100 for customer CUS01
- Check stock level for item XYZ
- Check credit available for customer CUS01
- Cancel order #1234
- Check stock level for item XYZ
  Check credit available for customer CUS01
- etc

Alongside these steps, write the expected results - ie how the tester will know that it worked as expected.

For example:

- 100
- £ 1000
- Order confirmation message confirms quantity 1 of item XYZ at price £100 for customer CUS01
- 99
- £900
- Order cancellation message confirms quantity 1 of item XYZ at price £100 for customer CUS01

- 100
- £1000
- etc

The remainder of this form is used as a checklist for running the test. For each step the tester either ticks the step to note that it worked or creates an test incident control record.

In this approach, we do not allow any other action. In other approaches a variety of other actions might be taken in an attempt to avoid noting the failure. Although this might seem desirable, the lack of control can be dangerous and counter-productive.

Encourage the expectation and belief that the purpose of a tester is to find discrepancies and that registering them is a good thing. In fact, you will find a majority of the problems are faults in the test scripts rather than the actual solution.

TEST CONTROL LOG

Progress will be tracked in a test control log. At any point in the process it should be clear what the status is for each test, along with the various incidents that were reported.

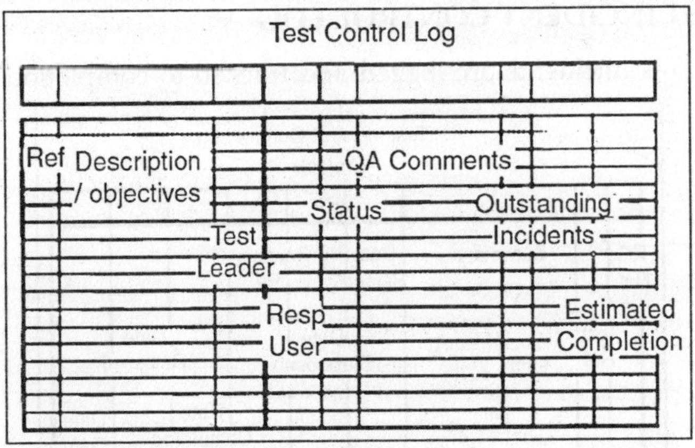

TEST INCIDENT CONTROL

For each discrepancy in the testing a test incident control form notes the details and tracks any remedial action.

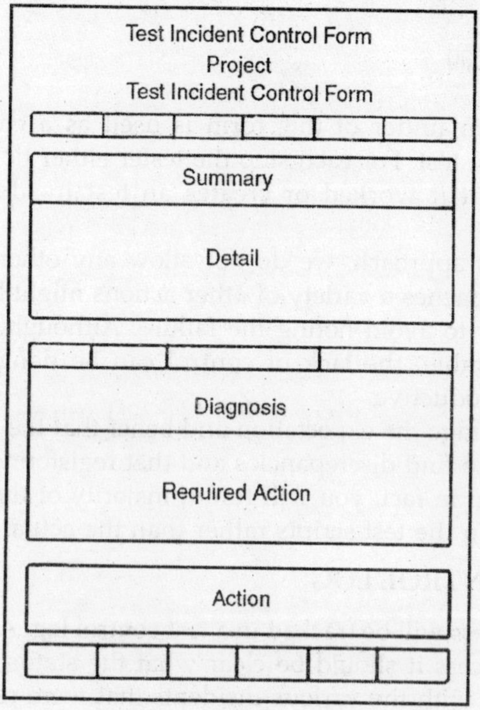

TEST INCIDENT CONTROL LOG

Test incidents are logged and tracked to completion.

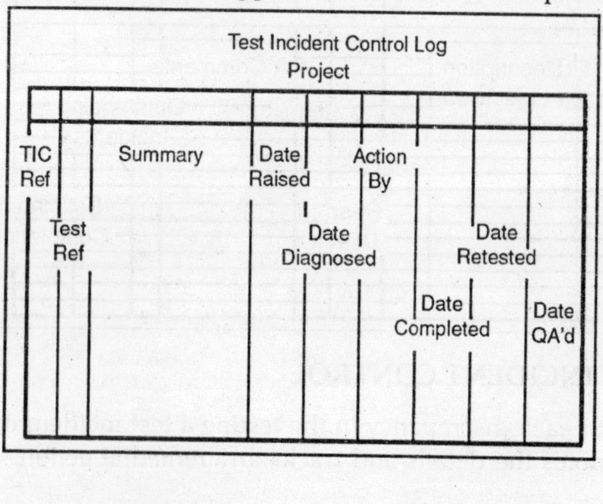

TEST SIGNOFF

When a test is completed, it should be reviewed and formally signed-off by the test leader, the responsible user manager and anyone else who is been identified as an authoritative reviewer.

In some cases you might note that a test was not entirely satisfactory although the problems were not sufficiently severe that you would wish to delay completing the tests or releasing the system. You should record what future action is required to remedy this problem. Ensure that appropriate remedial actions are defined and agreed for action at an appropriate time.

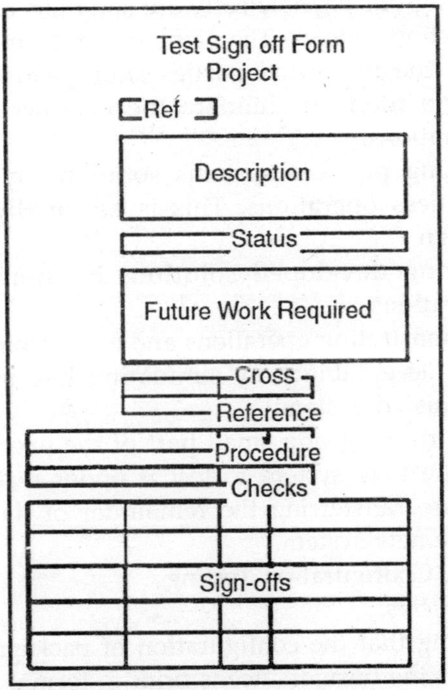

SPECIFIC TYPES OF TESTING

Here is a non-exhaustive list showing several types of testing. Consider which of these would be appropriate in your circumstances.

Note also that these types may have different characteristics when applied to different aspects of the overall solution.

For example, you could pilot a new computer system, a training course or a new workgroup structure.

Specific methodologies will use their own terminology. You should note that several expressions can mean more than one thing. The best example here is "Conference Room Pilot" where we list five different usages we have heard, each at a different stage in the lifecycle.

Type: Conference Room Pilot

Comments:

- Trying out possible software solutions as part of the selection process. The name comes from the concept that the interested parties shut themselves into a single room to simulate the conduct of business operations.
- Testing possible systems solutions by simulating business operations. This is essentially a form of design.
- Testing developed solutions by simulating live operations.
- Demonstrating operations and ascertaining business/ user acceptability by simulating live usage of the completed system.
- Live running of a small part of the overall business on the new system to test it under real conditions before transferring the remainder of the enterprise to the new system.

Type: Configuration Testing

Comments:

- Testing that the configuration of packaged software meets the business needs prior to formal testing.

*Type:*Data Load/Data Conversion Tests

Comments:

- Tests that data prepared for the new system is acceptable, for example, controls, comparisons with pre-converted data, integrity checking of linked records, validation of standard fields. Data may have been converted or loaded manually.

Type: Data Purification/Integrity/Quality

Comments:

- Review by the end-user departments that the operational data they hold is complete and correct. This exercise will often be conducted over a period of several months prior to data conversion for the new system. The data review might be supported by computer systems that highlight incomplete data and inconsistencies.

*Type:*Disaster Recovery Testing

Comments:

- Test the ability to re-instate the systems using off-site data and resources.
- Test the overall disaster recovery procedures and facilities from a business perspective.

Type: Fallback Testing

Comments:

- *Fallback Testing*: Test the contingency plan for reverting to the old system or to an alternative emergency solution (eg manual operation) in the event of a failure of the new system.

Type: Informal tests

Comments:

- Trying out ideas as a design aid.
- Checking that a developed component is fit to be released for formal testing.

Type: Integration Testing

Comments:

- Test of the sharing or transfer of transactions and data between the technical solution and all related systems.
- Overall testing of the business solution in conjunction with all other related operations and systems.

Type: Link Test

Comments:

- Test input, output and shared data are correctly

transferred between associated programs and databases.

Type: Live Pilot

Comments:

- Live running of a small part of the overall business on the new system to test it under real conditions before transferring the remainder of the enterprise to the new system.

Type: Model Office or Simulated Live Running

Comments:

- Informal testing where users try out the system as if it were real, testing that the processes, procedures, and operational support operate correctly and work in harmony using simulated normal work and volumes.

Type: Module Tests

Comments:

- Test that a developed module meets its technical specification.

Type: Operational Acceptance Testing

Comments:

- Formal tests to satisfy the IT operations department that the developed system is of adequate quality to enter the live environment and go into live production.

Type: Operations Testing

Comments:

- Testing of technical operational procedures such as start-up, shut-down, batch processing, special stationery handling, output handling, controls, error recovery, system backup and recovery procedures etc.

Type: Parallel Pilot

Comments:

- Test running of a small part of the overall business on the new system to test it under real conditions. Differs from Parallel Running in that not all input need be duplicated with the existing system and there is no attempt to reconcile the overall results between the two systems in a controlled manner.

Type: Parallel Running

Comments:

- Form of testing whereby the results on the new system are compared with identical real data passing through the old systems. This is normally achieved by duplicating the transactions for a specific time period and reconciling the results with the existing system. Very often it is not possible to get parallel results because the new system is not a duplicate copy of the old one. Where it is possible, parallel running may require a great deal of user effort to do things in duplicate and to reconcile the results.

Type: Pilot

Comments::

- Completion and live usage of a solution such that it can be tried out in a limited part of the organisation or marketplace. It is intended as a proof of concept. The eventual solution will probably be developed further or modified to take advantage of the lessons learned.

Type: Programme Tests

Comments:

- Test that a developed programme meets its technical specification.

Type: Prototyping

Comments:

- Development of a limited technical model of a component that can be used as a design tool to validate the concept. A prototype may use technology or techniques that are of no use beyond the prototyping work (eg screens simulated using PowerPoint).
- Development of the technical solution in stages such that each degree of refinement can be validated before moving to the next stage.
- The configuration of packaged software to apply the

org nisation's requirements and validate that they are properly addressed. When completed, the configured version will be the complete version ready for testing.

Type: Regression testing

Comments:

- Returning to earlier tests after a change has been made, both to check that the change was correct and to ensure no unforeseen impact has occurred. This is vital to maintain the integrity of prior testing during formalised, controlled testing. During formal testing, the environment should be designed to allow reversion and repeats. Timescales should assume a number of repeat cycles will be required.
- Re-testing a system following changes such as bug fixes or upgrades. Ideally, the original tests will have been preserved and be relatively easy to repeat and reconcile.

Type: Security Testing

Comments:

- Test overall protection from unauthorised access or usage. It should include physical access, access through external network links, firewalls, improper access by internal users, encryption, trusted third-parties, electronic emissions of physical and wireless networks, etc.
- Testing the mapping of individual users' access to specific functions, data and authorisation levels.

Type: System Testing

Comments:

- Main formal test of the overall technical solution.
- Main formal test of the functionality of an overall solution.

Type: Tiger Team Attack

Comments:

- Attempt to break through security measures by specialist external team.

Type: Unit Testing

Comments:

- Formal Tests applied to each "unit" of functionality within the system.
  Type: User Acceptance Testing
  Comments:
- Testing of the full solution by the business/users to validate that it operates correctly and meets requirements. The implication is that this is the point at which the business agrees to take the solution as produced by the developers (whether internal or external).
  Type:
  Comments:
- Volume Testing/Load Testing Creating sufficient hit rates, network loading, transactions and data volumes to simulate normal and peak loads thus verifying that response times and processing times will be satisfactory and that file sizes are sufficiently large. This also gives a firm basis for effective scheduling, operational capacity and tuning requirements.

SOFTWARE TESTING OBJECTIVES

INTRODUCTION

Establishing Software testing Objectives is a critical part of planning the Software testing process. Defining testing objectives is also one of the most difficult test planning activities. It is difficult because humans frequently do not have a clear idea of what they want to do until they begin to do it.

This means the best laid test plans change during test process execution. This is a problem without a solution, but there are some actions testers can take which will improve test planning.

The establishment of clear testing objectives goes a long way toward offsetting future execution problems. Before the tester can do this s/he must understand what we mean by the word objective.

An objective is a testing "goal." It is a statement of what the tester wants to accomplish when implementing a specific testing activity. Each testing activity may have several objectives and there are two levels of objective specification.

A test plan should contain both high-level general objectives in the overview section, and specific low-level "provable" objectives for each particular type of testing being implemented. The latter kind being operational goals for specific testing tasks. A good set of operational objectives can intuitively explain why we are executing a particular step in the testing process.

INPUTS

- System Requirements Document
- Software Design Description Document
- Risk Score Analysis Results (Task II.II)

Three methods can be used to specify test objectives. The first is brainstorming. The test team uses "creative" interaction to construct a list of test objectives.

The second approach is to identify "key" System functions. Next, specify test objectives for each function.

The third method is to identify business transactions and base objectives on them. This can also be thought of as Scenario-based as business cycles could be used to drive the process.

OUTPUT

Statement of Test Objectives - The statement of the test objectives is really a statement of the test requirements. It can be created using any word processing package or spread sheet. It can also be implemented with automated testing tools. As an example, in SQA's Manager product the test objects/requirements are input as a test requirements hierarchy and are stored in the test repository.

Each branch within the requirements tree can have sub-branches, and sub-branches can also have sub-branches. SQA is only one example. Other automated testing tools will have their own type of test objectives/requirements documentation.

COMPLETION CRITERIA

A completion criterion is the standard by which a test objective is measured. Completion criteria can be either quantitative or qualitative. The important point is that the test team must some how be able to determine when a test objective has been satisfied. One or more completion criteria must be specified for each test objective.

OUTPUT

Statement of Objective Completion Criteria - The important consideration is that each requirement and how it is validated is documented. Test requirements are completely useless unless they can be satisfied. Important test metrics that should be calculated and reported are the percentage of test requirements that have be covered by test cases, and the percentage of test requirements that have been successfully validated.

The statement of objective completion criteria does not have to be a separate document. It can simply be an addendum to the statement of test objectives. For example, if using SQA's Manager product, The description field that is included for each requirement could contain a statement of the requirement's validation rules.

The test objectives should be prioritized based on the risk analysis findings. Priority should be assigned using this scale.

High: Most important tests: must be executed

Medium: Second-level objectives: should be executed only after high-priority tests

Low: Least important: should be tested last and only if there is enough time

High and Medium: test objectives should be assigned more resources than Low priority objectives.

Output: Prioritized Test Objectives

Manual: Test objectives should be implemented manually in the form of quality checklists, with one or more checklist items satisfying a specific objective. (Single checklist items can also satisfy more than one objective, as is the case for the date field objectives).

Automated: Test objectives should be translated into an appropriate form for the automated test tool being used. For example, when using SQA TeamTest Test Manager a test requirements hierarchy would be created. Automated test requirements would be stored in the tool's test repository and would be used as the basis for constructing automated test scripts.

Chapter 3

Scope and Objectives

SCOPE AND OBJECTIVES TEST APPROACH

INCLUSIONS

The contents of this release are as follows:

Phase 1 Deliverables

- New & revised Transaction Processing with automated support
- New Customer Query Processes and systems
- Revised Inter-Office Audit process
- Relocate Exceptions to Head Office
- New centralised Agency Management system
- Revised Query Management process
- Revised Retrievals process
- New International Reconciliation process
- New Account Reconciliation process

EXCLUSIONS

When the scope of each Phase has been agreed and signed off, no further inclusions will be considered for inclusion in this release, except:

- Where there is the express permission and agreement of the Business Analyst and the System Test Controller;
- Where the changes/inclusions will not require significant effort on behalf of the test team (i.e. requiring extra preparation - new test conditions etc.) and will not adversely affect the test schedule.

Specific Exclusions

- Cash management is not included in this phase
- Sign On/Sign Off functions are excluded - this will be addressed by existing processes
- The existing Special Order facility will not be replaced
- Foreign Currency Transactions
- International Data Exchanges
- Accounting or reporting of Euro transactions

TESTING PROCESS

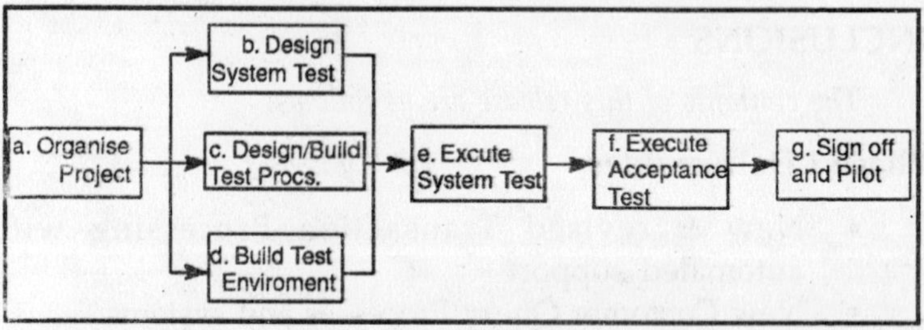

The diagram above outlines the Test Process approach that will be followed.

- Organise Project involves creating a System Test Plan, Schedule & Test Approach, and requesting/assigning resources.
- Design/Build System Test involves identifying Test Cycles, Test Cases, Entrance & Exit Criteria, Expected Results, etc. In general, test conditions/expected results will be identified by the Test Team in conjunction with the Project Business Analyst or Business Expert. The Test Team will then identify Test Cases and the Data required. The Test conditions are derived from the Business Design and the Transaction Requirements Documents
- Design/Build Test Procedures includes setting up procedures such as Error Management systems and Status reporting, and setting up the data tables for the Automated Testing Tool.

- Build Test Environment includes requesting/building hardware, software and data set-ups.
- Execute Project Integration Test - See Section 3 - Test Phases & Cycles
- Execute Operations Acceptance Test - See Section 3 - Test Phases & Cycles
- Signoff - Signoff happens when all pre-defined exit criteria have been achieved. See Section 2.4.

Exclusions

SQA will not deal directly with the business design regarding any design/functional issues/queries. The development team is the supplier to SQA - if design/functional issues arise they should be resolved by the development team and its suppliers.

TESTING SCOPE

Outlined below are the main test types that will be performed for this release. All system test plans and conditions will be developed from the functional specification and the requirements catalogue.

Functional Testing

The objective of this test is to ensure that each element of the application meets the functional requirements of the business as outlined in the:

- Requirements Catalogue
- Business Design Specification
- Year 2000 Development Standards
- Other functional documents produced during the course of the project i.e. resolution to issues/change requests/feedback.

This stage will also include Validation Testing - which is intensive testing of the new Front end fields and screens. Windows GUI Standards; valid, invalid and limit data input; screen & field look and appearance, and overall consistency with the rest of the application.

The third stage includes Specific Functional testing - these are low-level tests which aim to test the individual processes and data flows.

Integration Testing

This test proves that all areas of the system interface with each other correctly and that there are no gaps in the data flow. Final Integration Test proves that system works as integrated unit when all the fixes are complete.

Business (User) Acceptance Test

This test, which is planned and executed by the Business Representative(s), ensures that the system operates in the manner expected, and any supporting material such as procedures, forms etc.

Are accurate and suitable for the purpose intended. It is high level testing, ensuring that there are no gaps in functionality.

Performance Testing

These tests ensure that the system provides acceptable response times.

Regression Testing

A Regression test will be performed after the release of each Phase to ensure that -

- There is no impact on previously released software, and
- To ensure that there is an increase in the functionality and stability of the software.

The regression testing will be automated using the automated testing tool.

Bash & Multi-User Testing

Multi-user testing will attempt to prove that it is possible for an acceptable number of users to work with the system at the same time. The object of Bash testing is an ad-hoc attempt to break the system.

Technical Testing

Technical Testing will be the responsibility of the Development Team.

Operations Acceptance Testing (OAT)

This phase of testing is to be performed by the Systems Installation and Support group, prior to implementing the system in a live site. The SIS team will define their own testing criteria, and carry out the tests.

SYSTEM TEST ENTRANCE/EXIT CRITERIA

Entrance Criteria

The Entrance Criteria specified by the system test controller, should be fulfilled before System Test can commence. In the event, that any criterion has not been achieved, the System Test may commence if Business Team and Test Controller are in full agreement that the risk is manageable.

- All developed code must be unit tested. Unit and Link Testing must be completed and signed off by development team.
- System Test plans must be signed off by Business Analyst and Test Controller.
- All human resources must be assigned and in place.
- All test hardware and environments must be in place, and free for System test use.
- The Acceptance Tests must be completed, with a pass rate of not less than 80%.

Acceptance Tests

25 test cases will be performed for the acceptance tests. To achieve the acceptance criteria 20 of the 25 cases should be completed successfully - i.e. a pass rate of 80% must be achieved before the software will be accepted for System Test proper to start. This means that any errors found during acceptance testing should not prevent the completion of 80% of the acceptance test applications.

Resumption Criteria

In the event that system testing is suspended resumption criteria will be specified and testing will not re-commence until the software reaches these criteria.

Exit Criteria

The Exit Criteria detailed below must be achieved before the Phase 1 software can be recommended for promotion to Operations Acceptance status. Furthermore, I recommend that there be *a minimum 2 days effort Final Integration testing AFTER the final fix/change has been retested.*

- All High Priority errors from System Test must be fixed and tested
- If any medium or low-priority errors are outstanding - the implementation risk must be signed off as acceptable by Business Analyst and Business Expert
- Project Integration Test must be signed off by Test Controller and Business Analyst.
- Business Acceptance Test must be signed off by Business Expert.

NEED FOR SOFTWARE TESTING

A primary purpose for testing is to detect software failures so that defects may be uncovered and corrected. The scope of software testing often includes examination of code as well as execution of that code in various environments and conditions as well as examining the quality aspects of code: does it do what it is supposed to do and do what it needs to do.

We test software because developers are unable to build defect free software. If the development processes were perfect, meaning no defects were produced, testing would not be necessary.

Testing by the individual who developed the work has not proven to be a substitute to building and following a detailed test plan. The disadvantages of a person checking their own work using their own documentation are as follows:

- Misunderstandings will not be detected, because the checker will assume that what the other individual heard from him was correct.

- Improper use of the development process may not be detected because the individual may not understand the process.
- The individual may be "blinded" into accepting erroneous system specifications and coding because he falls into the same trap during testing that led to the introduction of the defect in the first place.
- Information services people are optimistic in their ability to do defect-free work and thus sometimes underestimate the need for extensive testing.
- Without a formal division between development and test, an individual may be tempted to improve the system structure and documentation, rather than allocate that time and effort to the test.

Testing unveils design defects as well as data defects of any product. All testing focuses on discovering and eliminating defects or variances from what is expected.

Testers need to identify these two types of defects:

- *Variance from Specifications*: A defect from the perspective of the builder of the product.
- *Variance from what is Desired*: A defect from a user (or customer) perspective.

BACKGROUND AND OBJECTIVES

Software testing is an integral and important activity in every software development environment. Software seems to have has permeated almost every equipment that we use in our daily lives. Companies that produce embedded systems for use in health care, transportation, and other critical segments of our society have embraced model based software testing by integrating them into their development environments.

- Software Testing is designed to establish that the software is working satisfactorily as per the requirements.
- Software Testing is a process designed to prove that the programme is error free.

- Software The job of testing is to certify that the software does its job correctly and can be used in production.

Because, with these as the guidelines, one would tend to operate the system in a normal manner to see if it works and one would unconsciously choose such normal/correct test data as would prevent the system from failing.

Besides, it is any way not possible to certify that a software has no errors, simply because it is almost impossible to detect all errors. In a way, we can say that software testing is basically a task of locating errors.

From the objective point of view, testing can be done in two ways:

Positive Testing

Operate application or software as it should be operated. Use proper variety of test data, including data values at boundries to test if it fails. Check actual test results with the expected and see

- Does it behave normally?
- Are results correct?
- Does the software function correctly?

Negative Testing

Test for abnormal operations. Test with illegal/abnormal test data. Intentionally attempt to make things go wrong and to discover/detect and see,

- Does the system fail/crash?
- Does the programme do what it should not?
- Does it fail to do what it should?

Positive view of Negative Testing

The job of testing is to discover errors before the user does. A good tester is one who is successfull in making the system fail. Mentality of the tester has to be destructive – opposite to that of the creator/developer which should be constructive. This chapter is designed to enable a clear understanding and knowledge of the foundations, techniques, and tools in the area of software testing and its practice in the industry. The course will prepare students to be leaders in software testing. Whether you are a developer or a tester, you must test software. This course is a unique opportunity to learn strengths and weaknesses of a variety of software testing techniques.

Applications of testing techniques in health care industry (e.g. pacemaker), nuclear industry (e.g. plant control), aerospace industry (e.g. Mars Polar Lander), security (e.g. smart card), automobile industry (e.g. automotive control systems), and others will be considered.

The chapter will focus on:

- Test process and continuous quality improvement
- Test generation from requirements
- Modeling techniques: UML: FSM and Statecharts, Combinatorial design; and others.
- Test generation from models.
- Test adequacy assessment.
- Industrial applications.

Discussion oriented lectures by the instructor, in-class group presentations by teams, laboratory exercises using advanced testing tools, and invited talks by experts from the industry will be the primary mechanisms for learning and the dissemination of knowledge.

CHAPTER DESCRIPTION

Fundamentals of software testing; software test proces and continuous quality improvement; Test generation using finite state models, Combinatorial design, and others; Test adequacy assessment using black box and white box criteria; Industrial applications of model based testing.

Students will be required to form small teams of three or four, preferably interdisciplinary, and make presentations to the class.The work of each team will be reviewed by the instructor and other teams.

Chapter 4

Unit Testing

DEFINITION

Unit testing refers to tests that verify the functionality of a specific chapter of code, usually at the function level. In an object-oriented environment, this is usually at the class level, and the minimal unit tests include the constructors and destructors.

These type of tests are usually written by developers as they work on code (white-box style), to ensure that the specific function is working as expected.

One function might have multiple tests, to catch corner cases or other branches in the code. Unit testing alone cannot verify the functionality of a piece of software, but rather is used to assure that the building blocks the software uses work independently of each other.

INTRODUCTION

Unit testing is a software development process in which the smallest testable parts of an application, called units, are individually and independently scrutinized for proper operation.This testing mode is a component of software development that takes a meticulous approach to building a product by means of continual testing and revision.

Once all of the units in a programme have been found to be working in the most efficient and error-free manner possible, larger components of the programme can be evaluated by means of integration testing. Unit testing must be done with an awareness that it may not be possible to test a unit for every input scenario that will occur when the programme is run in a real-world environment.

TESTING RULES

- Write the test first
- Never write a test that succeeds the first time
- Start with the null case, or something that doesn't work
- Don't be afraid of doing something trivial to make the test work
- Loose coupling and testability go hand in hand
- Use mock objects. A mock object is an object that pretends to be a particular type, but is really just a sink, recording the methods that have been called on it
- A test is not a pure unit test if: It talks to the database
  - It communicates across the network
  - It touches the file system
  - It can't run at the same time as any of your other unit tests
  - You have to do special things to your environment (such as editing config files) to run it. Tests that do these things should be kept aside from the regular unit test suit to run the test cases faster whenever we make changes.

Unit testing deals with testing a unit as a whole. This would test the interaction of many functions but confine the test within one unit. The exact scope of a unit is left to interpretation.

Supporting test code, sometimes called scaffolding, may be necessary to support an individual test. This type of testing is driven by the architecture and implementation teams. This focus is also called black-box testing because only the details of the interface are visible to the test. Limits that are global to a unit are tested here.

In the construction industry, scaffolding is a temporary, easy to assemble and disassemble, frame placed around a building to facilitate the construction of the building. The construction workers first build the scaffolding and then the building. Later the scaffolding is removed, exposing the completed building. Similarly, in software testing, one particular test may need some supporting software.

This software establishes an environment around the test. Only when this environment is established can a correct evaluation of the test take place. The scaffolding software may establish state and values for data structures as well as providing dummy external functions for the test. Different scaffolding software may be needed from one test to another test. Scaffolding software rarely is considered part of the system.

Sometimes the scaffolding software becomes larger than the system software being tested. Usually the scaffolding software is not of the same quality as the system software and frequently is quite fragile. A small change in the test may lead to much larger changes in the scaffolding.

Internal and unit testing can be automated with the help of coverage tools. A coverage tool analyses the source code and generates a test that will execute every alternative thread of execution. It is still up to the programmer to combine these test into meaningful cases to validate the result of each thread of execution. Typically, the coverage tool is used in a slightly different way.

First the coverage tool is used to augment the source by placing informational prints after each line of code. Then the testing suite is executed generating an audit trail. This audit trail is analysed and reports the per cent of the total system code executed during the test suite. If the coverage is high and the untested source lines are of low impact to the system's overall quality, then no more additional tests are required.

The idea behind unit testing is elegant and simple, but can be expanded to enable sophisticated series of tests for code validation and regression testing. A unit test is strictly something that 'exercises' or runs the code under test.

Many developers manually perform unit testing on a regular basis in the course of working on a segment of code. In other words, it can be as simple as *'I know the code should perform this task when I supply this input; I'll try it and see what happens.'* If it doesn't behave as expected, the developer would likely modify the code and repeat this iterative process until it works.

The problem with doing this manually is that it can easily overlook large ranges of values or different combinations of inputs and it offers no insight into how much of the code was actually executed during testing. Additionally, it does not help us with the important task of proving to someone else that it worked and that it worked *correctly*.

The cost and time required is compounded by the reality that one round of testing is rarely enough; besides fixing bugs, any changes that are made to code later in the development process may require additional investment of time and resources to ensure it's working properly.

Large projects typically augment manual procedures with tools such as the Framework to automate and improve this process. Automation mitigates risk of undetected errors, saves costs by detecting problems early, and saves time by keeping developers focused on the task of writing the software, instead of performing the tests themselves.

The idea behind unit testing is that once you have a unit that you think works, you set up a test case where you specify some input to the unit and compare the result of your unit with your expected result. You know about the expected result, because you know what your unit is doing (or you should know it).

Well, you better know what your unit is supposed to do, or else you should not do programming in the first place...;) Then you run the tests and the CakePHP/«insert your framework here» test suite tells you if they passed or if not, with some graceful message where the error occurred.

Now you have that testcase. Now you add testcases for t h a t input and this one. The advantage of this is that once you wrote the tests down they are there (cool, huh?) and you can hold on to them. There is no need anymore for you to open the browser and test everything manually again when you change your system. Instead, you add functionality, run the automated unit tests again, if they pass you are good to go, if they don't pass you broke something. Well, what if you broke something but your tests don't catch it? That's something that UT cannot do for you. You must make sure you have a good test coverage

Typically, the order of the running of the tests should not matter. There might be special cases, but in well over 90% it does not. This should also be your goal, too, to have two different problems if two test cases fail.

Keep them all isolated and you will sleep well. For most tests there is also not much configuration to be done. You specify the input, your expected result, crank the handle and evaluate how well you have done.

You should typically be able to group tests together, too. When you run these groups you can get a good overview over large components of your system.

TESTING PHASE

The first test in the development process is the unit test. The source code is normally divided into modules, which in turn are divided into smaller units called units. These units have specific behaviour. The test done on these units of code is called unit test. Unit test depends upon the language on which the project is developed. Unit tests ensure that each unique path of the project performs accurately to the documented specifications and contains clearly defined inputs and expected results.

Table. The Testing Phase: Improve Quality.

Phase	Deliverable
Testing	Regression Test
	Internal Testing
	Unit Testing
	Application Testing
	Stress Testing

Simply stated, quality is very important. Many companies have not learned that quality is important and deliver more claimed functionality but at a lower quality level.

It is much easier to explain to a customer why there is a missing feature than to explain to a customer why the product lacks quality. A customer satisfied with the quality of a product will remain loyal and wait for new functionality in the next version. Quality is a distinguishing attribute of a system indicating the degree of excellence.

In many software engineering methodologies, the testing phase is a separate phase which is performed by a different team after the implementation is completed. There is merit in this approach; it is hard to see one's own mistakes, and a fresh eye can discover obvious errors much faster than the person who has read and re-read the material many times. Unfortunately, delegating testing to another team leads to a slack attitude regarding quality by the implementation team.

Alternatively, another approach is to delegate testing to the the whole organization. If the teams are to be known as craftsmen, then the teams should be responsible for establishing high quality across all phases. Sometimes, an attitude change must take place to guarantee quality.

Regardless if testing is done after-the-fact or continuously, testing is usually based on a regression technique split into several major focuses, namely internal, unit,application, and stress.The testing technique is from the perspective of the system provider.

Because it is nearly impossible to duplicate every possible customer's environment and because systems are released with yet-to-be-discovered errors, the customer plays an important, though reluctant, role in testing. As will be established later in the thesis, in the Water Sluice methodology this is accomplished in the alpha and beta release of the system.

WORKING

Unit Testing generally works with assertions that take two parameters - at least most of them do. The first one is your known expected result and the second one is the output of your unit based on your input. The test suite then compares the expected result with the output of your unit.

Assertion	What it does	Example
assertTrue($x)	Fail if $x is false	$this->assertTrue(1 == true);
assertFalse($x)	Fail if $x is true	$this->assert False (1 === true);
assertNull($x)	Fail if $x is set	$variable = null; $this->assertNull($variable);
assertNot Null($x)	Fail if $x not set	$variable = 'something but not null'; $this->assertNotNull($variable);
assertIsA ($x, $t)	Fail if $x is not the class or type $t	$tim = new Person; $this->assert IsA($tim, 'Person');
assertNotA ($x, $t)	Fail if $x is of the class or type	Stim = new Person; $this>assertNotA ($tim, 'Animal');//or maybe I am? o_O
assertEqual ($x, $y)	Fail if $x == $y is false	$fahrenheit = 50; $celsius = (5/9)*($fahrenheit-32); $this->assertEqual(10, $celsius);
assertNotEqual ($x, $y)	Fail if $x == $y is true	$this->assertNotEqual('5', 5); // fails, they are equal but not identical
assert WithinMargin ($x, $y, $m)	Fail if abs($x - $y) < $m is false	$this- >assertWithinMargin (10, 50, 60); //passes $this->assert WithinMargin (10, 50, 30); //fails
assertOutside Margin ($x, $y, $m)	Fail if abs($x - $y) < $m is true	$this->>assertOutsideMargin (10, 50, 60); //fails $this- >assertOutsideMargin (10, 50, 30); //true
assertIdentical ($x, $y)	Fail if $x == $y is false or a type mismatch	$this->assertIdentical(0, false); / /will fail since 0 is not false
assert NotIdentical ($x, $y)	Fail if $x == $y is true and types match	$this->assertIdentical(10, 100/ 10*5 - 40);
assert Reference ($x, $y)	Fail unless $x and $y are the same	$a = 5; $b =& $a; $this->assertReference($a, $b);

	variable	
assertClone ($x, $y)	Fail unless $x and $y are identical copies, that means they are identical but not referenced	$a = 5; $b = 5; $this->assertClone($a, $b); //passes, 5 equals 5, but $a and $b are not references to each other
assertPattern ($p, $x)	Fail unless the regex $p matches $x	$this->assertPattern ('/hello/i', 'Hello world');
assertNo Pattern ($p,$x)	Fail if the regex $p matches $x	$this->assertNoPattern ('/heppo/i', 'Hello world'); //passes
expectError ($x)	Swallows any upcoming matching error	trigger_error ('Catastrophe'); $this->expectError();

assert($e)	Fail on failed expectation object $e; use SimpleTest's built in expectation objects to have fun here	<?php
		class TestOfNetworking extends UnitTestCase{
		...
		function assertValidIp ($ip, $message = '%s'){
		$this->assert(new ValidIp (), $ip, $message); //uses validIp expectation
		}
		function testGetValidIp(){
		$server = &new Server();
		$this->assertValidIp(
		$server->getIp(),
		'Server IP address->%s');
		}
		}
		?>

So, with the custom assert() function, mentioned last in the table, you can build your own assertions keeping your code really clean. The others should be straightforward. If not, head on over to http://simpletest.org and read the documentation there.

When any of these assertions fail, you will be presented an error message telling you which test failed, on which line and what the error is

USES

Forget for a moment that there is something called XP (Extreme Programming) that coined the Unit Test term. The most of the projects developed today are always under tight development schedules and usually have only its developers as the tester of their code. By writing the unit tests themselves they can have a head start towards bug-free and quality code.

One will argue that if the developer is writing all the unit tests, it is quite possible to get the set of unit tests that are passable, because these unit tests are developed based either on the foreknowledge of application code or the assumptions made in the application code.

However, do not be fooled with this, imagine what will happen if developer decides to change the application, her old test cases will break. That will force her to either re-think her changes or re-write the unit tests.

The application architect or analyst can write all the unit test cases upfront (Not what XP recommend, but we are not worried about it) and test the developed code against these cases and functionalities. The advantage is well defined deliverable for the developer and more quantifiable progress. A developer can also use this to disciple their work habits e.g. she can write a set of unit test that she wants to accomplish in a days work. Once tests ready, she can start developing the application and check her progress against the unit test. Now she has a meter to check her progress.

NUNIT FRAMEWORK

NUnit framework is port of JUnit framework from java and Extreme Programming (XP). This is an open source product. You can download it from http://www.nunit.org. The NUnit framework is developed from ground up to make use of.NET framework functionalities. It uses an Attribute based programming model. It loads test assemblies in separate application domain hence we can test an application without restarting the NUnit test tools.

The NUnit further watches a file/assembly change events and reload it as soon as they are changed. With these features in hand a developer can perform develop and test cycles sides by side.

Before we dig deeper, we should understand what NUnit Framework is not:

- It is not Automated GUI tester.
- It is not a scripting language, all test are written in.NET supported language e.g. C#, VC, VB.NET, J# etc.
- It is not a benchmark tool.
- Passing the entire unit test suite does not mean software is production ready.

IMPLEMENTING THE TEST

You can write the test anywhere you like, for example:

- A test method in application code class, you can use #if-#endif directives to include/exclude the code.
- A test class in application assembly, or
- A separate test assembly.

EFFECTIVE UNIT TESTING

- Careful and extreme programmers test early and test often.
- The unit test should motivate the code that you write. It should guide the design document.
- Define the scope of unit test carefully, neither too narrow nor too broad.
- Start with a feature that is described in the requirements document and work down until a method doesn't need a unit test. That way, tests are grouped according to major feature and should include as many unit tests that deal with the feature in question as are necessary.
- Select the appropriate and required methods for unit testing.If the code is simple enough that the

developer can just look at it and verify its correctness then it is simple enough to not require a unit test.Generally, any method that can break is a good candidate for having a unit test, because it may break at some time, and then the unit test will be there to help you fix it.

- Unit testing checks for the direct functionality and it can only uncover 40% of the defects at the design level.Best practices suggest that the ratio of test code to code under test required to achieve at least 90% code coverage is between 2/1 and 4/1. This means that to thoroughly test a 100-line class requires 200 to 400 lines of test code.
- Calculate the Cost Benefits of Unit Testing to decide the demand of testing.
- In order to get the full benefit from unit tests, the test suite should be run as part of the build process
- Maintain a strict process to keep the versioning and the documentation up-to-date with the development process.
- To maximize, the cost benefits of unit testing; start writing tests early. Focus on "quality" assertions where assertions are performed against relevant data.

BENEFITS

- Unit Testing allows us to refractor our code later with real confidence. If we break something and have plenty of tests there should be a test failing, we fix it up and the entire system should work again (that means all units independently of each other). Great!
- It forces you to think about what your code is really supposed to do. You finally get rid of the script kiddy attitude that hacks something together fast and does not even lose a second on thinking if his unit even returns an integer or if there could not be a division by zero error. I am not sure how it happens, but you will think about the edge cases, the most important cases, automatically. It's so difficult to think about

them without automated tests, but with UT you approach the problem from a more theoretical and mathematical side.

- Automatic testing is faster than browser testing. Period.
- UT provides living documentation. If you develop in a team with several people and someone wrote a unit without phpdoc comments and you have no idea what it does, you can frequent the tests for it. Understanding code from tests is ultra easy and fast and most of the time better than any discussion. You could even picture the code in your head (if you are smart enough) just looking at the tests.
- It helps you separate interface from implementation. Code that uses your code works with your interface, that is the unit name and the parameter signature and your return type. If you don't change that you can do what you want in the unit implementation. It's so great because it gives you so much freedom. Also as long as the original tests still run, you ensure backwards compatibility of your code, too.
- Make the CakePHP Core Team happy. Many people submit tickets to CakePHP to make us aware of bugs. That's a good thing. However, if more people submitted tests alongside their bugreports that would help even more.

There are plenty of other benefits such as:

- Unit tests find problems early in the development cycle.
- Unit testing allows the programmer to refractor code at a later date, and make sure the module still works correctly.
- Unit testing simplifies integration.
- Unit testing provides a living documentation of the system.
- Unit testing documents indicate appropriate/ inappropriate use of a unit as well as negative behaviors that are to be trapped by the unit.

- In a test-driven software development Unit-Test may take the place of formal design. Each unit test can be seen as a design element specifying classes, methods, and observable behaviour.
- An automated unit test suite watches over the code in two dimensions: time and space.
- The development process becomes more flexible and making change becomes easier, as controls are in place.
- Bringing new developers on board becomes easier and improve teamwork. Unit tests document the code.
- Software development will become more predictable and repeatable.

LIMITATIONS

- UT as such does not prove there are no errors in your system. It is not a theoretical/mathematical prove that a particular unit is bug free. Yes it shows the presence of errors if you have good and enough tests. However, it does not show the absence of errors.
- Besides that, unit testing tests the units of your system independently of each other (for the most part). So if your system suffers from performance problems or integration problems, unit testing will not catch them. Also it will not prove that your system is not vulnerable to any security attack from the outside.
- What's more? Well, many people don't implement unit testing yet, because it takes a rigorous amount of discipline to do it consistently. Especially in a team environment with clients paying, tight deadlines and all sorts of other interruptions, testing seems to be the first thing to cut on. However, in the long term it will prove to be much more productive to do it. The drawback stays, though: You write extra code that does not add any "real" features to your application. Don't get me wrong - I love to do it, but

I can partly understand the clients, too. Some other limitations are:

- Unit Testing cannot be expected to catch every error in the programme - it is impossible to evaluate all execution paths for all.
- Unit testing will not catch the integration errors, or broader system level errors (such as functions performed across multiple units,complex functional test areas or non-functional test areas).
- Unit tests can only show the presence of errors; it cannot show the absence of errors.
- It is essential to keep careful records not only of the tests that have been performed, but also of all changes that have been made to the source code of this or any other units in the software.The test case failures should be reviewed daily and addressed immediately.
- The cost factor due to unit testing may increase the overall cost without showing much visible results in a definite time frame.

EXAMPLE

Okay so before we are going to jump onto the cake test wagon let's look at a real world simpletest example. That way it will be easier for us to deal with cake's testsuite later.

You want to calculate the costs for a given trip (to a cakefest). You get: $flightPrice, $hotelCosts and expenses for food and drinks ($otherExpenses).

You know you will need more money since gwoo (the president of the Cake Software foundation) will come along persuading you to do sling shot (and yes we had a lot of fun at Cakefest in Orlando:]) although you are already a little drunk.

So we take on a 10% buffer that we add to the sum. Our total expenses are:

Formula: $total = 110% of ($flightPrice + $hotelCosts + $otherExpenses)

So, we might end up with:

```
<?php
require_once('simpletest/unit_tester.php'); /
/install simpletest into/vendors after you
downloaded it.
require_once('simpletest/reporter.php');
define('BUFFER_RATE', 0.1);
function calcTravelExpenses
($flightPrice, $hotelCosts, $otherExpenses)
{
$sum = $flightPrice + $hotelCosts + $otherExpenses;
$sum = (BUFFER_RATE) * $sum;
}
class TestOfTravelExpenses extends Unit
TestCase {
   function testExceededTravelExpenses() {
      $this->assertEqual(1320,
calcTravelExpenses(600, 400, 200), 'Okay
so this is a pretty exciting test %s
message end');
   }
}
$test = &new TestOfTravelExpenses();
$test->run(new HtmlReporter());
?>
```

When you run this you see you get a red bar with the message that "Integer" differs from "NUll". So 1320 is obviously an integer and the output of our function is NULL. Uh oh, okay, so there is no return statement!

Let's add it:

```
function calcTravel Expenses ($flightPrice,
$hotelCosts, $otherExpenses) {
   $sum = $flightPrice + $hotelCosts + $other
   Expenses;
   $sum = (BUFFER_RATE) * $sum;
   return $sum; //here
}
```

Now the value is not quite right. Ah okay, because we are taking 10% of the sum instead of 110%:

```
$sum = (1+BUFFER_RATE) * $sum;
```

TEST-DRIVEN DEVELOPMENT

So, when do you write the tests? From what you have read so far, you must have the idea that you write the tests after you wrote the code. However, with that "interface-over-implementation" and that "think-about-it-before-you-start-it" benefits, wouldn't it be cool to write the tests before you write the code? Test-driven Development - also known as TDD - does that.

Essentially TDD is a software development technique consisting of short iterations where new tests covering the desired improvement or new functionality are written first. Then you implement the production code necessary to pass the tests. TDD helps a lot, to make your code design nice and to accommodate changes you refactor.

The availability of tests before actual development ensures rapid feedback after any change. Remember that green-bar-means-you-are-done and red-bar-means-work? TDD ultimately boils down to those.

TDD is actually a method of designing your software instead of testing it. Why? Because with TDD you REALLY think about the stuff you do before you do it. If you have a problem you cannot tackle, you write the simplest possible test, make it work, and go from there.

As you write more tests and as you think about how people should use your code (ie, what your interface shall look like), you design your software well automatically. Yeah, it's not always that easy, but you get the idea.

In TDD you have a rough cycle that should take just minutes, if not seconds: Add a test -> see it failing -> make it work -> see the green bar -> refactor -> still see the green bar - > add a test -> see it failing ->...

MOCK OBJECTS

Mock Objects are objects that simulate real objects that would normally be difficult to construct or time consuming to set up for a test. The most common use of mock objects is the mocking of a database connection object. Setting up a test database at the start of each test would slow testing to a crawl and would require the installation of the database engine and test data on the test machine. If the connection can be simulated you can return data of your choosing. By that you not only win on the pragmatics of testing, but can also feed your code spurious data to see how it responds.

You could simulate databases being down or other extremes without having to create a broken database for real. In other words, you get greater control of the test environment.

However, the mock objects not only play a part (by supplying chosen return values on demand) they are also sensitive to the messages sent to them (via expectations). By setting expected parameters for a method call they act as a guard that the calls upon them are made correctly. If expectations are not met they save you the effort of writing a failed test assertion by performing that duty on our behalf. This can be very useful, because with standard Unit Testing you just test the interfaces of your objects. Mock Objects give you a means to test the inner implementation of them.

Chapter 5

Automated Testing

TEST AUTOMATION

- Test automation is the use of software to control the execution of tests, the comparison of actual outcomes to predicted outcomes, the setting up of test preconditions, and other test control and test reporting functions.
- Commonly, test automation involves automating a manual process already in place that uses a formalized testing process.
- Test automation is expensive and it is an addition, not a replacement, to manual testing. It can be made cost effective in the longer term though, especially in regression testing.

OBJECTIVES

The following points elucidate the reasons behind the need for automation (selective and not exhaustive):

- Running the existing tests on a new version(s) of a programme/application
- More number of tests can be run in a lesser period of time
- Bugs that can be uncovered only with long runs
- Better use of resources
- Testers can do better jobs, machines can be run all the time
- Consistency, Reliability and Repeatability of tests
- The same tests can be repeated exactly in the same

manner, every time when the automated scripts are executed thus eliminating manual testing error

AUTOMATE TEST CASES

- Tests that need to be run for every build of the application (sanity check, regression test)
- Tests that use multiple data values for the same actions (data driven tests)
- Stress/load testing
- Tests requiring a great deal of precision

TEST CASES NOT TO AUTOMATE

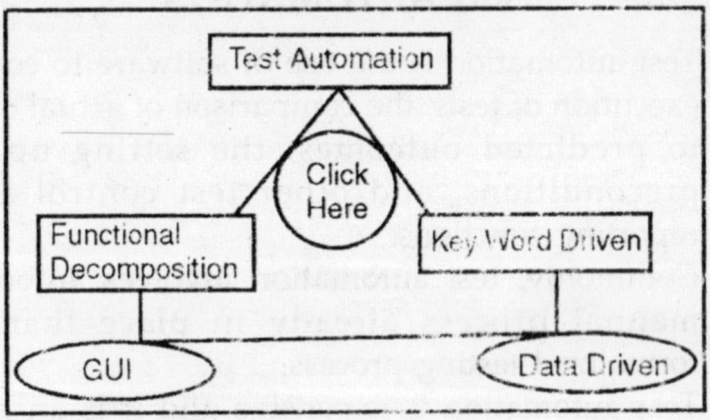

- Usability testing
  - "How easy is the application to use?"
- One-time testing
- "ASAP" testing
  - "We need to test NOW!"
- Ad hoc/random testing
  - Based on intuition and knowledge of application

ADVANTAGES OF AUTOMATION

- Unattended execution of large test sets
- Relief from tedious, routinely test activities
- Increased test coverage
- Accelerated test process
- Continuous quality control
- *Reliable*: Tests perform precisely the same operations each time they are run, thereby eliminating human error

- Reusable: You can reuse tests on different versions of an application, even if the user interfaces changes.

DISADVANTAGES OF AUTOMATION

- Automation is expensive to create
- Automation is limited in scope. All applications cannot be automated.
- Bugs in an automated test may mask a bug in the product and go unnoticed for long periods of time.
- Proficiency is required to write the automation test scripts.
- Debugging the test script is major issue. If any error is present in the test script, sometimes it may lead to deadly consequences.
- Test maintenance is costly in case of playback methods. Even though a minor change occurs in the GUI, the test script has to be re recorded or replaced by a new test script.
- Maintenance of test data files is difficult, if the test script tests more screens.

Chapter 6

Integration Testing

DEFINITION

Integration testing is the testing of a partially integrated application to identify defects involving the interaction of collaborating components. Integration tests (After Leung and White) for procedural languages. This is easily generalized for OO languages by using the equivalent constructs for message passing.

In the following, the word "call" is to be understood in the most general sense of a data flow and is not restricted to just formal subroutine calls and returns – for example, passage of data through global data structures and/or the use of pointers. Let A and B be two components in which A calls B. Let Ta be the component level tests of A Let Tb be the component level tests of B Tab The tests in A's suite that cause A to call B.

Tbsa The tests in B's suite for which it is possible to sensitize A – the inputs are to A, not B. Tbsa + Tab == the integration test suite (+ = union). Note: Sensitize is a technical term. It means inputs that will cause a routine to go down a specified path. The inputs are to A. Not every input to A will cause A to traverse a path in which B is called. Tbsa is the set of tests which do cause A to follow a path in which B is called.

The outcome of the test of B may or may not be affected. There have been variations on these definitions, but the key point is that it is pretty darn formal and there's a goodly hunk of testing theory, especially as concerns integration testing, OO testing, and regression testing, based on them. As to the difference between integration testing and system testing. System testing specifically goes after behaviors and bugs that are properties of the entire system as distinct from properties attributable to components (unless, of course, the component in question is the entire system). Examples of system testing issues: resource loss bugs, throughput bugs, performance, security, recovery, transaction synchronization bugs (often misnamed "timing bugs").

Objective of Integration testing is to make sure that the interaction of two or more components produces results that satisfy functional requirement. In integration testing, test cases are developed with the express purpose of exercising the interface between the components. Integration testing can also be treated as testing assumption of fellow programmer. During the coding phase, lots of assumptions are made. Assumptions can be made for how you will receive data from different components and how you have to pass data to different components.

During Unit Testing, these assumptions are not tested. Purpose of unit testing is also to make sure that these assumptions are valid. There could be many reasons for integration to go wrong, it could be because

- *Interface Misuse*: A calling component calls another component and makes an error in its use of interface, probably by calling/passing parameters in the wrong sequence.
- *Interface Misunderstanding*: A calling component makes some assumption about the other components behaviour which are incorrect.

Integration Testing can be performed in three different ways based on the from where you start testing and in which direction you are progressing.

- Big Bang Integration Testing
- Top Down Integration Testing
- Bottom Up Integration Testing
- Hybrid Integration testing

Top down testing can proceed in a depth-first or a breadth-first manner. For depth-first integration each module is tested in increasing detail, replacing more and more levels of detail with actual code rather than stubs. Alternatively breadth-first would proceed by refining all the modules at the same level of control throughout the application. In practice a combination of the two techniques would be used.

ENTRY CRITERIA

Main entry criteria for Integration testing is the completion of Unit Testing. If individual units are not tested properly for their functionality, then Integration testing should not be started.

EXIT CRITERIA

Integration testing is complete when you make sure that all the interfaces where components interact with each other are covered. It is important to cover negative cases as well because components might make assumption with respect to the data.

INTEGRATION STRATEGIES

One of the most significant aspects of a software development project is the integration strategy. Integration may be performed all at once, top-down, bottom-up, critical piece first, or by first integrating functional subsystems and then integrating the subsystems in separate phases using any of the basic strategies. In general, the larger the project, the more important the integration strategy.

Very small systems are often assembled and tested in one phase. For most real systems, this is impractical for two major reasons.

First, the system would fail in so many places at once that the debugging and retesting effort would be impractical. Second, satisfying any white box testing criterion would be very difficult, because of the vast amount of detail separating the input data from the individual code modules.

In fact, most integration testing has been traditionally limited to "black box" techniques. Large systems may require many integration phases, beginning with assembling modules into low-level subsystems, then assembling subsystems into larger subsystems, and finally assembling the highest level subsystems into the complete system.

To be most effective, an integration testing technique should fit well with the overall integration strategy. In a multi-phase integration, testing at each phase helps detect errors early and keep the system under control. Performing only cursory testing at early integration phases and then applying a more rigorous criterion for the final stage is really just a variant of the high-risk "big bang" approach.

However, performing rigorous testing of the entire software involved in each integration phase involves a lot of wasteful duplication of effort across phases. The key is to leverage the overall integration structure to allow rigorous testing at each phase while minimizing duplication of effort.

It is important to understand the relationship between module testing and integration testing. In one view, modules are rigorously tested in isolation using stubs and drivers before any integration is attempted. Then, integration testing concentrates entirely on module interactions, assuming that the details within each module are accurate.

At the other extreme, module and integration testing can be combined, verifying the details of each module's implementation in an integration context. Many projects compromise, combining module testing with the lowest level of subsystem integration testing, and then performing pure integration testing at higher levels.

MODULE TESTING AND INTEGRATION TESTING

The simplest application of structured testing to integration is to combine module testing with integration testing so that a basis set of paths through each module is executed in an integration context.

This means that the techniques can be used without modification to measure the level of testing. However, this method is only suitable for a subset of integration strategies.

The most obvious combined strategy is pure "big bang" integration, in which the entire system is assembled and tested in one step without even prior module testing. As discussed earlier, this strategy is not practical for most real systems. However, at least in theory, it makes efficient use of testing resources.

First, there is no overhead associated with constructing stubs and drivers to perform module testing or partial integration. Second, no additional integration-specific tests are required beyond the module tests as determined by structured testing.

Thus, despite its impracticality, this strategy clarifies the benefits of combining module testing with integration testing to the greatest feasible extent.

It is also possible to combine module and integration testing with the bottom-up integration strategy. In this strategy, using test drivers but not stubs, begin by performing module-level structured testing on the lowest-level modules using test drivers.

Then, perform module-level structured testing in a similar fashion at each successive level of the design hierarchy, using test drivers for each new module being tested in integration with all lower-level modules.

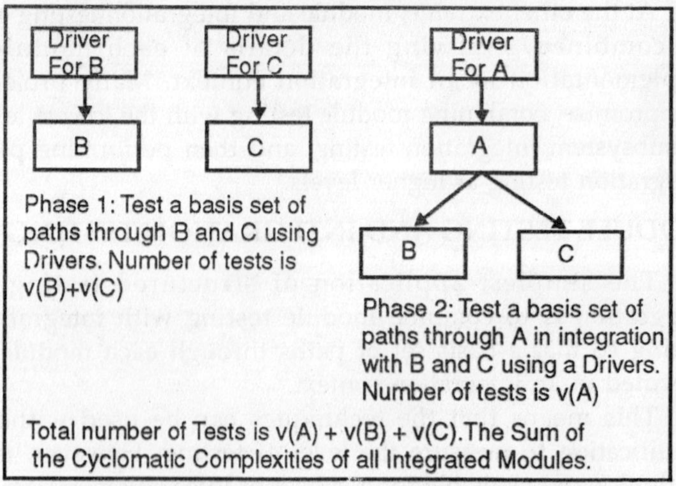

Fig. Combining Module Testing with Bottom-up Integration.

Illustrates the technique. First, the lowest-level modules

"B" and "C" are tested with drivers. Next, the higher-level module "A" is tested with a driver in integration with modules "B" and "C." Finally, integration could continue until the top-level module of the programme is tested (with real input data) in integration with the entire programme.

As shown, the total number of tests required by this technique is the sum of the cyclomatic complexities of all modules being integrated.

As expected, this is the same number of tests that would be required to perform structured testing on each module in isolation using stubs and drivers.

GENERALIZATION OF MODULE TESTING

Module testing criteria can often be generalized in several possible ways to support integration testing. As discussed in the previous subsection, the most obvious generalization is to satisfy the module testing criterion in an integration context, in effect using the entire programme as a test driver environment for each module.

However, this trivial kind of generalization does not take advantage of the differences between module and integration testing. Applying it to each phase of a multi-phase integration strategy, for example, leads to an excessive amount of redundant testing.

More useful generalizations adapt the module testing criterion to focus on interactions between modules rather than attempting to test all of the details of each module's implementation in an integration context.

The statement coverage module testing criterion, in which each statement is required to be exercised during module testing, can be generalized to require each module call statement to be exercised during integration testing.

Although the specifics of the generalization of structured testing are more detailed, the approach is the same. Since structured testing at the module level requires that all the decision logic in a module's control flow graph be tested independently, the appropriate generalization to the integration level requires that just the decision logic involved with calls to other modules be tested independently. The following subsections explore this approach in detail.

MODULE DESIGN COMPLEXITY

Rather than testing all decision outcomes within a module independently, structured testing at the integration level focuses on the decision outcomes that are involved with module calls. The *design reduction* technique helps identify those decision outcomes, so that it is possible to exercise them independently during integration testing.

The idea behind design reduction is to start with a module control flow graph, remove all control structures that are not involved with module calls, and then use the resultant "reduced" flow graph to drive integration testing.

Figureshows a systematic set of rules for performing design reduction. Although not strictly a reduction rule, the *call* rule states that function call ("black dot") nodes cannot be reduced.

The remaining rules work together to eliminate the parts of the flow graph that are not involved with module calls. The *sequential* rule eliminates sequences of non-call nodes.

Since application of this rule removes one node and one edge from the flow graph, it leaves the cyclomatic complexity unchanged. However, it does simplify the graph so that the other rules can be applied.

The *repetitive* rule eliminates top-test loops that are not involved with module calls. The *conditional* rule eliminates conditional statements that do not contain calls in their bodies.

The *looping* rule eliminates bottom-test loops that are not involved with module calls. It is important to preserve the module's connectivity when using the looping rule, since for poorly-structured code it may be hard to distinguish the ``top'' of the loop from the ``bottom.''

For the rule to apply, there must be a path from the module entry to the top of the loop and a path from the bottom of the loop to the module exit. Since the repetitive, conditional, and looping rules each remove one edge from the flow graph, they each reduce cyclomatic complexity by one. Rules 1 through 4 are intended to be applied iteratively until none of them can be applied, at which point the design reduction is complete. By this process, even very complex logic can be eliminated as long as it does not involve any module calls.

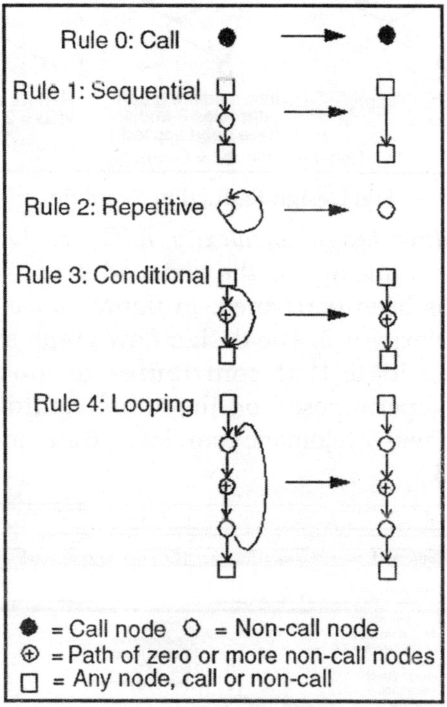

Fig. Design Reduction Rules.

Figure above shows a control flow graph before and after design reduction. Rules 3 and 4 can be applied immediately to the original graph, yielding the intermediate graph.

Then rule 1 can be applied three times to the left conditional branch, at which point rule 3 can be applied again, after which five more applications of rule 1 complete the reduction. The second application of rule 3 illustrates that a conditional structure may be eliminated even if its body contains a call node, as long as there is at least one path through its body that does not contain any call nodes.

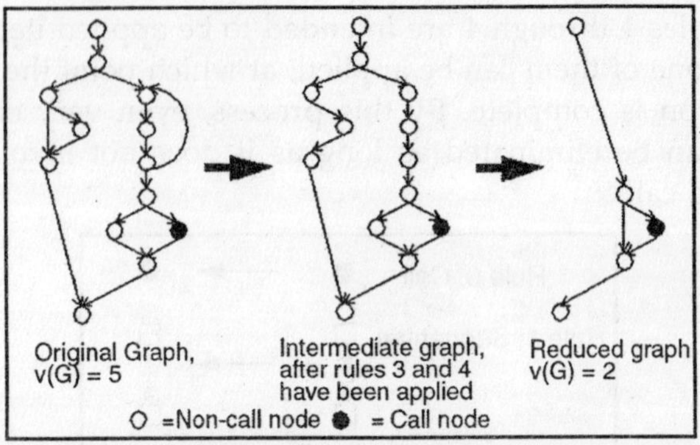

Fig. Design Reduction Example.

The *module design complexity, iv(G),* is defined as the cyclomatic complexity of the reduced graph after design reduction has been performed. In figure above, the module design complexity is 2. The design flow graph shown above, displays the logic that contributes to module design complexity superimposed on the entire control flow graph for a module with cyclomatic complexity 6 and module design complexity 3.

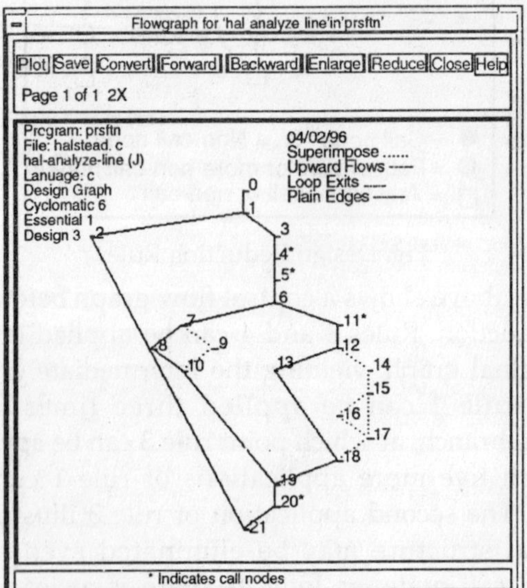

Fig. Design Graph With v(G) = 6, iv(G) = 3.

When structured testing has already been performed at the module level, module design complexity can be used to drive integration testing, requiring a basis set of paths through each module's reduced graph to be tested in integration.

Since module design complexity can be significantly less than cyclomatic complexity, this technique reduces the number of integration tests.

It also simplifies the process of deriving data for each test path, since there are fewer constraints on paths through the reduced graph than on paths through the full graph.

INTEGRATION COMPLEXITY

The *integration complexity, S1,* is defined for a programme with n modules (G_1 through G_n) by the formula: S_1 = (SUM iv(G_i)) - n + 1.

Integration complexity measures the number of independent integration tests through an entire program's design. The analogous integration-level method generates a set of independent tests through the program's design.

Begin with a baseline test, which contributes 1 to the S_1 formula and exercises one path through the program's main module. Then, make each successive test exercise exactly one new decision outcome in exactly one module's design-reduced graph.

Since the first "mini-baseline" path through each module comes as a result of exercising a path in a higher-level module (except for the main module, which gets its first path from the baseline test), each module contributes a number of new integration tests equal to one less than its module design complexity, for a total contribution of SUM (iv(G_i) - 1), which (since there are n modules) equals (SUM iv(G_i)) - n.

Adding the 1 for the baseline test gives the full S_1 formula. A similar argument shows that substituting v(G) for iv(G) in the S_1 formula gives the number of tests necessary to test every decision outcome in the entire programme independently.

Figure below shows an example programme with integration complexity 4, giving the control structure, cyclomatic complexity, and module design complexity for each module and a set of four independent integration tests.

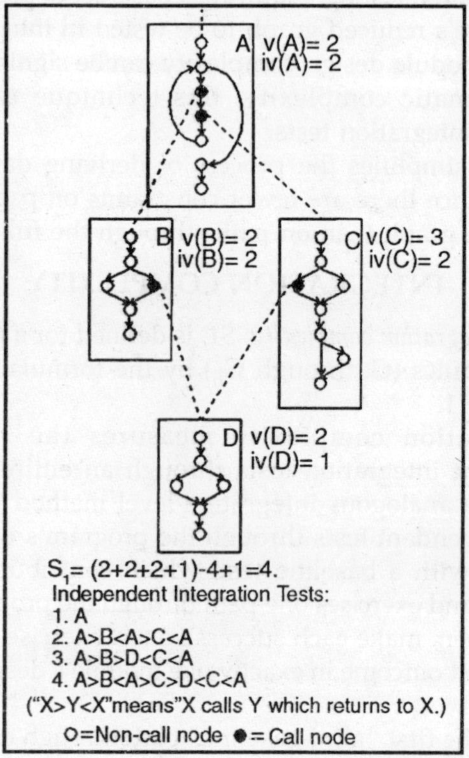

Fig. Integration Complexity Example.

Although a basis set of paths through each module's design-reduced control flow graph can typically be exercised with fewer than S_1 integration tests, more tests are never required. For the most rigorous level of structured testing, a complete basis set of S_1 integration tests should be performed.

Integration complexity can be approximated from a structured design, allowing integration test effort to be predicted before coding begins. The number of design predicates in a structure chart (conditional and iterative calls) can be used to approximate the eventual integration complexity.

Recall the simplified formula for cyclomatic complexity, which states that for modules with only binary decisions and p decision predicates, v(G) = p + 1. The corresponding formula for integration complexity is that for programs with d design predicates, S_1 will be approximately d + 1.

The reason is that each design predicate (conditional or iterative call) tends to be implemented by a decision predicate in the design-reduced graph of a module in the eventual implemented programme.

Hence, recalling that iv(G) is the cyclomatic complexity of the design-reduced graph, combine the v(G) and S_1 formulas to calculate the approximation that S_1 = SUM iv(G) - n + 1 = SUM (iv(G) - 1) + 1 = SUM $(v(G_{Reduced}) - 1) + 1$ = d + 1, where d is the total number of decision predicates in the design-reduced graphs of the modules of the implemented programme, and approximately equal to the number of design predicates in the original programme design.

Figure below shows a structured design representation with three design predicates and therefore an expected integration complexity of four.

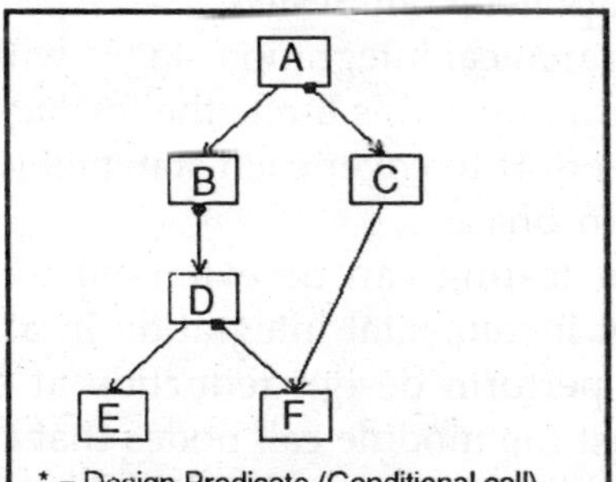

* = Design Predicate (Conditional call)
Since there are three design [predicates,
The expected integration complexity is Four.

Fig. Predicting Integration Complexity.

INCREMENTAL INTEGRATION

Hierarchical system design limits each stage of development to a manageable effort, and it is important to limit the corresponding stages of testing as well. Hierarchical design is most effective when the coupling among sibling components decreases as the component size increases, which simplifies the derivation of data sets that test interactions among components.

The key principle is to test just the interaction among components at each integration stage, avoiding redundant testing of previously integrated sub-components. Although this criterion is certainly not as rigorous as structured testing, its simplicity makes it easy to extend to support incremental integration.

Although the generalization of structured testing is more detailed, the basic approach is the same. To extend statement coverage to support incremental integration, it is required that all module call statements from one component into a different component be exercised at each integration stage.

To form a completely flexible "statement testing" criterion, it is required that each statement be executed during the first phase (which may be anything from single modules to the entire programme), and that at each integration phase all call statements that cross the boundaries of previously integrated components are tested.

Given hierarchical integration stages with good cohesive partitioning properties, this limits the testing effort to a small fraction of the effort to cover each statement of the system at each integration phase.

Structured testing can be extended to cover the fully general case of incremental integration in a similar manner. The key is to perform design reduction at each integration phase using just the module call nodes that cross component boundaries, yielding component-reduced graphs, and exclude from consideration all modules that do not contain any cross-component calls.

The complete testing method is to test a basis set of paths through each module at the first phase (which can be either single modules, subsystems, or the entire programme, depending on the underlying integration strategy), and then test a basis set of paths through each component-reduced graph at each successive integration phase.

However, for incremental integration, the integration complexity formula may not give the precise number of independent tests. The reason is that the modules with cross-component calls may not be connected in the design structure, so it is not necessarily the case that one path through each module is a result of exercising a path in its caller. However, at most one additional test per module is required, so using the S_1 formula still gives a reasonable approximation to the testing effort at each phase.

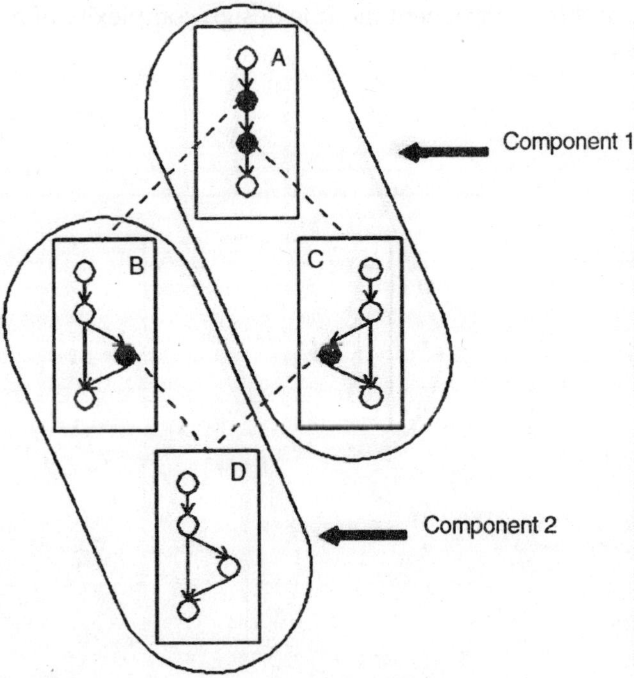

Independent Component Integration Tests:
Test 1: A>B<A>C<A
Test 2: A>B<A>C>D<C<A
("X>Y<X"mean "X calls Y which returns to X.")

○ = Non-call node
● = Cross-Component call node
● = Call Node within a Component

Figure above illustrates the structured testing approach to incremental integration. Modules A and C have been previously integrated, as have modules B and D. It would take three tests to integrate this system in a single phase.

However, since the design predicate decision to call module D from module B has been tested in a previous phase, only two additional tests are required to complete the integration testing. Modules B and D are removed from consideration because they do not contain cross-component calls, the component module design complexity of module A is 1, and the component module design complexity of module C is 2.

Chapter 7

Acceptance Testing

INTRODUCTION

Acceptance testing (also known as user acceptance testing) is a type of testing carried out in order to verify if the product is developed as per the standards and specified criteria and meets all the requirements specified by customer.

This type of testing is generally carried out by a user/ customer where the product is developed externally by another party. Acceptance testing falls under black box testing methodology where the user is not very much interested in internal working/coding of the system, but evaluates the overall functioning of the system and compares it with the requirements specified by them.

User acceptance testing is considered to be one of the most important testing by user before the system is finally delivered or handed over to the end user.

Acceptance testing is also known as validation testing, final testing, QA testing, factory acceptance testing and application testing etc.

And in software engineering, acceptance testing may be carried out at two different levels; one at the system provider level and another at the end user level (hence called user acceptance testing, field acceptance testing or end-user testing).

Acceptance testing in software engineering generally involves execution of number test cases which constitute to a particular functionality based on the requirements specified by the user. During acceptance testing, the system has to pass through or operate in a computing environment that imitates the actual operating environment existing with user. The user may choose to perform the testing in an iterative manner or in the form of a set of varying parameters (for example: missile guidance software can be tested under varying payload, different weather conditions etc.).

The outcome of the acceptance testing can be termed as success or failure based on the critical operating conditions the system passes through successfully/unsuccessfully and the user's final evaluation of the system.

The test cases and test criterion in acceptance testing are generally created by end user and cannot be achieved without business scenario criteria input by user. This type of testing and test case creation involves most experienced people from both sides (developers and users) like business analysts, specialized testers, developers, end users etc.

Acceptance testing is a black-box testing performed on a software prior to its delivery. It involves running a suite of tests on a completed system).

These test suites are made up of multiple tests or test cases. Each test case consists of a sequence of steps to perform which emulate the use case that is being tested; it also contains input data (if required) as well as the expected output. The result of a test case is either a pass or a fail.

OVERVIEW

For software delivered to ING we break down the types of test into two broad categories:

1. *Functional tests*: Tests designed to verify and validate the detailed functional behaviour of the delivered software system.
2. *Acceptance tests*: Tests designed to verify and validate the sustained integrated use of the delivered software system by either an astronomer or an engineer at the telescope (according to the user requirements); and tests designed to verify and validate the maintainability of the delivered software system (with reference to ING requirements).

We expect the funtional tests to be designed and used by the software development team during the development exercise, and that these tests are documented and delivered as part of the software system. These tests include unit (or module) tests, subsystem tests and system tests - where appropriate. On delivery, these tests may be performed in part or in full by LPO software staff as part of the acceptance exercise.

We expect acceptance tests to be designed and documented by LPO software staff, with reference to the user requirements, and that they will normally be performed during commissioning. The design of these tests will normally begin once a detailed design is available and they will be designed to reflect the continued integrated use of the software system in an operational environment. In addition, a maintainability audit of the delivered software system will also be performed.

This audit will test the use of ING guidlines for maintainability provided to the developers during the development phase. Any tools used for the maintainability audit will be available to developers during the development process. The acceptance tests will be fully documented in the Software Acceptance Test Plan and made available to the development team for pre-delivery system testing.

A report of the results of the software acceptance tests, the Software Acceptance Test Report, for the system will be prepared either during commissioning or immediately after by a member of the ING software staff. This report will uniquely identify the circumstances and nature of each non-conformity (either to the user requirements or existing ING software requirements) or software failure.

Software non-conformities or failures which are severe enough to affect the successful functioning of the delivered system may result in a recommendation that the software system not be accepted for operational use at ING until further development work has been carried out. Corrected software will, as a minimum, successfully complete a sub-set of the functional and acceptance tests.

WHY?

Although acceptance testing traditionally takes place at the end of development or major milestones, in agile software development acceptance testing needs to be performed at the user story level.

There are several reasons for why this is important:

- A passed test case becomes a measure of completeness of a user story; that is, a user story cannot be considered complete till it has passed all acceptance tests associated with it.
- Even though there is thorough unit testing performed, this is not enough. Unit tests, by their nature, test for a localized used case and are not concerned about the overall system.
- When we have iterations longer than a couple of weeks, it becomes easy to loose focus on initial agreements; acceptance test cases made for each story at the beginning of each iteration help the developers to keep things within the expectations.
- Acceptance test cases can serve as an excellent guide to developers to better interpret the requirements from a user story

TEST CASE

An acceptance test case has the following primary objectives:

- The Product Owner should be able to verify and validate that the user story has been implemented as it was supposed to.
- The developers should be able to check if what they have developed is in accordance with the requirements.
- We do no development that cannot be verified.

An acceptance test case is a human level test which determines whether the product meets the expectations of the end user.

HOW?

When creating acceptance test cases, the following points (some obvious) should be covered:

- All scenarios of the User Story should be covered in the test cases, and the expected outcome mentioned so that a tester can verify each function and use case.
- The acceptance test case needs to be at a broad overview level and not have details su ch as field validations, etc. because those will be covered by unit test cases.
- The test cases should precisely define the steps and their sequence that the tester should take; the inputs; and the expected outputs.
- When testing a non-UI based module, an acceptance test case can be an automated test case which also records the response. This will allow you to examine the output and see if it is acceptable.
- The acceptance test cases need to be reviewed and approved by the Product Owner in order to ensure that the coverage is complete.

Once test cases are created and approved, they should be given to the developer prior to start of development work. This allows the developers to get better understanding of the requirements as compared to what they might otherwise understand from just the User Story. This implies that the test cases need to be made before the actual development starts.

ACCEPTANCE TESTING PROCESS

- Test cases are created with the help of business analysts, business customers (end users), developers, test specialists etc.
- Test cases suites are run against the input data provided by the user and for the number of iterations that the customer sets as base/minimum required test runs.
- The outputs of the test cases run are evaluated against the criterion/requirements specified by user.
- Depending upon the outcome if it is as desired by the user or consistent over the number of test suites run or non conclusive, user may call it successful/ unsuccessful or suggest some more test case runs.

- Based on the outcome of the test runs, the system may get rejected or accepted by the user with or without any specific condition.

Acceptance testing is done in order to demonstrate the ability of system/product to perform as per the expectations of the user and induce confidence in the newly developed system/product. A sign-off on contract stating the system as satisfactory is possible only after successful acceptance testing.

TYPES OF ACCEPTANCE TESTING

USER ACCEPTANCE TESTING

User acceptance testing in software engineering is considered to be an essential step before the system is finally accepted by the end user. In general terms, user acceptance testing is a process of testing the system before it is finally accepted by user.

User

Users means the real business users, who will have to operate the system; normally the staff of an organization, but it could be your suppliers or customers. They are the only people who understand exactly what the business is, and how it operates. Therefore they are the only people qualified to check a system to see if it will deliver any benefit to the business or organization.

System developers cannot do it, as although they are expert in writing software, they are unlikely to know anything about the realities of running the organisation, other then what they have acquired from requirements specifications, and similar documents. In addition they have been closely involved in the design compromises that always take place when a system is being developed, and so have a commitment to the system as it is.

Acceptance

The acceptance of a system means you are confident it will give benefit to the organization. It does not mean that it only meets the original specification as requested. A system may very well meet all the specifications asked of it, but when trying to see how it will work in the business it is realized that it will not give anything positive to the organization, or may even damage the organization. This may be for a number of reasons such as a change in the business or business environment, such as a takeover.

The point is that a system may not be acceptable, even if it meets specification. You may still have to pay the supplier, but you will not incur any costs to implement it. Of course it may not even work to specification, which makes the question of acceptance even harder to answer. There are cases where it is worth implementing and paying for systems, which are imperfect, but that deliver real business value.

Testing

Whenever people are asked what testing is, many of them say it is to prove the system works. This is the key problem with the way UAT is employed in many organizations, as it is impossible to prove any system is correct. In fact a lot of effort is expended, and wasted, in trying to get right answers.

There is much literature on the subject of testing, and most writers agree that all you can prove is if a system is wrong. Therefore a good test is one that is designed to try and make a system fail, so as to expose its faults before it goes live. This type of testing is the only type worth doing.

UAT

Bringing the three words together shows that the point of UAT is for business users to try and make a system fail, taking into account the real organization it will be working in. It is checking the system in the context of the business environment it will operate in.

EXPLANATION OF ACCEPTANCE TESTING

Acceptance Testing is the formal testing conducted to determine whether a software system satisfies its acceptance criteria and to enable buyer to determine whether to accept the system or not. Acceptance testing is designed to determine whether software is fit for use or not.

Apart from functionality of application, other factors related to business environment also plays an important role. User acceptance testing is different from System Testing.

System testing is invariably performed by the development team which includes developer and tester. User acceptance testing on the other hand should be carried out by the end user.

ALPHA TESTING

- Here test are conducted at the development site by the end users. Environment can be controlled a little bit in this case.

BETA TESTING

- Where test are conducted at customer site and development team do not have any control on the test environment.

In both the cases, these testing might be assisted by software testers.

It is very important to define acceptance criteria with the buyer during the various phases of SDLC. A well defined acceptance plan will help development/QE teams by identifying user's need during software development. Acceptance Test plan must be created or reviewed by customer. *Development team and customer should work together and make sure that they have*:

- Identify interim and final products for acceptance, acceptance criteria and schedule.
- Plan how and by whom each acceptance activities will be performed.
- Schedule adequate time for buyer's staff to examine and review the product
- Prepare the acceptance plan.
- Perform formal acceptance testing at delivery
- Make a decision based on the results of acceptance testing.

Entry Criteria

- System Testing is completed and defects identified are either fixed or documented.
- Acceptance plan is prepared and resources have been identified.
- Test environment for the acceptance testing is available

Exit Criteria

- Acceptance decision is made for the software
- In case of any caveats, development team is notified

ALPHA TESTING & BETA TESTING

Alpha testing is a type of acceptance testing carried out at developer's site by users (internal staff). In this type of testing, the user goes on testing the system and the outcome is noted and observed by the developer simultaneously.

ALPHA TESTING

Alpha testing is the software prototype stage when the software is first able to run. It will not have all the intended functionality, but it will have core functions and will be able to accept inputs and generate outputs. An alpha test usually takes place in the developer's offices on a separate system.

The first testing should occur in-house with different operating systems and different hardware configurations. An alpha version may not yet contain all of the planned features, and may lack documentation. Use virtual systems or test drives to fully test software with various operating systems and patches.

Thorough alpha testing will make beta testing run smoother.

- Use people within your organization that are unfamiliar with your software. If you don't have anyone available in your organization consider asking family and friends.
- Before moving an alpha product, to a beta product consider having an "ignorant" user do a complete

install. Silently watching the tester, will give you a birdseye view into user habits and potential problems during the install process.

Any software that will be run on customer equipment must first be reviewed and approved by EPRI Corporate Software Quality. Be sure to discuss any exceptions with the Software Quality Manager for your EPRI sector.

The EPRI project manager utilizes this prototype to evaluate and provide input to the developer as the design evolves. Although software is usually not distributed to users prior to beta testing, selected end-users may also be involved. Usually, the most complex or most used parts of the code are developed more completely in the alpha, in order to enable early resolution of design questions.

The project manager collaborates with the developer to determine specific goals for alpha testing, and to integrate the results into evolving project plans. In-depth software reliability testing, installation testing, and documentation testing are not done at alpha test time, as the software is only a prototype. Alpha tester feedback forms are not used, although the developer does request feedback on specific aspects of the software.

Setting Customer Expectations

If customers will receive alpha software, they must understand that the product will be only minimally functional, and is likely to have problems. The required review by EPRI Corporate Software Quality checks for the most serious problems, but customers must still be prepared for unexpected or frustrating experiences.

A letter or e-mail accompanying alpha software is strongly recommended.

This letter should make customers aware of:

- The software's limited functionality at this early stage
- The likelihood of experiencing problems
- Their mission: Find problems and provide feedback

It is understood that alpha software is not fully functional. However, EPRI Corporate Software Quality tests all software that is to be sent to users or run on customer equipment so that possible serious errors can be removed. Examples of such errors are software behaviour that compromises a user's system, or presence of a virus. This pre-testing of alpha software that is sent to users will protect the reputation of EPRI software with customers.

If any end-users or customers will receive software for alpha evaluation, or if software will be run on customer equipment, be sure to send it first to EPRI Corporate Software Quality. This prior review and approval is required. Be sure to discuss any exceptions with the Software Quality Manager for your EPRI sector.

BETA TESTING

Is a type of testing done at user's site. The users provide their feedback to the developer for the outcome of testing. This type of testing is also known as field testing. Feedback from users is used to improve the system/product before it is released to other users/customers.

BETA TESTING OVERVIEW

The software has reached "beta" stage when it is operating with most of its functionality, and is ready for user feedback.

Beta tests enable the software to be tested in customer environments, giving users the opportunity to exercise the software, find errors, and correct them before a product is released. For beta test, the software is delivered to customers' sites, along with instructions on what features to exercise in the software. The developer records, tracks, and addresses reported bugs.

BETA TESTING

Beta testing provides important input from users. EPRI expects beta testing to evaluate:

- Software functionality
- Algorithms used
- Procedures

- Solved example problems or tutorial
- Subject matter technical content
- Ease of use
- Installation instructions
- User documentation

EPRI requires at least one beta tester to be an actual user of the software outside EPRI. Three or more beta testers are recommended. Ideally, the EPRI project manager identifies five to ten beta testers who represent various classes or types of future end users.

The beta testers will need to check the technical accuracy of the software, and will need to use it with their own computer setups, data and workflows to make sure that the software will perform as desired in their own environments.

The beta testers will use the software and respond in writing to the assessment points. In some cases, EPRI Corporate Software Quality or the EPRI project manager may specify that certain persons or groups inside or outside EPRI be included in beta testing.

Key Questions to Consider

In planning for beta testing, consider the following questions:

- Who will we invite to participate?
- How many testers do we plan to have?
- What tasks should each tester perform using the software? (develop a task list for beta testers)
- Have we included usability-oriented tasks and asked for user input on items such as installation, draft documentation, on-line help, and ease of use?
- What feedback shall we gather?
- What action will we take based on what we discover?
- What is the timetable?

Beta Test Timetable

Time needs to be allowed for the beta testers to get started and install the product, as well as time for the tests to take place. Beta testers are typically busy professionals, with many other tasks to complete besides EPRI beta testing. Beta testing with users may often take 60-90 days to complete.

Common Problems

- Solved examples do not cover all the major functions of the software code.
- Beta testers do not review the User Interface features and User Documentation.
- Beta testers do not exercise the software in their actual environments, using their actual data sets.
- Insufficient time is allowed for the beta test to be completed.

Beta Test Plan

During the implementation step, the software developer prepares a Beta Test Plan. This plan is much more specific than the general description of the Beta Testing Approach included in the Software Development Project Plan. Suggested contents appear below.

- Beta Plan Description
  - Plan Objectives
  - Scope of Work
  - Overview of Participating Organizations
  - Platforms and Configurations to Test
  - Key Software Properties and Functions to be Evaluated
- Tasks to be Performed
  - Obtain consent from beta testers
  - Prepare instructions for beta testers to follow, including a list of the functions and features to be tested utilizing actual data.
  - Develop or customise Beta Tester Feedback Form (Also, see this Example EPRI Beta Tester Package for a project)
  - Ship beta software and evaluation materials to EPRI Corporate Software Quality for review before sending to beta testers
  - Prepare supporting systems

  - List of Individual Beta Testers, their Organizations, and Contact Information
  - Procedures for Submitting and Tracking Bug Reports
  - Consider and integrate customer beta feedback received
  - Thank beta testers and request permission to name them in the Acknowledgments section of the User Manual
  - More on Beta Implementation
- Schedule
  - Major Milestones
  - Individuals and Responsibilities

OPERATIONAL ACCEPTANCE TESTING

This type of testing is also known as operational readiness/preparedness testing. It is a process of ensuring all the required components (processes and procedures) of the system are in place in order to allow user/tester to use it. Operational Acceptance Testing ensures that all the non-functional aspects of a system are tested to ensure that the system is within the specified parameters.

The original requirements of the project are examined and testing to ensure these requirements are being met is undertaken. Load and performance tests that assess the ability of the system to operate at the desired levels are performed and results collated and presented in an easy to understand format.

The ability of the system to perform reliably and to recover from problems is also tested. Backup recovery and data integration tests are performed to test that system data is recovered properly. The contingency plan for disaster recovery is tested and implemented to test that the system can recover effectively. The supportability of the complete system is also tested.

Also within the umbrella of Operational Acceptance Testing, non-functional testing disciplines such as Soak and Penetration Tests are conducted. SQA Consulting has the technical expertise and experience to fulfil these all these testing requirements.

OPERATIONAL ACCEPTANCE TESTING (OAT)

I becoming critically important to organizations that deliver and maintain complete software systems and complex IT infrastructures. In general, OAT addresses the non-functional attributes of a system. With the specific exclusions of performance and security, which we consider to be areas of specialty in their own right, OAT concentrates on such areas as maintainability, reliability, recoverability, installability, compatibility and conformance, to name a few.

In order to support and develop our capabilities in OAT, AppLabs' software testing consultants are drawn from all areas of discipline within IT. As well as being trained in our CMMI Level 5 certified software testing methodology, they bring with them, and continue to develop, their skills and experience of major hardware and software vendors' products, services and major corporate operational IT methodologies such as ITIL and COBIT.

AppLabs' experience in OAT, across all major industry segments and technology platforms, can help you measure, manage and control the operational attributes of the software projects you are expected to support and maintain.

CONTACT AND REGULATION ACCEPTANCE TESTING

In contract and regulation acceptance testing, the system is tested against the specified criteria as mentioned in the contract document and also tested to check if it meets/obeys all the government and local authority regulations and laws and also all the basic standards.

EXPRESS PROVISIONS

'Acceptance' is a significant stage in the contractual process; commercially, it is likely to operate as a payment milestone; legally it will affect the application of any warranty provisions and potential remedies which may be available to the customer. Principles of good commercial practice prescribe that express provisions for any acceptance testing procedure should be clearly set out, determining under which circumstances and upon what basis 'acceptance' of the software will be deemed to have occurred.

The scope and application of the acceptance testing procedure (the ATP) will vary considerably, depending upon the type of project and the nature of the software which is being supplied. For example, the supply of a standard off-the-shelf software package to meet a straightforward software requirement, such as the supply of a word processing package, may employ a relatively simple acceptance test.

In this instance, the acceptance test may be passed if the software has been used in a live environment for a period of thirty days without rejection. In contrast, a complex bespoke software development project is likely to demand detailed acceptance testing.

A bespoke software development project is likely to require extensive testing against a series of specified functions and facilities, each of which is to be achieved within particular performance requirements.

Testing the software against specific acceptance criteria will enable the customer to determine whether the software which has been delivered is in conformity with that for which he had contracted.

To define and draft the ATP in respect of the supply of bespoke software may prove to be a difficult and intricate task for the contracting parties. Each project will demand individualised testing criteria, although in general terms it can be noted that in any ATP it will be necessary to show the required levels of functionality and standards of performance which are to be demonstrated by the software being supplied.

The acceptance testing may be a lengthy procedure comprising of the testing of several components in a variety of circumstances and with a range of information and test data. The standards to be met will need to be clearly defined and expressed, hopefully serving as an accurate reflection of the customer's requirements of the software.[4]

However, of equal importance to defining the basis upon which the software will be accepted, the ATP will also need to address what will happen in the possible event of any failure to pass any part or indeed, all of the prescribed acceptance tests.

The circumstances under which the supplier may be afforded the opportunity to rectify any defects, to retest the software and of particular relevance, the time allowed in which to carry out this corrective work, should be clearly laid out in the contractual documentation.

For this reason, it can be seen that incorporating detailed and thorough acceptance test clauses into the contractual documentation will serve to promote the contract itself as a highly effective project management tool; the contract can be used as a point of reference for all involved in the implementation and continual monitoring of the project.

If the scope of the ATP is clearly laid out, everyone involved in the project should be in a position to know, for example how the tests are to be carried out, what is to be done in order to successfully complete the tests, and what is to be done in the event of failure of any part of the tests.

In the event that there is repeated failure of the acceptance tests, despite the supplier having been given a further period for rectification of any problems with the software, the contract is likely to provide that the customer may choose to reject the software and receive a refund of all monies paid.

If however, the software successfully passes the ATP, this is likely to activate a payment milestone, whereby the customer will be required to pay either the full fee for the software or the final instalment if there has been a staggered payment profile. It is possible that at this stage the contract may enter a warranty period.

The scope of the warranty provision will obviously vary from contract to contract, but a common practice is to offer a 90-day warranty period which will commence immediately upon acceptance of the software.

During the warranty period there will be the opportunity to identify any software bugs, not previously detected during the acceptance tests and these will often be corrected free of charge.[5] The level of severity of these errors will be such that they would not have been fundamental in preventing the customer from accepting the software during the acceptance tests but rather will be minor software bugs which were beyond the scope of acceptance testing.

Indeed, case law recognises that software will inevitably require testing and modification.However, the concept that software can be delivered, with both property and risk passing to the customer, while allowing the supplier time to improve the software so that it complies with, for example, statutory implied terms, creates significant uncertainties for determining the time at which a system may be in breach.[6]

In the *St. Albans* case,[7] Nourse LJ disapproved of such an approach and in doing so, appeared to lend support for contractual provisions clearly defining what constitutes acceptance of a computer system.

Nourse LJ stated: 'Parties who respectively agree to supply and acquire a system recognising that it is still in the course of development cannot be taken, merely by virtue of that recognition, to intend that the supplier shall be at liberty to supply software which cannot perform the function expected of it at the stage of development at which it is supplied. Such a dictum can be seen to lend support for the use of detailed express contractual provisions covering the ATP.

Clearly, if the ATP is set out comprehensively within the contract, this will have the effect of preventing the customer from delaying the contract progressing from the acceptance testing stage into the warranty period on the basis of there being minor software errors. It can be seen that from a supplier's perspective, detailed ATP, setting out decisively the basis on which the software is to be accepted and therefore for what and when payment is to be received, are valuable express provisions in any software contract.

TERMS IMPLIED BY STATUTE

Invariably, contracts for the supply of bespoke software

and from a more broader perspective, system supply contracts in general, will contain details of acts which will constitute an acceptance; specifying the criteria to be met and the consequences arising from that acceptance, such as payments due and the commencement of any warranty provisions.

However, the ATP and the corresponding notion of acceptance as expressly provided for in the contract may evoke a different effect to any 'acceptance' under statutory provisions; and the implications of this should be considered.

Sale of Goods Act 1979, as amended by the Sale and Supply of Goods Act 1994, sets out three ways in which the buyer is deemed to have accepted the goods. These are:

- When he intimates to the seller that he has accepted them;[9] or
- When the goods have been delivered to him and he does any act in relation to them which is inconsistent with the ownership of the seller;[10] or
- After the lapse of a reasonable time, he retains the goods without intimating to the seller that he has rejected them.[11]

Each of the three grounds for accepting the goods are subject to the buyer's right to examine the goods. In the event that the buyer has had this opportunity, the legislation provides that each method of acceptance will have the effect of removing the buyer's right to reject the goods.

Therefore, in a contract for the sale of goods, if the goods are 'accepted', any breach of a condition will merely be treated as a breach of warranty, and on this basis, the breach will not give rise to a ground for rejecting the goods.

Having a reasonable opportunity to examine the goods is a decisive factor in determining the application of the sale of goods legislation. Moreover, a consumer buyer will be afforded the right to a reasonable opportunity to examine the goods and this is a right which cannot be lost by 'agreement, waiver, or otherwise'.

On this basis, if the buyer does any act inconsistent with the seller's ownership, or even if he informs the seller that he has accepted the goods, this will not be binding until the buyer has had a reasonable opportunity to examine those goods. This factor may have particular significance in relation to the contract for the supply of a computing system, given that an opportunity to examine the constituent parts of the system by the customer through means of individual and separate testing may prove to be difficult.

A 'commercial unit' is defined to be a unit, 'division of which would materially impair the value of the goods or the character of the unit'.[16] It can be seen that a contract for the supply of a complete computing system may fall within the definition of a 'commercial unit' and that the delivery of a number of goods under the contract, 'such as CPUs, monitors, printers, cabling and software media'[17] may serve to represent unit divisions of that commercial unit.

From this perspective, the legislation provides that acceptance of any of the goods, for example, acceptance of the CPUs will constitute acceptance of the whole system

DELIVERABLES

All identified deliverables for the system must be present and of an acceptable standard. By acceptable, it is meant that they must conform to any documentary standard made available to the developers during the project. Specified deliverables which are absent at the time of acceptance testing will be regarded as a failure of the delivered system.

CODING STANDARDS

The delivered software source code will be audited for conformance to any written coding standard supplied to the developers during the development programmed. Any delivered C source code will be audited for ANSI C compliance using the lint tool.

Any delivered Fortran source code will be audited for Fortran 77 compliance using the ftnchk tool. All delivered source code will be audited for maintainability using published maintainability metrics.

Other software quality tests may be carried out on the delivered source code at the discretion of the tester.

COMMAND-LINE INTERFACE VALIDATION

All commands will be tested for the following:

- A legal command should complete the required action successfully. On completion, the user interface should indicate the successful completion of the action.
- Where a command requires a parameter and one is not given, the user interface should deliver an error message to this effect and not act. The user interface should tell the user how to obtain a list of valid parameters interactively.
- Where a command requires a numeric parameter and a non-numeric parameter is given, the user interface should deliver an error message to this effect and not act. The user interface should also tell the user the valid numerical range of the parameter.
- If a command requires a numeric parameter and is given a value that is out of range, the user interface should deliver an error message to this effect and not act. The user interface should also tell the user the valid numerical range of the parameter.
- If a command requires one of a predefined set of of strings and is given a string outside this set, the user interface should deliver an error message to this effect and not act. The user interface should also tell the user the valid values for the parameter.

All commands must conform to any command name conventions provided by ING during the development process.

All error messages reported by the software system must conform to any error reporting conventions provided by ING during the development process. All informational messages reported must conform to any error reporting conventions provided by ING during the development process.

ERROR HANDLING

Designers of software systems intended for delivery to ING must ensure that they plan and design effectively for failures. Software systems must be designed to be robust to illegal input, erroneous or missing data files, network failures, instrument failures (where applicable), dynamic memory failures and predictable numerical failures.

Here, classic programming misjudgements are programs which need not be sensitive to alphabetic case, but which fail to perform string comparisons in a case-insensitve way, or do not strip unnecessary white space off strings which are to be compared.

In an operational environment where software systems are frequently used by non-specialists it is safe to assume that if any of the above can happen, then sooner or later they will. It is the responsibility of the programmer to ensure that these predictable errors are checked for at run-time and that an informative error message is delivered to the user if an error occurs.

In such cases, the aim of the programmer should be to have the software system recover from the failure and to leave the system in a known and usable state. If a successful recovery is not possible, then an error message describing the failure and informing the user that the failure is not recoverable should be delivered before closing the system down in a controlled way.

The software system's robustness to illegal input, erroneous or missing data files, network failures will be tested in detail. The software system must be able to recover from the failure and deliver an error message via the user interface. The error message must indicate the nature of the failure in enough detail to isolate its cause.

If the software system is a control system, each instrument mechanism will be induced to fail and the resulting behaviour of the software system observed. The software system must not fail - it must be able to recover from the failure and deliver an error message via the user interface. The error message must indicate which mechanism has failed and, where appropriate, how it has failed. Any MIMIC display must also be updated to indicate that the mechanism has failed.

ACCEPTANCE TEST REPORT

The Software Acceptance Test Report is primarily addressed to the software developers and summarises the tests performed and their results. The report should attempt to classify the severity of each test non-conformity or failure and must identify each test uniquely. Recommendations resulting from the acceptance tests will be addressed to the Director of ING or a deputy.

The test report will include the following:

- The titles of all test scripts executed and definitions of any other software tests performed.
- The name of the tester and the time the tests were performed.
- The location of all test logs.
- Summaries of the results of each test non-conformity.
- Summaries of the results of each test failure.
- The details of any code changes made during testing and the location of the modified source code.
- Recommendations of any action to be taken as a result of the acceptance tests, where applicable.

Chapter 8

Regression Testing

DEFINITION

Regression testing is the process of testing changes to computer programs to make sure that the older programming still works with the new changes. Regression testing is a normal part of the programme development process and, in larger companies, is done by code testing specialists. Test department coders develop code test scenarios and exercises that will test new units of code after they have been written. These test cases form what becomes the *test bucket*.

Before a new version of a software product is released, the old test cases are run against the new version to make sure that all the old capabilities still work. The reason they might not work is because changing or adding new code to a programme can easily introduce errors into code that is not intended to be changed.

The selective retesting of a software system that has been modified to ensure that any bugs have been fixed and that no other previously working functions have failed as a result of the reparations and that newly added features have not created problems with previous versions of the software.

Also referred to as *verification testing,* regression testing is initiated after a programmer has attempted to fix a recognized problem or has added source code to a programme that may have inadvertently introduced errors. It is a quality control measure to ensure that the newly modified code still complies with its specified requirements and that unmodified code has not been affected by the maintenance activity.

Any time you modify an implementation within a programme, you should also do regression testing. You can do so by rerunning existing tests against the modified code to determine whether the changes break anything that worked prior to the change and by writing new tests where necessary.

Adequate coverage without wasting time should be a primary consideration when conducting regression tests. Try to spend as little time as possible doing regression testing without reducing the probability that you will detect new failures in old, already tested code.

Some strategies and factors to consider during this process include the following:

- *Test fixed bugs promptly*: The programmer might have handled the symptoms but not have gotten to the underlying cause.
- *Watch for side effects of fixes*: The bug itself might be fixed but the fix might create other bugs.
- Write a regression test for each bug fixed.
- If two or more tests are similar, determine which is less effective and get rid of it.
- Identify tests that the programme consistently passes and archive them.
- Focus on functional issues, not those related to design.
- Make changes (small and large) to data and find any resulting corruption.
- Trace the effects of the changes on programme memory.

BUILDING A LIBRARY

The most effective approach to regression testing is based on developing a library of tests made up of a standard battery of test cases that can be run every time you build a new version of the programme. The most difficult aspect involved in building a library of test cases is determining which test cases to include.

The most common suggestion from authorities in the field of software testing is to avoid spending excessive amounts of time trying to decide and err on the side of caution. Automated tests, as well as test cases involving boundary conditions and timing almost definitely belong in your library.

Some software development companies include only tests that have actually found bugs. The problem with that rationale is that the particular bug may have been found and fixed in the distant past.

Periodically review the regression test library to eliminate redundant or unnecessary tests. Do this about every third testing cycle. Duplication is quite common when more than one person is writing test code. An example that causes this problem is the concentration of tests that often develop when a bug or variants of it are particularly persistent and are present across many cycles of testing.

Numerous tests might be written and added to the regression test library. These multiple tests are useful for fixing the bug, but when all traces of the bug and its variants are eliminated from the programme, select the best of the tests associated with the bug and remove the rest from the library.

INFORMATION

If a piece of Software is modified for any reason testing needs to be done to ensure that it works as specified and that it has not negatively impacted any functionality that it offered previously. This is known as Regression Testing.

WHEN IS REGRESSION TESTING NECESSARY

Regression Testing plays an important role in any Scenario where a change has been made to a previously tested software code. Regression Testing is hence an important aspect in various Software Methodologies where software changes enhancements occur frequently.

Any Software Development Project is invariably faced with requests for changing Design, code, features or all of them. Some Development Methodologies embrace change. For example 'Extreme Programming' Methodology advocates applying small incremental changes to the system based on the end user feedback.

Each change implies more Regression Testing needs to be done to ensure that the System meets the Project Goals.

IMPORTANCE

Any Software change can cause existing functionality to break. Changes to a Software component could impact dependent Components. It is commonly observed that a Software fix could cause other bugs.

All this affects the quality and reliability of the system. Hence Regression Testing, since it aims to verify all this, is very important.

COST EFFECTIVE

Every time a change occurs one or more of the following scenarios may occur:

- More Functionality may be added to the system
- More complexity may be added to the system
- New bugs may be introduced
- New vulnerabilities may be introduced in the system
- System may tend to become more and more fragile with each change

After the change the new functionality may have to be tested along with all the original functionality. With each change Regression Testing could become more and more costly. To make the Regression Testing Cost Effective and yet ensure good coverage one or more of the following techniques may be applied:

TEST AUTOMATION

If the Test cases are automated the test cases may be executed using scripts after each change is introduced in the system. The execution of test cases in this way helps eliminate oversight, human errors. It may also result in faster and cheaper execution of Test cases. However there is cost involved in building the scripts.

SELECTIVE TESTING

Some Teams choose execute the test cases selectively.

They do not execute all the Test Cases during the Regression Testing. They test only what they decide is relevant. This helps reduce the Testing Time and Effort.

REGRESSION TESTING – WHAT TO TEST MH]

Since Regression Testing tends to verify the software application after a change has been made everything that may be impacted by the change should be tested duringRegression Testing.

Generally the following areas are covered during Regression Testing:

- Any functionality that was addressed by the change
- Original Functionality of the system
- Performance of the System after the change was introduced

REGRESSION TESTING – HOW TO TEST

Like any other Testing Regression Testing Needs proper planning. For an Effective Regression Testing to be done the following ingredients are necessary:

CREATE A REGRESSION TEST PLAN

Test Plan identified Focus Areas, Strategy, Test Entry and Exit Criteria. It can also outline Testing Prerequisites, Responsibilities, etc.

CREATE TEST CASES

Test Cases that cover all the necessary areas are important. They describe what to Test, Steps needed to test, Inputs and Expected Outputs. Test Cases used for Regression Testing should specifically cover the functionality addressed by the change and all components affected by the change.

The Regression Test case may also include the testing of the performance of the components and the application after the change(s) were done.

DEFECT TRACKING

As in all other Testing Levels and Types It is important Defects are tracked systematically, otherwise it undermines the Testing Effort.

REGRESSION TEST A RELATIONAL DATABASE

Relational database management systems (RDBMSs) often persist mission-critical data which is updated by many applications and potentially thousands if not millions of end users. Furthermore, they implement important functionality in the form of database methods (stored procedures, stored functions, and/or triggers) and database objects (e.g. Java or C# instances).

The best way to ensure the continuing quality of these assets, at least from a technical point of view, you should have a full regression test suite which you can run on a regular basis. In this article I argue for a fully automated, continuous regression testing based approach to database testing.

Just as agile software developers take this approach to their application code, we should also do the same for our databases.

TESTING RDBMS

There are several reasons why you need to develop a comprehensive testing strategy for your RDBMS:

Data is an Important Corporate Asset

Doesn't it make sense to invest the effort required to validate the quality of data via effective testing? My July 2006 survey into the current state of data management indicates that 95.7% of respondents believe that data is a corporate asset.

Yet of them only 40.3% had a database test suite in place to validate the data and of those without a test suite only 31.6% had even discussed the concept.

Implementation in RDBMSs

In the survey, 63.7% of respondents indicated that their organizations did this, but of those only 46% had regression tests in place to validate the logic. Shouldn't we be doing better?

Current Approaches

The current state of the art in many organizations is for data professionals to control changes to the database schemas, for developers to visually inspect the database during construction, and to perform some form of formal testing during the test phase at the end of the lifecycle. Unfortunately, none of these approaches prove effective.

Application developers will often go around their organization's data management group because they find them too difficult to work with, too slow in the way they work, or sometimes they don't even know they should be working together. The end result is that the teams don't follow the desired data quality procedures and as a result quality suffers. Although visual inspection of query results is a good start it is little more than a debugging technique in practice that will help you to find problems but not prevent them. Testing late in the lifecycle is better than nothing, but as Barry Boehm noted in the early 80s it's incredibly expensive to fix any defects you find at that point.

Concrete Feedback

How do you know how good the quality of your source data actually is without an effective test suite which you can run whenever you need to?

Support for Evolutionary Development

Many evolutionary development techniques, in particular database refactoring, are predicated upon the idea that it must be possible to determine if something in the database has been broken when a change has been made. The easiest way to do that is to simply run your regression test suite.

Uncomfortable Question

Isn't it time that we stopped talking about data quality and actually started doing something about it?

Here's a few interesting questions to ask someone who isn't convinced that you need to test the DB:

- If you're implementing code in the DB in the form of stored procedures, triggers,... shouldn't you test that code to the same level that you test your app code?
- Think of all the data quality problems you've run into over the years. Wouldn't it have been nice if someone had originally tested and discovered those problems before you did?
- Wouldn't it be nice to have a test suite to run so that you could determine how (and if) the DB actually works?

OBJECTIVES OF TEST

Figure below indicates what to consider in testing when it comes to relational databases. The diagram is drawn from the point of view of a single database, the dashed lines indicate threat boundaries, indicating that you need to consider threats both within the database (clear box testing) and at the interface to the database (black box testing). Table 1 lists the issues which you should consider testing for both internally within the database and at the interface to it. For details, read the article What To Test in an RDBMS.

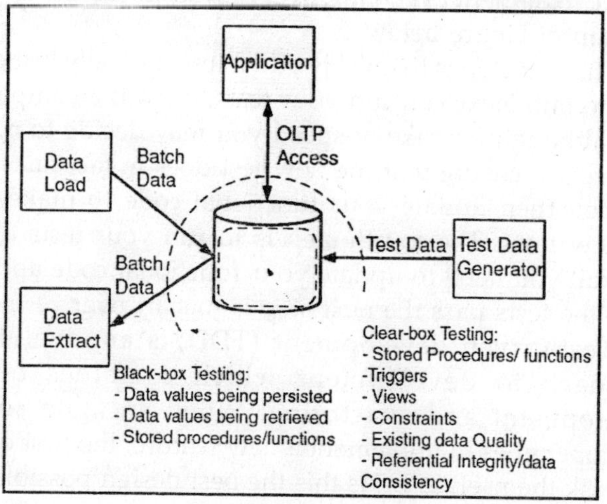

Fig. What to Test.

Table. What to Test in an RDBMS

Black-Box Testing at the Interface	White/Clear-Box Testing Internally Within the Database
O/R mappings (including the meta data)	Scaffolding code (e.g. triggers or updateable views) which support refactorings·
Incoming data values	Typical tests for your Stored producers, Functions and triggers
Outgoing data values (from queries, stored functions, views...)	Existence tests for database schema elements (tables, procedures,...)
	View definitions•
	Referential integrity (RI) rules•
	Default values for a column•
	Data invariants for a single column•
	Data invariants involving several columns.

WHEN TO TEST

Agile software developers take a test-first approach to development where they write a test before you write just enough production code to fulfill that test. The steps of test first development (TFD) are overviewed in the UML activity diagram of Figure below.

The first step is to quickly add a test, basically just enough code to fail. Next you run your tests, often the complete test suite although for sake of speed you may decide to run only a subset, to ensure that the new test does in fact fail.

You then update your functional code to make it pass the new tests. The fourth step is to run your tests again. If they fail you need to update your functional code and retest. Once the tests pass the next step is to start over.

Test-driven development (TDD) is an evolutionary approach to development which combines test-first development and refactoring. When an agile software developer goes to implement a new feature, the first question they ask themselves is "Is this the best design possible which enables me to add this feature?"

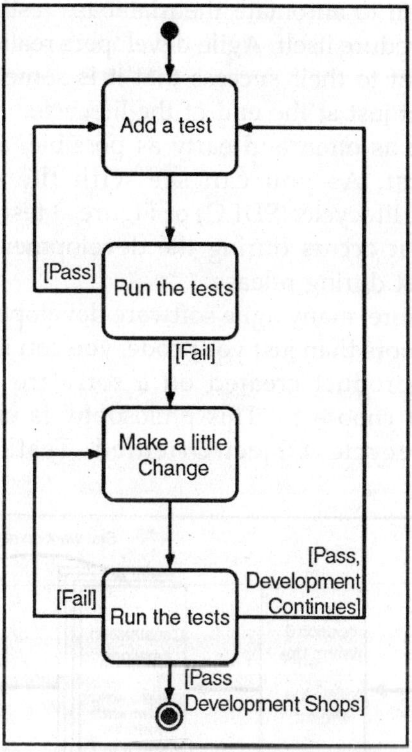

Fig. The Process of Test First Development (TFD).

If the answer is yes, then they do the work to add the feature. If the answer is no then they refactor the design to make it the best possible then they continue with a TFD approach. This strategy is applicable to developing both your application code and your database schema, two things that you would work on in parallel.

When you first start following a TDD approach to development you quickly discover that to make it successful you need to automate as much of the process as possible?

Do you really want to manually run the same build script(s) and the same testing script(s) over and over again? Of course not. So, agile developers have created OSS tools such as ANT, Maven, and Cruise Control (to name a few) which enable them to automate these tasks. More importantly, it enables them to automate theirdatabase testing script into the build procedure itself. Agile developers realise that testing is so important to their success that it is something they do every day, not just at the end of the lifecycle.

They test as often and early as possible, and better yet they test first. As you can see with the agile system development lifecycle (SDLC) of Figure 3 testing is in fact something that occurs during the development and release cycles, not just during release.

Furthermore, many agile software developers realise that you can test more than just your code, you can in fact validate every work product created on a software development project if you choose to. This philosophy is exemplified by the Full Lifecycle Object-Oriented Testing (FLOOT) Methodology.

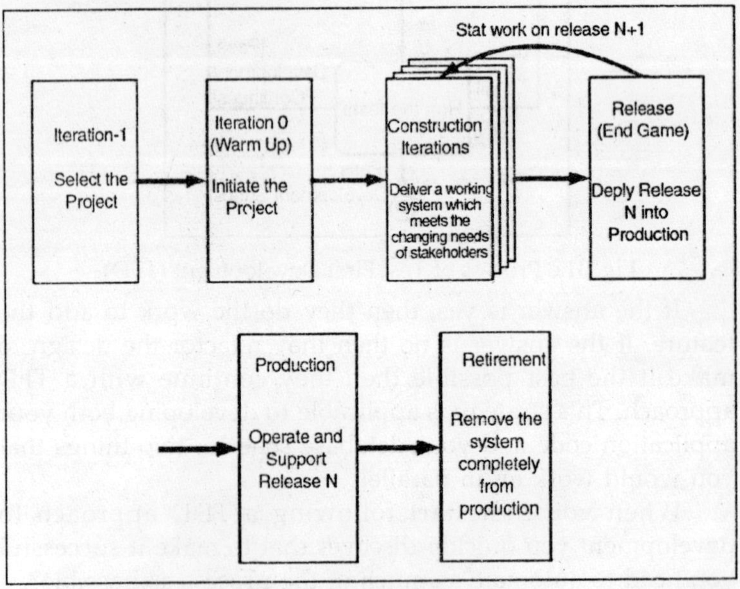

Fig. The Agile Lifecycle.

HOW TO TEST

Although you want to keep your database testing efforts

as simple as possible, at first you will discover that you have a fair bit of both learning and set up to do. In this section I discuss the need for various database sandboxes in which people will test: in short, if you want to do database testing then you're going to need test databases (sandboxes) to work in. I then overview how to write a database test and more importantly describe setup strategies for database tests.

Database Sandboxes

A common best practice on agile teams is to ensure that developers have their own "sandboxes" to work in. A sandbox is basically a technical environment whose scope is well defined and respected. Figure below depicts the various types of sandboxes which your team may choose to work in.

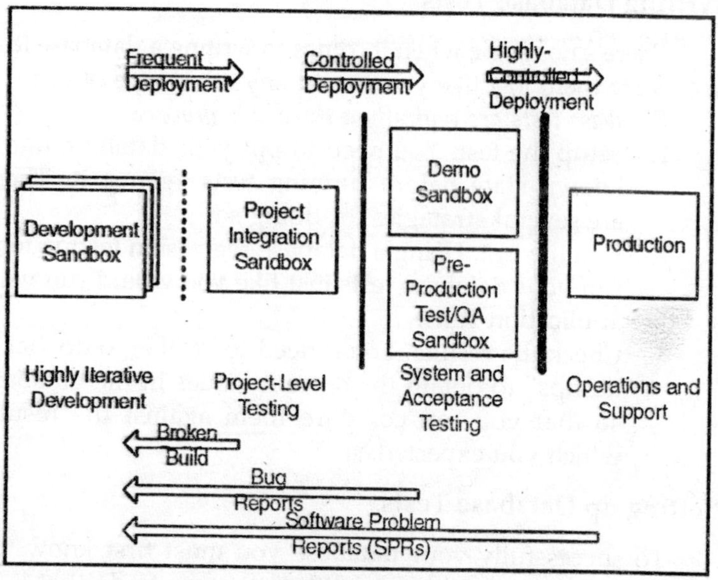

Fig. Sandboxes.

In the development sandbox you'll experiment, implement new functionality, and refactor existing functionality, validate your changes through testing, and then eventually you'll promote your work once you're happy with it to the project integration sandbox. In this sandbox you will rebuild your system and then run all the tests to ensure you haven't broken anything (if so, then back to the development sandbox).

Occasionally, at least once an iteration/cycle, you'll deploy your work to the level (demo and pre-production testing), and rerun your test suite (including database tests) each time that you do so to ensure that your changes integrate with the changes made by other developers.

Every so often (perhaps once every six to twelve months) into production. The primary advantage of sandboxes are that they help to reduce the risk of technical errors adversely affecting a larger group of people than is absolutely necessary at the time.

Writing Database Tests

There's no magic when it comes to writing a database test, you write them just like you would any other type of test.

Database tests are typically a three-step process:

1. Setup the test. You need to put your database into a known state before running tests against it. There are several strategies for doing so.
2. Run the test. Using a database regression testing tool, run your database tests just like you would run your application tests.
3. Check the results. You'll need to be able to do "table dumps" to obtain the current values in the database so that you can compare them against the results which you expected.

Setting up Database Tests

To successfully your database you must first know the exact state of the database, and the best way to do that is to simply put the database in a known state before running your test suite.

There are two common strategies for doing this:

1. *Fresh start:* A common practice is to rebuild the database, including both creation of the schema as well as loading of initial test data, for every major

test run (e.g. testing that you do in your project integration or pre-production test sandboxes).

2. *Data reinitialization*: For testing in developer sandboxes, something that you should do every time you rebuild the system, you may want to forgo dropping and rebuilding the database in favour of simply reinitializing the source data. You can do this either by erasing all existing data and then inserting the initial data vales back into the database, or you can simple run updates to reset the data values. The first approach is less risky and may even be faster for large amounts of data.

An important part of writing database tests is the creation of test data. You have several strategies for doing so:

- Have source test data. You can maintain an external definition of the test data, perhaps in flat files, XML files, or a secondary set of tables. This data would be loaded in from the external source as needed.
- Test data creation scripts. You develop and maintain scripts, perhaps using data manipulation language (DML) SQL code or simply application source code (e.g. Java or C#), which does the necessary deletions, insertions, and/or updates required to create the test data.
- Self-contained test cases. Each individual test case puts the database into a known state required for the test.

These approaches to creating test data can be used alone or in combination. A significant advantage of writing creation scripts and self-contained test cases is that it is much more likely that the developers of that code will place it under configuration management (CM) control.

Although it is possible to put test data itself under CM control, worst case you generate an export file that you check in, this isn't a common practice and therefore may not occur as frequently as required.

Choose an approach that reflects the culture of your organization. Where does test data come from? For unit testing, I prefer to create sample data with known values. This way I can predict the actual results for the tests that I do write and I know I have the appropriate data values for those tests. For other forms of testing — particularly load/stress, system integration, and function testing,

TESTING TOOLS

I believe that there are several critical features which you need to successfully test RDBMSs. There are two categories of database testing tools, one for interface tests and one for internal database tests. Second, these testing tools should support the language that you're developing in. For example, for internal database testing if you're a Microsoft SQL Server developer, your T-SQL procedures should likely be tested using some form of T-SQL framework.

Similarly, Oracle DBAs should have a PL-SQL-based unit testing framework. Third, you need tools which help you to put your database into a known state, which implies the need not only for test data generation but also for managing that data.

To make a long story short, although we're starting to see a glimmer of hope when it comes to database testing tools, as you can see in Table, but we still have a long way to go. Luckily there are some good tools being developed by the open source software (OSS) community and there are some commercial tools available as well. Having said that, IMHO there is still significant opportunity for tool vendors to improve their database testing offerings.

Table. Some Database Testing Tools.

Category	Description	Examples
Unit testing tools	Tools which enable you to regression test your database	AnyDbTest DBFit DBUnit NDbUnit OUnit for Oracle (being replaced soon by Qute) • SQLUnit TSQLUnit (for

		testing T-SQL in MS SQL Server) Visual Studio Team Edition for Database Professionals includes testing capabilities XTUnit
Testing tools for load testing	Tools simulate high usage loads on your database, enabling you to determine whether your system'sarchitecture will stand up to your true production needs.	Empirix Mercury Interactive RadView Rational Suite Test Studio Web Performance
Test Data Generator	Developers need test data against which to validate their systems. Test data generators can be particularly useful when you need large amounts of data, perhaps for stress and load testing.	Data Factory Datatect DTM Data Generator Turbo Data

WHO SHOULD TEST

During development cycles, the primary people responsible for doing database testing are application developers and agile DBAs. They will typically pair together, and because they are hopefully taking a TDD-approach to development the implication is that they'll be doing database unit testing on a continuous basis.

During the release cycle your testers, if you have any, will be responsible for the final system testing efforts and therefore they will also be doing database testing.

The role of your data management (DM) group, or IT management if your organization has no DM group, should be to support your database testing efforts. They should promote the concept that database testing is important, should help people get the requisite training that they require, and should help obtain database testing tools for your organization.

As you have seen, database testing is something that is done continuously by the people on development teams, it isn't something that is done by another group (except of course for system testing efforts). In short, the DM group needs to support database testing efforts and then get out of the way of the people who are actually doing the work.

Introducing Database Regression Testing into Your Organization

Database testing is new to many people, and as a result you are likely to face several challenges:

- Insufficient testing skills. This problem can be overcome through training, through pairing with someone with good testing skills (pairing a DBA without testing skills and a tester without DBA skills still works), or simply through trial and error. The important thing is that you recognize that you need to pick up these skills.
- Insufficient unit tests for existing databases. Few organizations have yet to adopt the practice of database testing, so it is likely that you will not have a sufficient test suite for your existing database(s). Although this is unfortunate, there is no better time than the present to start writing your test suite.
- Insufficient database testing tools. As I said earlier, we still have a way to go with respect to tools.
- Reticent DM groups. My experience is that some data management (DM) groups may see the introduction of database regression testing, and agile techniques such as test-first development (TFD) and refactoring, as a threat. Or, as my July 2006 "state of data

management" survey shows, a large percentage of organizations are not only not doing any database testing at all they haven't even discussed it. For many in the data management community the idea of doing database testing is rather new and it's simply going to take a while for them to think it through.

DATABASE TESTING AND DATA INSPECTION

A common quality technique s to use data inspection tools to examine existing data within a database. You might use something as simple as a SQL-based query tool such as DB Inspect to select a subset of the data within a database to visually inspect the results.

For example, you may choose to view the unique values in a column to determine what values are stored in it, or compare the row count of a table with the count of the resulting rows from joining the table with another one. If the two counts are the same then you don't have an RI problem across the join.

As Richard Dallaway points out, the problem with data inspection is that it is often done manually and on an irregular basis. When you make changes later, sometimes months or years later, you need to redo your inspection efforts. This is costly, time consuming, and error prone.

Data inspection is more of a debugging technique than it is a testing technique. It is clearly an important technique, but it's not something that will greatly contribute to your efforts to ensure data quality within your organization.

Best Practices

I'd like to conclude this article by sharing a few database testing "best practices" with you:

- Use an in-memory database for regression testing. You can dramatically speed up your database tests by running them, or at least portions of them, against an in-memory database such as HSQLDB. The challenge with this approach is that because database methods are implemented differently across database vendors that any method tests will still need to run against the actual database server.

- Start fresh each major test run. To ensure a clean database, a common strategy is that at the beginning of each test run you drop the database, then rebuild it from scratch taking into account all database refactorings and transformations to that point, then reload the test data, and then run your tests. Of course, you wouldn't do this to your production database. ;-)
- Take a continuous approach to regression testing. I can't say this enough, a TDD approach to development is an incredibly effective way to work.
- Train people in testing. Many developers and DBAs have not been trained in testing skills, and they almost certainly haven't been trained in database testing skills. Invest in your people, and give them the training and education they need to do their jobs.
- Pair with novices with people that have database testing experience. One of the easiest ways to gain database testing skills is to pair programme with someone who already has them.

REGRESSION TESTING WITH TEST COMPLETE

Regression testing means re-testing an application after its code has been modified to verify that it still functions correctly. Regression testing consists of re-running existing test cases and checking that code changes did not break any previously working functions, inadvertently introduce errors or cause earlier fixed issues to reappear. These test cases should be run as often as possible (fox example, after each new software build), so that code modifications that damaged how application works can be quickly identified and fixed.

Regression testing starts as soon as there is anything to test at all. The regression test suite grows as the application moves ahead and test engineers add test cases that test new or rewritten code. Soon the suite may extend to thousands of test cases that cover various application functions. Obviously, by this point, automation of regression tests becomes essential because it is humanly impossible to rapidly and reliably repeat all of the test cases and analyse their results.

This is where Test Complete is very helpful and provides you with maximum return on your automated testing investment. Test omplete has all of the features needed to make regression testing fully automated and thus to help you produce high-quality products:

Automate Regression Tests [SH

TestComplete lets you perform regression testing by re-running automated functional tests of desktop and web applications as well as load, stress and scalability tests of web applications as developers add new functionality to the application. Regression tests can be composed of any successful keyword, scripted or low-level functional tests or load tests that have earlier verified the desired application functionality and behaviour.

Verify Applications with Checkpoints

To verify the tested application's functionality and behaviour, your regression testing should include checkpoints that compare the application characteristics and outputs against baselines. With TestComplete, you can easily capture, store or update baselines and insert the appropriate comparison instructions into regression tests with a few button clicks.

Manage Regression Tests

TestComplete makes it easy to maintain the list of regression test cases included in the regression test suite, select the test or test collections to run and specify their execution order.

Analyse Regression Testing

Test completes' test logs clearly identify whether the regression test passed or failed and what went wrong, where the problem is and how it happened. This helps developers easily detect which recent code modifications caused the problems and fix them quickly. Detected issues can automatically be reported to an issue-tracking database during or after the regression test run.

Run Regression Tests with Automated Builds

Regression testing with TestComplete can be run as part of automated builds (for example, nightly builds) to ensure that problems caused by recent code modifications are identified and fixed as soon as possible. TestComplete is integrated with Automated Build Studio and MSBuild and supports command-line and COM integration with any other build tools.

Distributed Regression Testing

You can distribute regression tests among multiple differently-configured machines and run them in parallel to shorten the regression testing cycle.

FEATURES

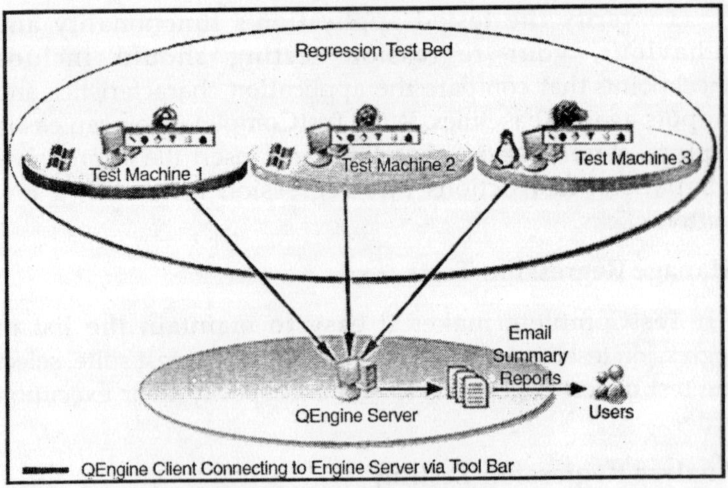

Fig. Regression Testing Architecture

The Regression testing capability helps to automate testing of functional, performance and load handling capability of web applications as new functionality is added to the software. In addition to being easy to setup and maintain, Engine supports a distributed architecture, which can scale to your organization needs and help your development team to produce high quality software.

NEED FOR REGRESSION TESTING

LOAD TESTING

Manage Engine QEngine Load testing tool helps ensure your web applications and web sites can handle the load conditions that it will face in production. It helps ensure that critical information and services are available at speeds your end-users expect. In addition to load tests for web applications, it supports Performance Testing and Stress Testing.

QEngine load testing provides flexible user scenarios and realistic load types to help application load testing. The load tests can help simulate real time user activities and load test hundreds or even thousands of concurrent users under dynamic load conditions.

PERFORMANCE TESTING

ManageEngine QEngine performance testing tool allows you to load test / stress test your web applications or web sites with accuracy and ease. Comprehensive reports helps you to identify critical performance issues and optimize the user experience of your web applications/web sites before it goes into production

MIXED FEATURES

- *Easy Test Setup and Execution*: Time taken to install the testing software in regression test machine is vastly reduced as it takes only seconds to install the toolbar.
- *Powerful Suite Components*: Provides set of interfaces that enables you to perform fine tuning of the test according to specific operating needs.

- *Easy Test Maintenance*: Object repository to accomodate changes that are made to the application's user interface.
- *Test Selection*: Provision to configure and activate filters to select individual or a group of tests to run in the test machine.
- *Test Scheduling*: Easy-to-use web UI to schedule test suite execution.
- *Distributed Testing*: Provision to run regression tests on multiple machines and different platforms at the same time.
- *Unattended Testing*: Individual and/or group of tests can be executed singly or in parallel from one or many workstations.

Chapter 9

Functionality and Performance Testing

INTRODUCTION

Functionality testing is employed to verify whether your product meets the intended specifications and functional requirements laid out in your development documentation.

Functionality testing is performed to verify that a software application performs and functions correctly according to design specifications. Whether you are in need of basic functionality tests to ensure that primary features function properly or you are in need of in depth verification of complex operations, TelSoft can meet your needs.

For Functionality testing of a software application, our Test Engineers analyse the application and develop a comprehensive Test Plan that outlines all features and functional areas of the application that will be tested. The Test Plan also includes Test Cases that outline how each feature and functional area will be tested.

Some of the functional tests that we perform include:

- Simple Functional Testing
- Task Feature Testing
- Boundary Testing
- Forced Error Condition Testing
- Exploratory Testing

The members of our Testing Department have extensive experience in testing software applications and their comprehensive testing techniques provide our clients with the assurance that their applications will perform and function properly.

We also offer our clients the use of TelTRACK, our proprietary, web-based, defect-tracker. This allows developers to start fixing errors as soon as they are detected by our QA Team, which saves a considerable amount of time in the software development life cycle.

PURPOSE OF FUNCTIONALITY TESTING

As competition in the software and hardware development arena intensifies, it becomes critical to deliver products that are virtually bug-free. Functionality testing helps your company provide products with a minimum amount of issues to an increasingly sophisticated pool of end users. Gone are the days when users will quietly find their own workarounds for bug-filled technology.

Potential purchasers of your products may find professional and consumer review sites online where honest and often brutal product reviews and bug reports deter them from buying your software. nResult will help ensure that your product functions as intended, keeping your service and support calls to a minimum.

Functional testing of software or hardware is testing conducted on a complete, integrated system to evaluate the system's compliance with its specified requirements. This testing falls within the scope of black box testing, and as such, should require no knowledge of the inner design of the code or logic.

TYPES OF FUNCTIONAL TESTING

Functional Testing	Description
GUI software testing	Process of testing a product that uses a graphical user interface, to ensure it meets its written specifications.
Usability testing	Technique used to evaluate a product by testing it on user
Performance testing	Process used to measure Qualitative

	attributes such as reliability, scalability, interoperability, speed, effectiveness etc.
Compatibility testing	Testing conducted on the application to evaluate the application's compatibility with the computing environment.
Load testing	Process of creating demand on a system or device and measuring its response.
Volume Testing	Volume testing refers to testing a software application for a certain data volume.
Stress testing	Form of testing that is used to determine the stability of a given system or entity
Security Testing	Process to determine that an Information System protects data and maintains functionality as intended.
Scalability Testing	Testing of a software application for measuring its capability to scale up or scale out.
Sanity testing	Basic test to quickly evaluate the validity of a claim or calculation.
Smoke testing	First test made after repairs or first assembly to provide some assurance that the system under test will not catastrophically fail.
Exploratory testing	An approach in software testing that is concisely described as simultaneous learning, test design and test execution
Ad hoc testing	Software testing performed without planning and documentation.
Regression testing	Type of software testing which seeks to uncover software regressions
Recovery testing	Activity of testing how well the

	software is able to recover from crashes, hardware failures and other similar problems.
Installation testing	Kind of quality assurance work in the software industry that focuses on what customers will need to do to install and set up the new software successfully.
Maintenance testing	Testing which is performed to either identify equipment problems, diagnose equipment problems or to confirm that repair measures have been effective
Accessibility testing	Process to evaluate the degree to which a product (e.g., device, service, environment) is accessible by as many people as possible.

GUI SOFTWARE TESTING

- GUI software testing is the process of testing a product that uses a graphical user interface, to ensure it meets its written specifications. This is normally done through the use of a variety of test cases.
- GUIs make testing systems more difficult for many reasons: the event-driven nature of GUIs, unsolicited events, many ways in/many ways out and the infinite input domain problems make it likely that the programmer has introduced errors because he could not test every path.
- GUI testing mostly focuses on using tools such as JUNIT.
- To generate a 'good' set of test cases, the test designer must be certain that their suite covers all the functionality of the system and also has to be sure that the suite fully exercises the GUI itself. Two main aspects to look into are domain size and sequences.
- A recent breakthrough in the field of automated GUI testing is a new graph model called the event-flow

graph that represents events and event interactions. A GUI is decomposed into a hierarchy of modal dialogues; this hierarchy is represented as an integration tree; each modal dialogue is represented as an event-flow graph that shows all possible event execution paths in the dialogue.

USABILITY TESTING

- Usability testing is a technique used to evaluate a product by testing it on users. This can be seen as an irreplaceable usability practice, since it gives direct input on how real users use the system.
- Usability testing focuses on measuring a human-made product's capacity to meet its intended purpose. Examples of products that commonly benefit from usability testing are web sites or web applications, computer interfaces, documents, or devices.
- Usability testing measures the usability, or ease of use, of a specific object or set of objects.

COMPATIBILITY TESTING

- Compatibility testing, part of software non-functional tests, is testing conducted on the application to evaluate the application's compatibility with the computing environment.

LOAD TESTING

- Load testing is the process of creating demand on a system or device and measuring its response. In mechanical systems
- Load testing generally refers to the practice of modeling the expected usage of a software programme by simulating multiple users accessing the program's services concurrently
- For example, a word processor or graphics editor can be forced to read an extremely large document; or a

financial package can be forced to generate a report based on several years' worth of data.

- The most accurate load testing occurs with actual, rather than theoretical, results.

VOLUME TESTING

- Volume testing refers to testing a software application for a certain data volume. This volume can in generic terms be the database size or it could also be the size of an interface file that is the subject of volume testing.

STRESS TESTING

- Stress testing is a form of testing that is used to determine the stability of a given system or entity. It involves testing beyond normal operational capacity, often to a breaking point, in order to observe the results.
- In software testing, stress testing often refers to tests that put a greater emphasis on robustness, availability, and error handling under a heavy load, rather than on what would be considered correct behaviour under normal circumstances.

SECURITY TESTING

- The process to determine that an Information System protects data and maintains functionality as intended.
- The six basic security concepts that need to be covered by security testing are: confidentiality, integrity, authentication, authorization, availability and non-repudiation.

SCALABILITY TESTING

- It is the testing of a software application for measuring its capability to scale up or scale out - in terms of any of its non-functional capability - be it the user load supported, the number of transactions, the data volume etc.

SANITY TESTING

- A sanity test or sanity check is a basic test to quickly evaluate the validity of a claim or calculation.
- In computer science it is a very brief run-through of the functionality of a computer programme, system, calculation, or other analysis, to assure that the system or methodology works as expected, often prior to a more exhaustive round of testing.

SMOKE TESTING

- Smoke testing is done by developers before the build is released or by testers before accepting a build for further testing.
- In software engineering, a smoke test generally consists of a collection of tests that can be applied to a newly created or repaired computer programme.
- This is also known as a build verification test.

EXPLORATORY TESTING

- Exploratory testing is an approach in software testing that is concisely described as simultaneous learning, test design and test execution
- Exploratory testing seeks to find out how the software actually works, and to ask questions about how it will handle difficult and easy cases. The testing is dependent on the tester's skill of inventing test cases and finding defects. The more the tester knows about the product and different test methods, the better the testing will be.
- When performing exploratory testing, there are no exact expected results; it is the tester that decides what will be verified, critically investigating the correctness of the result.

AD HOC TESTING

- Ad hoc testing is a part of exploratory testing, being the least formal of test methods.

- The tests are intended to be run only once, unless a defect is discovered.
- Ad hoc testing is most often used as a complement to other types of testing.

REGRESSION TESTING

- Regression testing can be used not only for testing the correctness of a programme, but it is also often used to track the quality of its output.
- Common methods of regression testing include re-running previously run tests and checking whether previously fixed faults have re-emerged.

RECOVERY TESTING

- In software testing, recovery testing is the activity of testing how well the software is able to recover from crashes, hardware failures and other similar problems.
- Recovery testing is the forced failure of the software in a variety of ways to verify that recovery is properly performed.
- Recovery testing should not be confused with Reliability testing, which is tries to discover the point at which failure occurs.
- For example, While the application is running, suddenly restart the computer and after that check the validness of application's data integrity.

INSTALLATION TESTING

- Installation testing is a kind of quality assurance work in the software industry that focuses on what customers will need to do to install and set up the new software successfully.
- The testing process may involve full, partial or upgrades install/uninstall processes.
- This can also be called as Implementation testing.
- This testing is typically done by the software testing

engineer in conjunction with the configuration manager.

MAINTENANCE TESTING

- Maintenance testing is that testing which is performed to either identify equipment problems, diagnose equipment problems or to confirm that repair measures have been effective.
- It can be performed at either the system level, or the component level.

ACCESSIBILITY TESTING

- It is the process to evaluate the degree to which a product (e.g., device, service, and environment) is accessible by as many people as possible.

TESTING TECHNIQUES :

AD HOC

Takes advantage of individual testing talents and intelligence based upon consideration of product goals, level of user capabilities and possible areas and features that may create confusion. The tester will generate test cases on the spur of the moment, as quickly as possible, as ideas occur to them. This kind of testing generally finds most bugs in new software in the shortest possible time.

EXPLORATORY

The tester designs and executes tests while learning the product. Test design is organized by a set of concise patterns designed to assure that testers don't miss anything important.

COMBINATION

The tester performs a sequence of events using different paths to complete tasks. This can uncover bugs related to order of events that are difficult to find using other methods.

SCRIPTED

The tester uses a test script that lays out the specific

functions to be tested. A test script can be provided by the customer/developer or constructed by nResult, depending on the needs of your organization.

Let nResult help you make sure that your hardware or software will function as intended. Our team will check for any anomalies or bugs in your product, through any or all stages of development, to help increase your confidence level in the product you are bringing to market.

Whether you want us to augment your internal test group, or if you are looking for a complete test source from alpha through gold master stages, nResult offers you a detailed, reasonably priced solution to meet your testing needs.

MASQ FUNCTIONALITY WITHOUT DNS

Now try TELNETing to a remote IP address (i.e. telnet 152.2.210.81 (this is technically the DNS name "metalab.unc.edu").

It might take a few seconds to get a login prompt since this is a VERY busy server. Did you get a login prompt like shown below? If so, it means that TCP Masquerading is running OK. If not, try TELNETing to some other hosts you think will support TELNET like 198.182.196.55 (www.linux.org). If this still doesn't work, make sure you are using the simple rc.firewall-* ruleset for this test. An example of this output might look like (hit Control-D to exit out of the TELNET):

```
masq-client# telnet 152.2.210.80
Trying 152.2.210.80...
Connected to 152.2.210.80.
Escape character is '^]'.
SunOS 5.7
            Welcome to MetaLab.unc.edu
 To login to MetaLab as a user, connect to
            login. metalab.unc.edu.
 This machine does not allow public telnet
                    logins.
login: Connection closed by foreign host.
```

MASQ FUNCTIONALITY WITH DNS RESOLUTION

Now try TELNETing to a remote machine by DNS name (i.e. "telnet metalab.unc.edu". If this works, the output should look like something below. With this test, this shows that UDP-based DNS is working fine.

```
masq-client# telnet MetaLab.unc.edu
Trying 152.2.210.80...
Connected to 152.2.210.80.
Escape character is '^]'.
SunOS 5.7
              Welcome to MetaLab.unc.edu
  To login to MetaLab as a user, connect to
           login.metalab.unc.edu.
  This machine does not allow public telnet
                   logins.
login: Connection closed by foreign host.
```

If this did not work, but Step EIGHT did work, make sure that you have one or more valid DNS servers configured on each of the MASQ CLIENT computer(s) as shown in Please note that these DNS servers will typically be your ISP's DNS servers and NOT your local MASQ server.

TESTING METHODOLOGIES

Our manual testing methodology and exploratory techniques are extremely effective, especially when operating to a compressed timescale, while test scripts and automated testing are used when projects demand a more formalised approach.

Frequently the optimum solution is a combination of the two. Test Partners can work with you to assess the testing requirements, develop the project plan and undertake the testing required, on time and on budget.

IN-HOUSE TESTING CAPABILITY?]

Can you afford the cost and management overhead associated with maintaining an effective in-house test facility that is often under-utilised or over-stretched? Test Partners can allocate dedicated resource for the duration of your project, altering the level of resources as required to maximise efficiency, ensuring you meet your targets as planned whilst containing the overall costs.

YOUR PLACE OR OURS

Our Test Centre is fully equipped to conduct almost any project, and it operates 24/7 so we can keep working when your day has finished. Of course some projects can only be run on your premises, in which case we will provide the skilled testers and any equipment that is needed.

TESTING FOR PERFORMANCE

DEFINITION

Performance testing is the process of determining the speed or effectiveness of a computer, network, software programme or device. This process can involve quantitative tests done in a lab, such as measuring the response time or the number of MIPS (millions of instructions per second) at which a system functions.

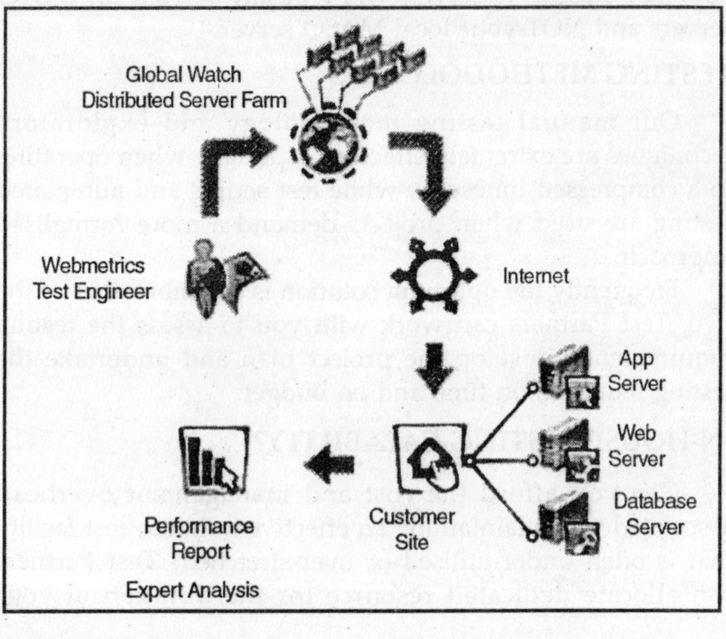

Qualitative attributes such as reliability, scalability and interoperability may also be evaluated. Performance testing is often done in conjunction with stress testing.

Performance testing can verify that a system meets the specifications claimed by its manufacturer or vendor. The process can compare two or more devices or programs in terms of parameters such as speed, data transfer rate, bandwidth, throughput, efficiency or reliability.

Performance testing can also be used as a diagnostic aid in locating communications bottlenecks. Often a system will work much better if a problem is resolved at a single point or in a single component. For example, even the fastest computer will function poorly on today's Web if the connection occurs at only 40 to 50 Kbps (kilobits per second).

Slow data transfer rate may be inherent in hardware but can also result from software-related problems, such as:

- Too many applications running at the same time
- A corrupted file in a Web browser
- A security exploit
- Heavy-handed antivirus software
- The existence of active malware on the hard disk.

Effective performance testing can quickly identify the nature or location of a software-related performance problem.

OVERVIEW

Our SiteStressSM service is a remotely executed, completely outsourced performance and load testing solution. Site Stress simulates end-user activity against designated web sites, challenging both performance capacities and infrastructure reliability. As a completely managed service there are no tool costs and no training overhead.

Following consultation all necessary tests are scripted and executed remotely from one or more of our 17 global points of presence, by our team of engineers. The results of the tests are analysed by our engineers and a detailed report of our findings is produced. SiteStress is used by companies, developers and service providers to ensure a positive online experience for end-users.

How it Works

A SiteStressSM test consists of one or more scenarios (typically up to 10 steps each) as defined by the client. Our engineers create scripts based on defined transactional scenarios, and simulate them with a prescribed number of virtual users over our GlobalWatch testing and monitoring network. On completion of each test we produce a detailed report of our findings.

Key Features

- *Simulated Traffic*: SiteStressSM can generate hundreds or thousands of virtual users that interact with a specified web site to assess how much load the applications and infrastructure can handle, providing performance rates at various loads and application breaking points.
- *Transactional Simulations*: Typically anywhere from one to five different user behaviours are executed simultaneously, precisely mimicking real end-user behaviour, such as Login, Checkout, Order Status etc.
- Service: Outsourced (Hosted/Managed) load testing service executed from our distributed load testing network with servers across North America, Asia and Europe.
- *Expertise*: A dedicated performance engineer is allocated to each load test customer to provide performance analysis, diagnosis and recommendations for optimising the performance of web sites, applications and systems.
- Reports: Detailed HTML/Flash reports are generated after each test iteration, which include detailed performance analysis by our testing experts.
- Schedule: Testing engagements usually consist of three executions and can be as short as a few days.

Key Benefits

- *Time Saver*: Outsourcing load testing saves time. In a typical 30-day engagement, the average customer spends fewer than four hours of their time involved with the load test. Time is money.

- *Cost Effective*: Eliminate the need to purchase expensive load testing software and infrastructure. Leverage our technology, GlobalWatch Network and engineering expertise.
- *Proof of Quality*: Load testing provides third party validation of the quality of online applications.
- *Benchmarking*: Know the potential of your systems by leveraging the experience of a team of engineers who have tested nearly every type of web system in use today.

PERFORMANCE TEST TOOLS

ALLMON

Remote Allmon collector agents are designed to harvest a range of metrics values coming from many areas of monitored infrastructure (i.e. application instrumentation, JMX, HTTP service checks, database, SNMP stats). Metrics are sent to the server and stored.

The collected data are base for quantitative and qualitative performance and availability analysis. Allmon collaborates with other analytical tools for OLAP multidimensional analysis and Data Mining processing. The tool can be used for continuous production monitoring/ auditing as well as for development (profiling) and QA (load testing) purposes.

Allmon schema is design to store hundreds of millions of raw metrics data rows. Allmon database can hold hundreds GB of data. Later on data can be aggregated by very flexible generic processes which can limit amount of allocated data and provide better prepared data for analysis.

DESCRIPTION

The main goal of the project is to create a distributed generic system collecting and storing various runtime metrics collections used for continuous system performance, health, quality and availability monitoring purposes. Allmon agents are designed to harvest a range of metrics values coming from many areas of monitored infrastructure (application instrumentation, JMX, HTTP health checks, SNMP). Collected data are base for quantitative and qualitative performance and availability analysis. Allmon collaborates with other analytical tools for OLAP analysis and Data Mining processing.

APACHE JMETER

Apache JMeter is open source software, a 100% pure Java desktop application designed to load test functional behaviour and measure performance. It was originally designed for testing Web Applications but has since expanded to other test functions.

Apache JMeter may be used to test performance both on static and dynamic resources (files, Servlets, Perl scripts, Java Objects, Data Bases and Queries, FTP Servers and more). It can be used to simulate a heavy load on a server, network or object to test its strength or to analyse overall performance under different load types.

You can use it to make a graphical analysis of performance or to test your server/script/object behaviour under heavy concurrent load.

Description

Apache JMeter is a 100% pure Java desktop application designed to load test functional behaviour and measure performance.

It was originally designed for testing Web Applications but has since expanded to other test functions. Apache JMeter may be used to test performance both on static and dynamic resources (files, Servlets, Perl scripts, Java Objects, Data Bases and Queries, FTP Servers and more).

It can be used to simulate a heavy load on a server, network or object to test its strength or to analyse overall performance under different load types. You can use it to make a graphical analysis of performance or to test your server/script/object behaviour under heavy concurrent load.

Benerator

Benerator supports you in performing realistic load and performance tests. It is a framework for generating realistic and valid high-volume test data for your system under test (avoiding the Datalite anti-pattern). benerator actually reduces the amount of time for creating a useful data setup of a medium sized enterprise application or XML Schema from 2-4 weeks to 1-2 days!

Since data representation and constraints are platform independent, benerator can provide you with a rich set of plugin interfaces for custom extensions and mappings, allowing virtually any platform to be targeted with data generation.

Out of the box benerator supports database systems, XML, XML Schema, CSV, Flat Files and Excel(TM) sheets. Domain packages provide reusable generators for creating domain-specific data as names and addresses internationalizable in language and region..

Description

Benerator is a framework for creating realistic and valid high-volume test data, used for (unit/integration/load) testing and showcase setup. Metadata constraints are imported from systems and/or configuration files. Data can be imported from and exported to files and systems, anonymized or generated from scratch.

Domain packages provide reusable generators for creating domain-specific data as names and addresses internationalizable in language and region. It is strongly customizable with plugins and configuration options.

CLIF is a Load Injection Framework

CLIF is a sub-project of OW2 JMOB project. CLIF is a Java framework dedicated to performance testing of any kind of system reachable from a JVM. CLIF framework aims at supporting the deployment and control of:

- Distributed load injectors, responsible for load/traffic generation on the system under test;

- As well as probes giving information about resource consumptions.

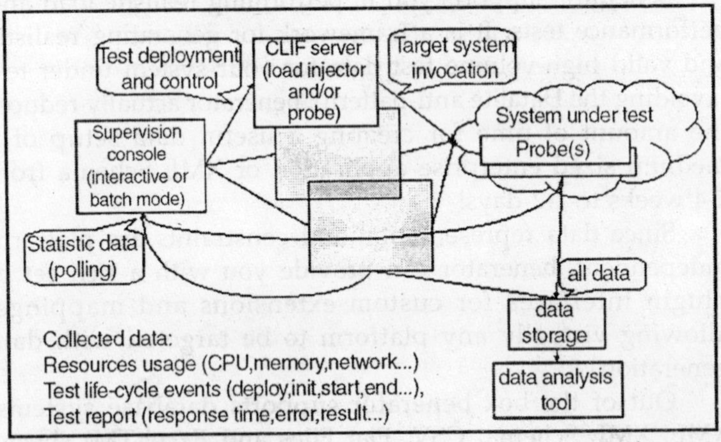

CLIF will also come with test supervision features (including monitoring of response times, throughput, error rate, computing resource consumptions), and analysis tools.

Key Features

- 3 user interfaces available: Swing-based GUI, Eclipse-based GUI, command line
- low footprint probes available for CPU, memory, disks, network, JVM
- graphical monitoring and execution control of all probes and load injectors
- advanced, generic, extensible scenario definition environment ISAC, coming with:
  - A graphical editor
  - Plug-ins for managing target protocols (HTTP, DNS, TCP, SIP, etc.) and miscellaneous utilities (counters, random timers, runtime parameter provisioning from an external data source...)
  - A powerful execution engine, able to manage a million virtual users and a million requests/second throughput per load injector *(the actual limits depend on the computing overhead of the target protocol management)*

Fractal Architecture

To provide a flexible architecture, CLIF makes use of the Fractal component model. For example, load injectors and probes are components that can be defined, plugged in and (un-/re-)deployed at runtime.

Thanks to the Fractal model, customizing CLIF does not require to know details about the whole framework, but only about a well-defined, reduced number of client and server interfaces.

Description

CLIF is a modular and flexible distributed load testing platform. It may address any target system that is reachable from a Java programme (HTTP, DNS, TCP/IP...) CLIF provides 3 user interfaces (Swing or Eclipse GUI, command line) to deploy, control and monitor a set of distributed load injectors and resource consumption probes (CPU, memory...)

An Eclipse wizard helps programming support for new protocols. Load scenarios are defined through XML-editing, using a GUI, or using a capture tool. The scenario execution engine allows the execution of up to millions of virtual users per load injector.

Curl-loader

Curl-loader (also known as "omes-nik" and "davilka") is an open-source tool written in C-language, simulating application load and application behaviour of thousands and tens of thousand HTTP/HTTPS and FTP/FTPS clients, each with its own source IP-address. In contrast to other tools curl-loader is using real C-written client protocol stacks, namely, HTTP and FTP stacks of libcurl and TLS/SSL of openssl, and simulates user behaviour with support for login and authentication flavors.

The goal of the project is to deliver a powerful and flexible open-source testing solution as a real alternative to Spirent Avalanche and IXIA IxLoad.

The tool is useful for performance loading of various application services, for testing web and ftp servers and traffic generation. Activities of each virtual client are logged and collected statistics includes information about resolving, connection establishment, sending of requests, receiving responses, headers and data received/sent, errors from network, TLS/SSL and application (HTTP, FTP) level events and errors.

Virtual clients are grouped together to the so-called batches of clients, performing the same sort of activities, like:

- Authentication login;
- User activity simulation by fetching several URLs with configurable timeouts in between;
- Logoff.

The tool can be easily extended to generate sftp, telnet, tftp, ldap, ssh, scp etc other application protocols, supported by the great libcurl library.

Features List

- *Virtual clients number*: The tool runs, depending on your HW and scenario, 2500-100 000 and more simultaneously loading clients, all from a single curl-loader process. Actual number of clients may be several times higher, and it is limited mainly by memory. Each client loads from its "personal" source IP-address, from the "common" IP-address shared by all clients, or from the IP-addresses shared by some clients, where a limited set of shared IP-addresses can be used by a batch of clients.
- Rampup of the virtual clients number at loading start in either automatic or manual mode;
- IPv4 and IPv6 addresses and URIs;
- HTTP 1.1. GET, POST and PUT, including file upload operations;
- HTTP user authentication login with POST or GET+POST methods. Unique configurable username and password for each virtual client as well as configurable posted string (post-forms) are the options. Another option is loading of users with credentials from a tokens text file;

- HTTP POST/GET forms with up to 16 tokens filled from a tokens text file;
- HTTP user logoff with POST, GET+POST, or GET (cookies); POST logoff with configurable posted string (post-forms);
- HTTP multipart form data POST-ing as in RFC1867;
- HTTP Web and Proxy Authentication (HTTP 401 and 407 responses) with Basic, Digest (RFC2617) and NTLM supported;
- HTTP 3xx redirections with unlimited number of redirections;
- HTTP cookies and DNS caches;
- FTP passive and active, FTP upload;
- Full customization of client request HTTP/FTP headers;
- Transfer limit rate for each client download or upload operation on a per url bases;
- URL fetching probability;
- TCP connections reuse or re-establishment on a per url bases;
- Unlimited configurable number of URLs. Mixing of HTTP, HTTPS, FTP and FTPS urls in a single batch (test plan) configuration;
- Connection establishment timers for each URL;
- URL completion timers monitoring and enforcement for each client;
- Inter/after URL "sleeping" timers, including random timers taken from a configurable interval;
- Logfile with tracing activities for each virtual client. The logfile is automatically rewinded, when reaching configurable size preventing disk crashes;
- Logging of responses (headers and bodies) to files.
- Pre-cooked batch configuration (test plan) examples;
- Load Status GUI at console and with output to file;
- Status and statistics for each virtual client, which are logged to file;

Here is a screenshot:

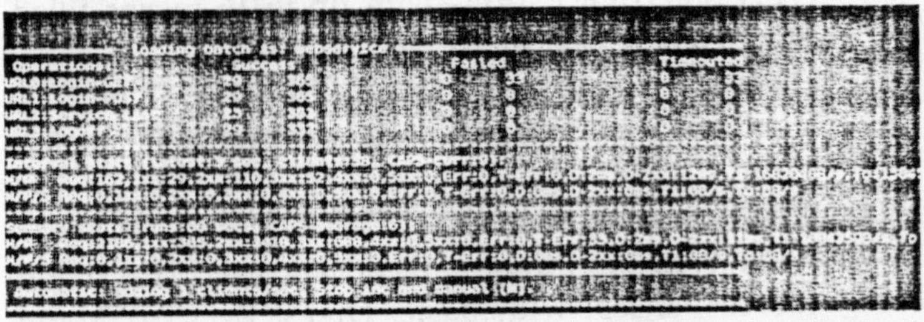

The tool is written and supported by Robert Iakobashvili and Michael Moser, both from Israel.

Please, use the link to the mailing list provided in Support section to contact us and to get support for the tool. Subscribe to the curl-loader-devel list and mail your filled PROBLEM-REPORTING form located in the curl-loader tarball to the list. Your suggestions, ideas and patches would be very much appreciated. The official language of the curl-loader-devel mailing list is English, whereas Russian and German written mails are also welcomed.

Successfully Used

To simulate HTTP/S load of thousands of clients against authentication gateway for testing of the gateway performance in various scenarios.

Curl-loader supplied HTTP/S client load against Apache web-server with the gateway in the middle, where the gateway made a browser hijacking and HTTP- redirection of the curl-clients to the HTTPS url at the gateway's own web-server. HTTPS page of the web-server provided a POST form to the user with username and password for the client/user authentication against an external AAA (RADIUS) server.

If the authentication was OK, user (a libcurl virtual client object) was allowed to enter the Internet and to perform some sort of simulated by curl-loader network activity, namely, fetching urls and sleeping in between them.

After enjoying Internet, user was coming to logoff. To test web-server pages, authenticating tens and hundred thousand of clients, where each client comes to a HTTPS url using GET method and is redirected by the web-server to another url, providing authentication POST form with username and password. After successful authentication of a client the web-server was setting to the client server-cookies. Client activities were further simulated by fetching urls and sleeping in between. Clients were doing logoff using GET-method to the web-server logoff-url, where the cookies were used by the web-server to verify client identity.

To generate Gbps traffic from thousands of TCP/HTTP clients and to test the impact of thousands of firewalling and NAT iptables/ipset rules and hundreds of the rules being added/deleted each second at performance of a gateway device. curl-loader provided client load against Apache web-server fetching a url with a gigabyte file, thus, creating a permanent heavy-load traffic, containing thousands of tcp-streams at the gateway in the middle.

Description

A C-written web application testing and load generating tool. The goal of the project is to provide a powerful open-source alternative to Spirent Avalanche and IXIA IxLoad. The loader uses real HTTP, FTP and TLS/SSL protocol stacks, simulating tens of thousand and hundred users/clients each with own IP-address. The tool supports user authentication, login and a range of statistics.

Database Open source Test Suite

Description

The Database Opensource Test Suite (DOTS) is a set of test cases designed for the purpose of stress-testing database server systems in order to measure database server performance and reliability.

DBMonster

Description

DBMonster is an application to generate random data for testing SQL database driven applications under heavy load.

Deluge

Description

An open-source web site stress test tool. Simulates multiple user types and counts. Includes proxy server for recording playback scripts, and log evaluator for generating result statistics. Note: this tool is no longer under active development although it is still available on Sourceforge.

Dieseltest

Dieseltest is an easy-to-use load testing tool for simulating hundreds or thousands of users on a website. It has a facility for recording scripts, playing them back, and showing the results in real time. Results can be exported for further analysis.

Description

Contains the high-end features common to packages costing $50,000 or more. Dieseltest is a Windows application that simulates hundreds or thousands of users hitting a website. To run a load test, you first create a test script using our script editor. The script contains all of the requests that a real-world user would make of a website. You then load the script and run the test. The system will show you real-time results while the script is running, and produce a report analyzing the results at the conclusion.

Faban

Faban is a facility for developing and running benchmarks. Faban supports multi-tier server benchmarks (such as web/cache/database benchmarks) run across dozens of machines. It also supports developing and running a simple micro-benchmark targeting a single component (such as an ftp server.) It has two major components, the Faban *Driver Framework* and the Faban *Harness*.

The Faban Driver Framework is an API-based framework and component model to help develop new benchmarks rapidly. The driver framework controls the lifecycle of the benchmark run as well as the stochastic model used to simulate users.

It provides built-in support for many servers such as Apache httpd, Sun Java System Web, Portal and Mail Servers, Oracle RDBMS, memcached etc. It provides a well-documented interface to add support for any other server.

The Faban Harness is a tool to automate running of server benchmarks. It also serves as a container to host benchmarks allowing new benchmarks to be deployed in a rapid manner. Faban provides an easy to use web interface to configure and queue runs, and includes extensive functionality to view, compare and graph run outputs.

The Faban Harness not only supports benchmarks developed using the Faban Driver Framework but also supports stand-alone benchmarks. Non-faban benchmarks are supported by defining a benchmark wrapper that identifies the processes involved in preparing and running the benchmark, and reporting results.

We summarize briefly, the features and attributes of Faban:

Faban Harness

- Web interface for controlling benchmark runs and viewing results
- Queuing of benchmark runs
- Benchmark process automation
- Automated collection of system and application statistics
- Manages the whole rig consisting of multiple systems across multiple teers
- Automated benchmark code distribution
- Centralized logging
- Pluggable services and tools to control and observe software components in the rig
- Analysis tools - post processes and graphs and compares detailed run results
- Automatically integrates and manages workloads defined using the Faban Driver Framework
- Integrates with any existing workload or benchmark

Faban Driver Framework

- Workload component model with high-level APIs and abstractions
- Driven by declarative workload model/specification
- Provides, and encourages the use of stochastic models
- Throughput-oriented measurements with response-time criteria
- Life-cycle control
- Time synchronization between all systems
- Extremely accurate timings with large number of time calibrations built in
- Automated timing measurements
- Lightweight and extremely scalable across large number of driver systems
- Standardized/extensible reporting

Description

Faban is a facility for developing and running benchmarks, developed by Sun. It has two major components, the Faban harness and the Faban driver framework. The Faban harness is a harness to automate running of server benchmarks as well as a container to host benchmarks allowing new benchmarks to be deployed in a rapid manner. Faban provides a web interface to launch & queue runs, and extensive functionality to view, compare and graph run outputs.

Requirement:

OS independent; JVM 1.5 or later.

Download data:

No data feed available

FunkLoad

FunkLoad is a functional and load web tester, written in Python, whose main use cases are:

- Functional testing of web projects, and thus regression testing as well.
- Performance testing: by loading the web application and monitoring your servers it helps you to pinpoint

bottlenecks, giving a detailed report of performance measurement.

- Load testing tool to expose bugs that do not surface in cursory testing, like volume testing or longevity testing.
- Stress testing tool to overwhelm the web application resources and test the application recoverability.
- Writing web agents by scripting any web repetitive task, like checking if a site is alive.

Main FunkLoad features are:

- FunkLoad is free software distributed under the GNU GPL.
- Functional test are pure Python scripts using the pyUnit framework like normal unit test. Python enable complex scenarios to handle real world applications.
- Truly emulates a web browser (single-threaded) using Richard Jones' webunit:
  - Basic authentication support
  - Cookies support
  - Referrer support
  - Fetching css, javascript and images
  - Emulating a browser cache
  - File upload and multipart/form-data submission
  - Post any kind of content type like application/xml
  - https support
  - http_proxy support
- Advanced test runner with many command-line options:
  - Set the target server url
  - Display the fetched page in real time in your browser
  - Debug mode
  - Check performance of a single page (or set of pages) inside a test
  - Green/red colour mode
  - Select or exclude tests cases using a regex

  - Support normal pyUnit test
  - Support doctest from a plain text file or embedded in python docstring
- Turn a functional test into a load test: just by invoking the bench runner you can identify scalability and performance problems.
- Detailed bench reports in ReST or HTML (and PDF via ps2pdf) containing:
  - The bench configuration
  - Tests, pages, requests stats and charts.
  - The 5 slowest requests.
  - Monitoring one or many servers cpu usage, load average, memory/swap usage and network traffic charts.
  - An http error summary list

Description

FunkLoad is a functional and load web tester, written in Python, whose main use cases are functional and regression testing of web projects, performance testing by loading the web application and monitoring your servers, load testing to expose bugs that do not surface in cursory testing, and stress testing to overwhelm the web application resources and test the application recoverability, and writing web agents by scripting any web repetitive task, like checking if a site is alive.

FWPTT Load Testing Web Applications

FWPTT it's a Web application tester programme for load testing web applications. It can record normal and ajax requests.

How does it work

FWPTT let's the user record his browsing actions. It does this by using a proxy server. After the recording is done the user save the recorded data into an xml format for later use or generate a c# class that will call all the http request that the user has previously recorded.

Than using the tests runner the user will be able to run the code from his c# testing class. Because it uses a proxy server you can record your browsing actions using any browser you like IE, Firefox Opera etc. Also becaues the actual test is a C# class you can modify it. The class has functions for handling the query/post params which you can use to easily add more or delete some of the existing ones and of course you'll have at your disposal all the.net classes so you can connect to a database open a file etc.

Description

fwptt is an open source Web application testing programme for load testing web applications. It can record normal and AJAX requests. It has been tested on ASP.Net applications, but it should work with JSP, PHP or other.

Grinder

The Grinder is a Java load testing framework that makes it easy to run a distributed test using many load injector machines. It is freely available under a BSD-style open-source license.

Key Features

- Generic Approach Load test anything that has a Java API. This includes common cases such as HTTP web servers, SOAP and REST web services, and application servers (CORBA, RMI, JMS, EJBs), as well as custom protocols.
- Flexible Scripting Tests are written in the powerful Jython scripting language.
- Distributed Framework A graphical console allows multiple load injectors to be monitored and controlled, and provides centralised script editing and distribution.
- Mature HTTP Support Automatic management of client connections and cookies. SSL. Proxy aware.

Description

The Grinder is a Java load-testing framework making it

easy to orchestrate the activities of a test script in many processes across many machines, using a graphical console application.

Hammerhead 2 - Web Testing Tool

Description

Hammerhead 2 is a stress testing tool designed to test out your web server and web site. It can initiate multiple connections from IP aliases and simulated numerous (256+) users at any given time. The rate at which Hammerhead 2 attempts to pound your site is fully configurable, there are numerous other options for trying to create problems with a web site.

Hammerora

Hammerora is an open source load generation tool for the Oracle Database, MySQL Database and HTML environments.

Description

Hammerora is a load generation tool for the Oracle Database and Web Applications. Hammerora includes pre-built schema creation and load tests based on the industry standard TPC-C and TPC-H benchmarks to deploy against the Oracle database with multiple users. Hammerora also converts and replays Oracle trace files and enables Web-tier testing to build bespoke load tests for your entire Oracle application environment.

HTTPERF

Httperf is a tool for measuring web server performance. It provides a flexible facility for generating various HTTP workloads and for measuring server performance. The focus of httperf is not on implementing one particular benchmark but on providing a robust, high-performance tool that facilitates the construction of both micro- and macro-level benchmarks.

The three distinguishing characteristics of httperf are its robustness, which includes the ability to generate and sustain server overload, support for the HTTP/1.1 and SSL protocols, and its extensibility to new workload generators and performance measurements.

Description

Httperf is a tool for measuring web server performance. It provides a flexible facility for generating various HTTP workloads and for measuring server performance.

The focus is not on implementing one particular benchmark but on providing a robust, high-performance tool that facilitates the construction of both micro and macro level benchmarks.

The three distinguishing characteristics of httperf are its robustness, which includes the ability to generate and sustain server overload, support for the HTTP/1.1 and SSL protocols, and its extensibility.

Http_load

http_load runs multiple http fetches in parallel, to test the throughput of a web server. However unlike most such test clients, it runs in a single process, so it doesn't bog down the client machine. It can be configured to do https fetches as well.

You give it a file containing a list of URLs that may be fetched, a flag specifying how to start connections (either by rate or by number of simulated users), and a flag specifying when to quit (either after a given number of fetches or a given elapsed time). There are also optional flags for checksums, throttling, random jitter, and progress reports.

Description

http_load runs multiple HTTP fetches in parallel, to test the throughput of a Web server. However, unlike most such test clients, it runs in a single process, to avoid bogging the client machine down. It can also be configured to do HTTPS fetches.

Requirement:
tbc
Download data:
No data feed available

IxoraRMS

IxoraRMS is a tool for gathering and visualizing monitoring data. It was developed in Java and has a Swing GUI. As part of my job I am involved in performance testing and I felt the need for a tool with the following characteristics:

- Quick to deploy
- Able to provide rich amounts of monitoring data
- Able to automatically update the customized data views when the topology changes
- Able to provide updates in almost real time
- And able to customise the following aspects by writing none or very little code:
  - Adding new monitoring agents
  - Data visualization
  - Adding complex reactions to trigger notifications and tuning/configuration advice

The project is open source, released under theApache License, Version 2.0 and is hosted on Google Code.

If you are a developer interested in this kind of work, I am looking for contributors willing to add or maintain monitoring agents. If you are an user and just want to share with others an interesting dashboard or data view that you designed,contact me to have it included in the project. I'm also looking for people willing to contribute tutorials.

Have a look at the screenshots and go through the documentationand tutorials to familiarize yourself with this tool. For a list of existing monitoring agents see this page in documentation.

Description

Monitoring tool with great visualization and customization capabilities. It's quick to install and suitable for use in performance labs.

JChav

Description

JChav is a way to see the change in performance of your web application over time, by running a benchmark test for each build you produce. JChav reads all the JMeter logs from each of your runs (one per build), and produces a set of charts for each test in each run.

Requirement:

JMeter

Download data:

No data feed available

JCrawler

JCrawler is an open-source (under the CPL) Stress-Testing Tool for web-applications. It comes with the crawling/ exploratory feature. You can give JCrawler a set of starting URLs and it will begin crawling from that point onwards, going through any URLs it can find on its way and generating load on the web application. The load parameters (hits/sec) are configurable.

Why

But, wait a second! Aren't there already a whole bunch of tools like that? Why would anybody write a new one? You could bet there are a number of such programs in the open-source and definitely have to be some kick-ass commercial ones.

Well, that's what we thought, too. Frankly, we had no desire to write a load-tester tool. We are writing a web-portal system (http://www.digijava.org) not load-testing tools. But then we had a problem with one of our portlets that would only occur on the production server, during a high load, and none of the existing tools we tried was able to recreate it. Log-replay tools were not much help either, because the problem would occur in several hours and we needed some tool to really stress the application so it would crash in more reasonable (i.e. less) time.

We spent a lot of time trying not to "reinvent the wheel" and find an existing wheel that would help us. There was none. We tried both OSS and commercial tools. None of them gave us the kind of result we needed. So we ended up with the JCrawler.

JCrawler was irreplaceable in helping us to identify and solve the problem we had. We have released it in under an open source license because we hope it may help somebody else, too and that somebody will not have to go through what we have gone. Also, it may be a good chance for the JCrawler itself to get enhancements. We are very open to the suggestions and especially - help:) We continue to use JCrawler for testing our applications and would not mind, of course, it to get as good as it can.

How

What features were missing in some of the similar tools, and what is the bundle that was in none of them together? Why did not any of them work for us?

Crawling - A lot of load-test tools allow you to indicate a set of URLs and they would just hit these URLs repeatedly. For a complex web-application it may not make much sense. There are too many URLs, for testing any limited number of them to give much confidence. You may hope that indicating "typical" ones may help, but if you use caching and stuff - the one "typical" URL will soon be cached, whereas in the real life hitting 10 different ones like that would have a surprisingly different effect.

"Human" pattern - Most of the existing tools allow you to indicate how many threads they start up for load-testing. This isn't always an accurate way to replicate real load. People measure performance in the terms of the number of hits per second on a website, not some geeky "number of threads". Having 200 threads hit your site does not mean that you are generating 200 hits/second.

The load tester tool may be generating just 2 hits per second with that setting, if your application pages are slow. Threads have to wait for the pages to load and not all pages load in 1/200th of a second, for example. We wish they did, of course but that wish is often far from the reality.

JCrawler follows hits-per-second pattern, guaranteeing indicated load and will fire-up as many threads, as needed to keep the load constant.

Http Redirects and Cookies - Some of the tools were not able to properly handle it. These can leave your application's authentication completely untested and give you another set of surprises in the production. This is especially true if you are using a single-sign-on system of some kind, which usually employs transparent HTTP Redirects.

OSS and tested - JCrawler is open-source and comes with thorough unit-tests. So, one has reasonable confidence that it is not buggy itself, as well as the ability to fix, customise, or enhance it. Some tools we tried (especially, proprietary ones, of course) - we could not even understand how exactly they worked and it was not clear if they were doing what the documentation claimed they would.

What are the features that may not be critical but we like having in the JCrawler?

Console mode - All these graphs and pie-charts look cool and can help for a presentation to the management but when you have a real problem to solve they are not the ones that matter. JCrawler is easy to run remotely and monitor, using little bandwidth. It can be very useful if your testing point is secured i.e. if you can access your testing environment only from a limited network, hence your test tool has to be in that network, too and the only access you get is SSH.

Also, GUI-based applications have this tendency of hanging up on you when application gets real busy, which can quickly become quite annoying. And a load-tester is definitely one very busy application.

Easy to configure - "Easy to configure - The entire configuration happens in a central XML file. You can keep different XML files in a handy place and have several configurations ready to go, whenever you need them. It may be just us, but we find using a neat XML file more convenient then jumping from one tab to another of an overloaded GUI configuration. (Also, by using an XML formatted file from the start, it will be easier to create a GUI configuration tool if others don't agree with us on the convenience of this.)

Platform independent - JCrawler is a tool for the developers and QAs. In our team, we found that people prefer different operating systems so having tool that runs on any of them was nice.

Description

Stress-Testing Tool for web-applications. It comes with the crawling/exploratory feature. You can give JCrawler a set of starting URLs and it will begin crawling from that point onwards, going through any URLs it can find on its way and generating load on the web application. The load parameters (hits/sec) are configurable.

Lobo, Continuous Tuning

Lobo is a performance monitoring tool. It is designed to track how the performance of your systems evolve. It is specially useful if you are using agile development since your code and architecture evolve; if you don't constantly track your performance you might get a few surprises in the end.

Benefits

What JUnit does to code accuracy, Lobo does to the code performance. With your continuous integration turned on and a good performance profiling suit, you'll be able to exactly pin-point the modifications that lead to a good or bad performance scenario. It increases the performance visibility so you have more information to make the right decision.

Description

Lobo is a tool for performance testing and monitoring that allows you to monitor the evolution of performance along the time-line of the project. It was specially designed to be used in agile-iterative and evolutionary approaches.

MessAdmin

MessAdmin is a light-weight and non-intrusive tool for

monitoring and interacting with Java. MessAdmin can be added to any J2EE application, with zero change to the monitored application.

With MessAdmin, you can:

- Display statistics about any Web Application
- Monitor all active HttpSessions (including their size)
- Interact with and see detailed information about any session
- Send html messages to any users

MessAdmin can be added to any J2EE application. And apart from a very minor change to your web.xml, you don't need to change anything at all in your web application! That's right, no coding, no application change!

Administration is done either with a built-in servlet, and/ or via JMX. MessAdmin brings you a lot of benefits, whether you are an IT manager, a system administrator or developer.

Description

MessAdmin is a light-weight and non-intrusive notification system and HttpSession administration for J2EE Web Applications, giving detailed statistics and informations on the application. It installs as a plug-in to any Java EE WebApp, and requires zero-code modification.

NTime

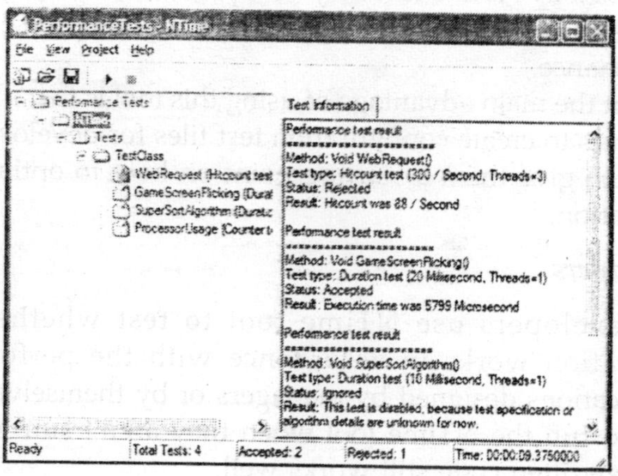

The NTime tool is very similar to NUnit tool - another unit testing tool, so the users of NUnit will find an almost similar GUI and functionality.

This is the first release of the tool that performs repeatable tasks to help managers, architects, developers and testers test an application against its performance. This version may not be very consistent and it may report errors under different situations. However, the tool was tested under many situations.

Tool Usage

This chapter provides information for the application management team that wishes to use NTime tool to keep applications working at the desired performance level.

Managers

Programme managers are welcome to specify application performance boundaries at the beginning of the application development process. They may also note which modules and functions of the application need to work and at which time frames. The performance specifications written by them may be helpful for developers when designing the application performance. Further, the NTime tool tests their performance specifications against real, developed applications. The tests performed by NTime tool may be reproduced at different time periods to see whether the application is giving the expected performance.

But the main advantage of using this tool is that it enables managers to create configuration test files for developers and testers to give them a starting point on how to optimize the application.

Developers

Developers use NTime tool to test whether their application works in accordance with the performance specifications designed by managers or by themselves. They need to run the NTime tool when they aren't sure whether their rewritten code still works well.

The NTime tool can also be made to remain open on the desktop even when the programmers develop, compile or debug their applications - every application that is built will be reloaded in NTime automatically and shown with the updated tests.

Testers

Testers are actively in the performance test stage. They run repeatable tests after every application's alpha release. Testers will review hundreds or thousands of tests and register them to the bug tracing applications.

Simultaneous Compile and Test Time

NTime tool may still be running even when the compilation process of the application that we want to test is going on. After the application has been built, NTime will reflect all the changes, you just need to run the tests and wait for the performance test results whether they are accepted or rejected.

Test Timings

Actually, NTime's timings are based on high frequency timers that rely on different onboard chipsets' architecture. This difference generates more or less precision in the performed tests. The disadvantages, while profiling the tests, include system processes and CPU load.

Even after closing the heavy loaded applications, there may be other bad things that can occur - like, NTime needs some CPU and threads to perform complex tests and therefore you can indicate about 10 microseconds overhead, so if you want to test high frequency running functions, then you need to write inside of the test code a "for" loop statement i.e. 100 loops, and then test the result for the specified time multiplied by 100.

SDK Documentation

NTime tool is supported by two documentation files. The NTime Framework SDK will be your starting point to test your applications against performance tests by adding.NET attributes into your code.

NTime framework SDK

NTime Framework SDK is the often used SDK documentation. This help file shows you the available.NET attributes that you can use in your testing applications. Many attributes are similar to that of NUnit attributes, so if you've used NUnit tool before, then working with NTime will be quite easy.

NTime GUI SDK

After the installation of NTime, you will find the NTime source documentation. This will help you to add some functionality to NTime, but remember every change that you make to this tool is only for your private and non-commercial use. Read*License.rtf* file for further information about NTime licensing.

Further Development

This NTime version is a GUI only application. In future, I plan to develop a console application to provide batch script usability. For further improvements, you may send comments to with your suggestions to help me make the application work better.

Bugs found in this release will be fixed in the next version, so the earlier found errors will be corrected as soon as possible. The source code of NTime will be soon available on the sourceforge.net website, so you can track the latest versions.

Using the Code

Below, you can see a sample code which uses all the attributes available with NTime framework. See the NTime framework SDK documentation for more information:

Collapse:

```
using System;
using NTime.Framework;
```

```
namespace NTime.Tests
{
    ///<SUMMARY>
    ///This is a tested class.
    ///</SUMMARY>
    [TimerFixture]
    public class TestClass
{
    [TimerFixtureSetUp]
    public void GlobalSetUp()
    {
      //initialize one-time initialization
      data in
      //this testfixture.
    }
    [TimerFixtureTearDown]
    public void GlobalTearDown()
    {
      //release one-time initialized data in
      //this testfixture.
    }
    [TimerSetUp]
    public void LocalSetUp()
    {
      //initialize data for every test found
      //in this testfixture class
    }
    [TimerTearDown]
    public void LocalTearDown()
    {
      //release data for every finished test
      //found in this testfixture class
    }
    [TimerHitCountTest(300, Threads = 3,
      Unit = TimePeriod.Second)]
    public void WebRequest()
    {
    //invoke some code from real application
```

```
    //to test its functions against specified
    //performance.
    //in example we will keep our fictional
    //web server's response at 10 milliseconds
    if(System.Threading.Thread.Current
Thread.Name == "NTimeThread_0")
    System.Threading.Thread.Sleep(5);
    else if (System.Threading. Thread.Current
Thread. Name == NTimeThread_1")
    System.Threading.Thread.Sleep(8);
else
    System.Threading.Thread.Sleep(10);
}
[TimerDurationTest(20, Unit = TimePeriod.
Millisecond)]public void GameScreenFlicking()
{
    //we want to calc game AI, 3d engine and
    //other stuff to keep it running at 50Hz
    //vertical screen sync.
    System.Threading.Thread.Sleep(5);
    }
    [TimerDurationTest(10, Unit =
       TimePeriod.Millisecond)]
       [TimerIgnore("This test is disabled.")]
    public void SuperSortAlgorithm()
    {
       //code here will not be profiled until
           TimerIgnore
       //flag was removed.
    }

    [TimerCounterTest("Process", "% Processor
    Time",
       Threads = 1, InstanceName = "NTimeGUI",
       MinimumValue = 0, MaximumValue = 50)]
    public void ProcessorUsage()
    {
       //we want to see whether our application
```

```
            is
            //optimized to work with minimal CPU
            usage.
            for(int i = 0; i < 150; i++)
            {
        System.Threading.Thread.Sleep(30);
            }
        }
    }
}
```

OpenSTA

OpenSTA is a distributed software testing architecture designed around CORBA, it was originally developed to be commercial software by CYRANO. The current toolset has the capability of performing scripted HTTP and HTTPS heavy load tests with performance measurements from Win32 platforms. However, the architectural design means it could be capable of much more.

The applications that make up the current OpenSTA toolset were designed to be used by performance testing consultants or other technically proficient individuals. This means testing is performed using the record and replay metaphor common in most other similar commercially available toolsets.

Recordings are made in the tester's own browser producing simple scripts that can be edited and controlled with a special high level scripting language. These scripted sessions can then be played back to simulate many users by a high performance load generation engine. Using this methodology a user can generate realistic heavy loads simulating the activity of hundreds to thousands of virtual users.

Results and statistics are collected during test runs by a variety of automatic and user controlled mechanisms. These can include scripted timers, SNMP data, Windows Performance Monitor stats and HTTP results & timings. Much of the data logged can be monitored live during the test runs;

once test runs are complete, logs can be viewed, graphed, filtered and exported for use by more sophisticated report generation software.

The OpenSTA toolset is Open Source software licensed under the GNU GPL (General Public License), this means it is free and will always remain free. If you wish to build your own customized version of OpenSTA or take part in its development then the complete toolset source code, buildable in Microsoft Visual Studio 6, and all related information is available fromOpenSTA.SourceForge.net, the developer home site.

Much more information can be found out about OpenSTA by checking the online documentation or simply downloading and installing the toolset. TheFAQ contains lots of other useful background information and helpful tips, this should be the first place you look if you need help with anything not covered in the documentation. There is no need to stop at reading the FAQ either, it is hosted on theOpenSTA Community Portal and, in common with every other resource on this site, it is user editable.

This site is a great place for every OpenSTA user to share their experiences with the product and help others learn and use OpenSTA: Remember, the toolset is completely free and any time the developers spend helping users is time they are not enhancing, or fixing problems with, the toolset. By helping other users you are in fact helping OpenSTA and its community become stronger.

The premier place for free OpenSTA support and discussions is the OpenSTA Users Mailing List, here the developers and many long time users of this toolset give as much help as their freetime will allow.

Description

A distributed software testing architecture based on CORBA. Using OpenSTA (Open System Testing Architecture) a user can generate realistic heavy loads simulating the activity of hundreds to thousands of virtual users. OpenSTA graphs both virtual user response times and resource utilization information from all Web Servers, Application Servers, Database Servers and Operating Platforms under test, so that precise performance measurements can be gathered during load tests and analysis on these measurements can be performed.

Open Web Load

Open Web Load is a tool for load testing web applications. It aims to be easy to use and providing near real-time performance measurements of the application under test. This is particulary useful when you are doing optimization as you can see the impact of your changes almost immediately.

Open Web Load is (currently) a commandline tool, that you execute from a prompt like this:

```
openload [options] http://testapp.site.com 10
```

The 2 parameters are:

- The url of the web page you want to test.
- Number of simultanous clients to simulate. This is optional and defaults to 5.
- A number of options is also available. You will then get output similar to this:

```
$ openload localhost 10
URL: http://localhost:80/
Clients: 10
MaTps 355.11, Tps 355.11, Resp Time 0.015,
Err 0%, Count 511
MaTps 339.50, Tps 199.00, Resp Time 0.051,
Err 0%, Count 711
MaTps 343.72, Tps 381.68, Resp Time 0.032,
Err 0%, Count 1111
MaTps 382.04, Tps 727.00, Resp Time 0.020,
Err 0%, Count 1838
MaTps 398.54, Tps 547.00, Resp Time 0.018,
Err 0%, Count 2385
MaTps 425.78, Tps 670.90, Resp Time 0.014,
Err 0%, Count 3072
Total TPS: 452.90
```

```
Avg. Response time: 0.021 sec.
Max Response time: 0.769 sec
```

Where:

- *MaTps*: a 20 second moving average of TPS.
- *Tps*: (Transactions Per Second) is the number of completed requests during that second.
- *Resp Time*: the average response time in seconds for the elapsed second.
- *Err*: the percentage of responses that was erronous, i.e. didn't return a HTTP 200 Ok staus.
- *Count*: The total number of completed requests.
- Total TPS is the average TPS for the whole run, i.e. (Total completed requests)/(Total elapsed time).
- *Avg*: Response time: the overall average response time in seconds.
- *Max Response time*: The highest response time during this run.

Description

OpenWebLoad is a tool for load testing web applications. It aims to be easy to use and providing near real-time performance measurements of the application under test.

Raw Load Tester

The RawLoadTester application is a free Open Source tool to load test websites. It does not have many features but it is useful in situations where using a more comprehensive load testing solution (e.g., Apache Flood) is not practical.

The application calls the URL you select as many times as you choose and tells you how long it took the server to respond.

It writes some additional runtime details to the PHP log file so you can optionally do more granular analysis afterwards. Although the server processes most of the statistics, all URL requests come from the browser.

You can run as many browsers and workstations simultaneously as you want. It is possible that non-programers can install and use this application (e.g., junior testers); but, these instructions and the programme itself assume the installer and user are familiar with their webserver configuration.

Description

This application calls the URL you select as many times as you choose and tells you how long it took the server to respond. It writes some additional runtime details to the PHP log file so you can optionally do more granular analysis afterwards.

Although the server processes most of the statistics, all URL requests come from the browser. You can run as many browsers and workstations simultaneously as you want.

Seagull

Seagull is a free, Open Source (GPL) multi-protocol traffic generator test tool. Primarily aimed at IMS (3GPP, TISPAN, CableLabs) protocols (and thus being the perfect complement to SIPp for IMS testing), Seagull is a powerful traffic generator for functional, load, endurance, stress and performance/ benchmark tests for almost any kind of protocol.

In addition, its openness allows to add the support of a brand new protocol in less than 2 hours - with no programming knowledge.

For that, Seagull comes with several protocol families embedded in the source code:

- Binary/TLV (Diameter, Radius and many 3GPP and IETF protocols)
- External library (TCAP, SCTP)
- Text (XCAP, HTTP, H248 ASCII)

Description

Seagull is a multi-protocol traffic generator test tool. Primary aimed at IMS protocols, Seagull is a powerful traffic generator for functional, load, endurance, stress and performance tests for almost any kind of protocol. Currently supports Diameter, XCAP over HTTP, TCAP (GSM Camel, MAP, Win) protocols.

Siege

SIEGE is an http load tester and benchmarking utility. It was designed to let web developers measure the performance of their code under duress, to see how it will stand up to load on the internet. It lets the user hit a web server with a configurable number of concurrent simulated users. Those users place the server "under siege."

Description

SIEGE is an http regression testing and benchmarking utility. It was designed to let web developers measure the performance of their code under duress, to see how it will stand up to load on the internet. It lets the user hit a webserver with a configurable number of concurrent simulated users. Those users place the webserver "under siege." SCOUT surveys a webserver and prepares the urls.txt file for a siege. In order to perform regression testing, siege loads URLs from a file and runs through them sequentially or randomly. Scout makes the process of populating that file easier. You should send out the scout, before you lay siege.

Sipp

SIPp is a free Open Source test tool/traffic generator for the SIP protocol. It includes a few basic SipStone user agent scenarios (UAC and UAS) and establishes and releases multiple calls with the INVITE and BYE methods. It can also readscustom XML scenario files describing from very simple to complex call flows.

It features the dynamic display of statistics about running tests (call rate, round trip delay, and message statistics), periodic CSV statistics dumps, TCP and UDP over multiple sockets or multiplexed with retransmission management and dynamically adjustable call rates.

Other advanced features include support of IPv6, TLS, SIP authentication, conditional scenarios, UDP retransmissions, error robustness (call timeout, protocol defence), call specific variable, Posix regular expression to extract and re-inject any protocol fields, custom actions (log, system command exec, call stop) on message receive, field injection from external CSVfile to emulate live users.

SIPp can also send media (RTP) traffic through RTP echo and RTP/pcap replay. Media can be audio or audio+video.While optimized for traffic, stress and performance testing, SIPp can be used to run one single call and exit, providing apassed/failed verdict. Last, but not least, SIPp has a comprehensive documentation available both in HTML and PDF format.

SIPp can be used to test many real SIP equipements like SIP proxies, B2BUAs, SIP media servers, SIP/x gateways, SIP PBX,... It is also very useful to emulate thousands of user agents calling your SIP system.

Here is a screenshot:

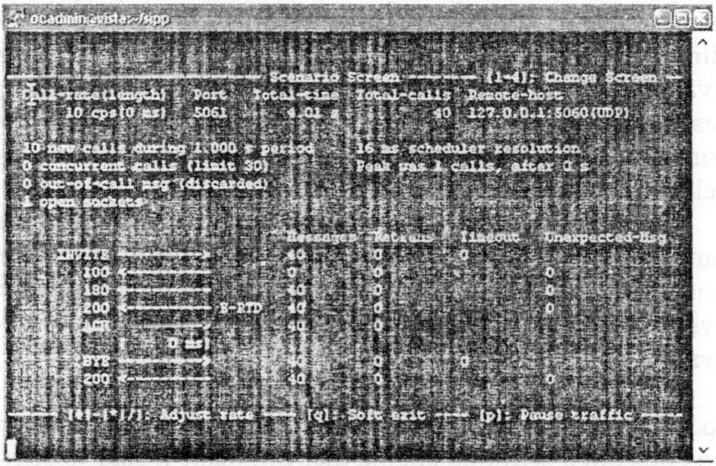

Description

SIPp is a performance testing tool for the SIP protocol. Its main features are basic SIPStone scenarios, TCP/UDP transport, customizable (xml based) scenarios, dynamic adjustement of call-rate and a comprehensive set of real-time statistics. It can also generate media (RTP) traffic for audio and video calls.

Requirement:

Linux/Unix/Win32-Cygwin

Download data:

Downloadable files: 216173 total downloads to date

SLAMD

The SLAMD Distributed Load Generation Engine (SLAMD) is a Java-based application designed for stress testing and performance analysis of network-based applications. Initial development of SLAMD was performed at Sun Microsystems, with recent development sponsored primarily by UnboundID Corp..

SLAMD is available under the terms of the Sun Public License, which is an OSI-approved open source license. The main site for obtaining information about SLAMD.

SLAMD was originally developed for the purpose of benchmarking and analyzing the performance of LDAP directory servers, and it is the most powerful and flexible tool available for this task. However, it is also well-suited for testing other kinds of network applications and has been used for things like Web servers and Web-based applications, relational databases, and mail servers.

It can also be used for non-network based applications (and in fact, it is used for comparing things like CPU power and memory latency across a number of different kinds of systems), although its distributed nature makes it ideal for systems that can be accessed remotely.

SLAMD provides a Java-based API to make it possible to quickly develop custom workloads, and it also contains an embedded scripting engine that can make it easy to stress applications using protocols like LDAP, HTTP, SMTP, IMAP, and POP, or any database that can be accessed via JDBC. It also includes tools for recording and playing back TCP traffic, and a utility for intercepting LDAP communication and writing it as a script that may be executed in the SLAMD scripting engine.

Description

SLAMD Distributed Load Generation Engine is a Java-based application designed for stress testing and performance analysis of network-based applications.

Requirement:

Any system with Java 1.4 or higher

Download data:

No data feed available

Soap-Stone

Soap-Stone is the network benchmark application which can answer these questions for you by putting your network under load and conducting automatic benchmark and recording activities.

Description

Network benchmark application which can put your network under load and conduct automatic benchmark and recording activities.

Requirement:

OS Independent

Download data:

Downloadable files: 7399 total downloads to date

Stress–driver

Description

General-purpose stress test tool.

Requirement:

Windows NT/2000, Linux

Download data:

Downloadable files: 7847 total downloads to date

TestMaker

Description

TestMaker from PushToTest.com delivers a rich environment for building and running intelligent test agents that test Web-enabled applications for scalability, functionality, and performance. It comes with a friendly graphical user environment, an object-oriented scripting language (Jython) to build intelligent test agents, an extensible library of protocol handlers (HTTP, HTTPS, SOAP, XML-RPC, SMTP, POP3, IMAP), a new agent wizard featuring an Agent Recorder to write scripts for you, a library of fully-functional sample test agents, and shell scripts to run test agents from the command line and from unit test utilities.

TPTEST

The purpose with TPTEST is to allow users to measure the speed of their Internet connection in a simple way. TPTEST measures the throughput speed to and from various reference servers on the Internet. The use of TPTEST may help increase the consumer/end user knowledge of how Internet services work.

TPTEST was originally developed by the Swedish ICT-commission, then later by the Foundation for Internet Infrastructure (iis.se), the Swedish Consumer Agency (konsumentverket.se), and the Swedish National Post- and Telecom Agency (pts.se).

The latest development has been to separate the platform-independent test method software (the test engine) from the platform-dependent user interface software in order to make it easier for anyone to write a test client or server that uses the TPTEST testing method.

The test engine code is to be regarded as a library module and is released under the LGPL license while the reference client/server applications is released under the GPL license.

TPTEST 3.0 does the following:

- Measures TCP throughput, incoming and outgoing
- Measures UDP throughput, incoming and outgoing
- Measures UDP packet loss, incoming and outgoing
- Measures UDP roundtrip times
- Measures UDP out-of-order packet reception

For a UDP test you can select test time, the number of packets to be transferred, and the packet size. For a TCP test you can only select the number of bytes to be transferred.

The Win32 and MacOS reference client applications include "auto" test modes that try to determine the performance of your particular Internet connection. The results are a good guesstimate for the not-so-technical user who wishes to see if s/he gets what s/he is paying for but for really accurate results you need to know what you're doing and do it manually.

The auto modes determine TCP throughput by sending increasingly large amounts of data over the connection until the reception time is long enough (currently ten seconds) that the programme judges the result to be fairly accurate. UDP throughput is determined by performing repeated 5-second tests with higher and higher data rates until the calculated reception speed doesn't increase anymore.

UDP throughput is usually significantly higher than TCP throughput, due to the TCP algorithm backing off when it encounters a congestion, thus "making way" for UDP transmissions.

Description

The purpose with TPTEST is to allow users to measure the speed of their Internet connection in a simple way. TPTEST measures the throughput speed to and from various reference servers on the Internet. The use of TPTEST may help increase the consumer/end user knowledge of how Internet services work.

Tsung

The purpose of Tsung is to simulate users in order to test the scalability and performance of IP based client/server applications. You can use it to do load and stress testing of your servers. Many protocols have been implemented and tested, and it can be easily extended. WebDAV, LDAP and MySQL support have been added recently (experimental).

Description

Tsung is a distributed load testing tool. It is protocol-independent and can currently be used to stress HTTP, SOAP and Jabber servers (SSL is supported). It simulates complex user's behaviour using an XML description file, reports many measurements in real time (including response times, CPU and memory usage from servers, customized transactions, etc.).

HTML reports (with graphics) can be generated during the load. For HTTP, it supports 1.0 and 1.1, has a proxy mode to record sessions, supports GET and POST methods, Cookies, and Basic WWW-authentication. It has already been used to simulate thousands of virtual users.

Valgrind

Valgrind is an award-winning instrumentation framework for building dynamic analysis tools. There are Valgrind tools that can automatically detect many memory management and threading bugs, and profile your programs in detail. You can also use Valgrind to build new tools.

The Valgrind distribution currently includes six production quality tools: a memory error detector, two thread error detectors, a cache and branch-prediction profiler, a call-graph generating cache profiler, and a heap profiler. It also includes two experimental tools: a heap/stack/global array overrun detector, and a SimPoint basic block vector generator. It runs on the following platforms: X86/Linux, AMD64/Linux, PPC32/Linux, PPC64/Linux, and X86/Darwin (Mac OS X).

Description

Valgrind is an award-winning suite of tools for debugging and profiling Linux programs. With the tools that come with Valgrind, you can automatically detect many memory management and threading bugs, avoiding hours of frustrating bug-hunting, making your programs more stable. You can also perform detailed profiling, to speed up and reduce memory use of your programs.

Web Application Load Simulator

Description

LoadSim is a web application load simulator. It allows you to create simulations and have those simulations run against your webserver.

Web Polygraph

Web Polygraph is a freely available performance testing tool for caching proxies, origin server accelerators, L4/7 switches, content filters, and other Web intermediaries. Polygraph's features include:

- High-performance HTTP clients and servers
- Realistic HTTP and SSL traffic generation
- HTTP Basic, NTLM, and Negotiate proxy authentication
- LDAP-friendly generation of user credentials
- Flexible content simulation
- Ready-to-use standard workloads for benchmarking
- Powerful domain-specific configuration language
- Portable open-source implementation
- Friendly commercial support

Description

Benchmarking tool for caching proxies, origin server accelerators, L4/7 switches, content filters, and other Web intermediaries.

WebLOAD

The WebLOAD Open Source Load Generation Engine is an open source project sponsored by RadView Software. This project is based on fourteen years of code development invested in WebLOAD Professional, the award winning performance testing solution. This project is intended for ISVs, SIs and software developers who need to integrate a professional load generation engine into their applications.

Description

WebLOAD Open Source is a fully functional, commercial-grade performance testing product based on WebLOAD, Radview's flagship product that is already deployed at 1,600 sites.

Available for free download and use, WebLOAD is a commercial-grade open source project with more than 250 engineering years of product development. Companies that require commercial support, additional productivity features and compatibility with third-party protocols have the option of purchasing WebLOAD Professional directly from RadView.

Requirement:

Windows NT/2000/XP

Download data:

Downloadable files: 115981 total downloads to date

Chapter 10

Top - Down and Bottom - up Testing Strategies

TEST STRATEGIES

Defining a test strategy helps you focus test resources on the right portions of code at the right time.

When developing medium to large applications, the first question that comes up is "Where do I start?", and then "What next?". Guidance is provided in the form of metrics that help you analyse the complexity and reliability of the methods, classes, and components-under-test (CUT) and decide your strategy.

Component testing, as opposed to functional testing, concentrates on individual software components: classes or methods as well as Enterprise JavaBeans (EJB) and Web service components. The point of component testing is to isolate each component in order to ensure that it functions properly.

If necessary, you can use stubs to replace other components, thus conditioning the test results only to the behaviour of the component-under-test. Once a reliable test suite has been created, you can rerun it on a regular basis to ensure non-regression of the CUT.

You can concentrate your component tests on the following areas:

- Multiple classes or methods integrated as a subsystem.
- A single class

- A single method
- A single Java interface, abstract class, or superclass
- EJBs
- Web services

SUBSYSTEM-LEVEL TESTING

The scope of subsystem-level testing (also called integration testing) is to test a set of integrated classes that must cooperate to provide some service. In a multi-tier environment, a subsystem might be one of the tiers. The focus of subsystem-level testing is to verify the interfaces between the component-under-test and other subsystems. These tests exercise the interactions between the different objects of the subsystem.

Although subsystem-level testing should play a significant role in your overall test effort, be sure to supplement subsystem-level testing with method-level and class-level testing. Focusing only on subsystem-level testing would provide superficial test coverage because it does not give you enough control over the individual classes.

TOP-DOWN TESTING

Top-down testing starts at the top of the programme hierarchy and travels down its branches. This can be done in either from the shortest path down to the deepest level, or across the hierarchy, before proceeding to the next level.

The main advantage of this type of testing is that the global architecture of the subsystem can be seen and tested early. The main disadvantage is the need to use stubs until the lower-level components are written, which may not necessarily provide reliable test results for the top-level components.

BOTTOM-UP TESTING

Bottom-up testing typically starts by testing the lowest-level components first on an individual basis and then in clusters. This ensures that each component is fully tested before it is used by its calling component. This method has the advantage of detecting errors in critical components earlier in the development process. The main disadvantage is that most or many components must be built before a working programme can be presented. Object-oriented languages lend themselves well to bottom-up testing.

A third option is to closely follow the design strategy. This means that each component is tested as it is built. Test definition is part of the design of the component. As part of this strategy, you can take either a top-down or bottom-up approach.

CLASS-LEVEL TESTING

Class-level testing exercises the interactions between the methods in a class or a small cluster of classes. The focus is to verify that the class supports all of the use cases required by its consumers and is robust enough to handle unexpected sequences of methods. For the following reasons, class-level testing is generally considered the most effective way to test object-oriented software:

- Testing at the class level is extremely effective in terms of code coverage. With just a few tests, you can reach 60% to 70% code coverage.
- Class-level testing reflects the services that the class provides to its consumers. The tests are easy to write and can be used as documentation for the class.
- Class-level testing is the optimal level of testing for finding bugs early in the design process.

METHOD-LEVEL TESTING

Method-level testing exercises the different conditions defined in the method code in isolation from any other methods. The focus is generally on ensuring that the method correctly processes all of its possible inputs.

In many cases, testing a series of methods in isolation provides incomplete test coverage, and some methods, such as private methods, cannot be tested in isolation. (Private methods can have a major impact on the state of an object and can change the behaviour of other method invocations.)

Interactions between the methods of a class are a common source of problems, and the best way to discover these problems is to exercise the methods in various scenarios.

Therefore, you should always combine method-level testing with class or subsystem-level testing, or both. In some cases, such as testing stateless classes, you can focus exclusively on method-level testing, but in other cases you might decide to avoid method-level testing and focus only on class-level testing.

The key to successful method-level testing is determining which methods to actually test. The following table provides answers to some frequently asked questions about method-level testing:

Question	Answer
What if the method is inherited from a superclass?	If the method is inherited from a superclass and has already been tested as part of the superclass, you do not need to do method-level testing of this method in the context of the inherited object. You should still use this method in the context of class-level testing of the inherited object.
What if the method overrides the method of a parent class?	If the method has been tested in the context of a parent class,you need to retest the overriding method.
What if the method is overloaded or overridden?	A method is overloaded when multiple methods in the same class have the same name but different parameters. A method is overridden when it is declared in a class and it's implementation is defined or altered in a subclass. Overridden methods allow an object type to be polymorphic in nature. In either case, be sure to

test each implementation of these class methods individually.

INTERFACE, ABSTRACT CLAS, AND SUPER CLASS TESTING

You can use abstract tests to test Java interfaces, abstract classes, and super classes. Although abstract classes cannot actually be run on their own, you can apply an abstract test to any class that implements an interface, realizes an abstract class, or inherits from a superclass.

EJB TESTING

Testing an Enterprise Java Bean (EJB) generally consists of verifying the EJB's business logic and the success or failure of its lifecycle methods. This is done by testing the methods defined in the bean class by calling the methods through their various interfaces. Tests can reside in the same container as the EJB or outside the application server.

The best way to test an EJB is to deploy it on an application server and run it in the context of its container. If the EJB has a local interface, you must test it from within the same application server, for example, using another EJB. If the EJB has a remote interface, you can test it with a Java client running outside the application server (at the expense of increased network traffic). Either way, you will need to stub out components called by the EJB-under-test so that you can isolate the behaviour of the EJB.

You can test both stateful and stateless session beans and entity beans with either container-managed or bean-managed persistence (CMP or BMP). To be tested, all beans must have either a remote or a local interface. Testing of message-driven beans is not currently supported.

WEB SERVICE TESTING

When testing distributed components such as Web services, the approach is basically the same as for testing any other component. The best approach is to submit a series of requests to the server and to verify that server responses match the expected return values. The Web service interface, as described in a Web service description document (WSDL), is a required input to automatically generate a component test for a Web service.

TOP-DOWN AND BOTTOM-UP STRATEGIES

Small and large scale studies ranging from "voluntary" to "mandatory" top-down strategies have consistently demonstrated that local implementation fails in the vast majority of cases. The best known study of the "voluntary" type is the Rand Change Agent study conducted by Berman and McLaughlin and associates (1978).

They investigated federally sponsored educational programs adopted in 293 sites. Berman and McLaughlin found that, even though adoption was voluntary, districts often took on change projects for 'opportunistic' rather than for substantial reasons.

Local school officials may view the adoption of a change agent project primarily as an opportunity to garner extra, short term resources. In this instance the availability of federal funds rather than the possibility of change in educational practice motivate project adoption.

Or, school managers may see change agent projects as a "low cost" way to cope with bureaucratic or political pressures. Innovation qua innovation often serves the purely bureaucratic objective of making the district appear up-to-date and progressive in the eyes of the community.

Or a change agent project may function to mollify political pressures from groups in the community to "do something" about their special interests. Whatever the particular motivation underlying opportunistic adoption there was an absence of serious educational concerns.

As dissatisfaction with failed implementation grew in the 1970s, states and districts turned more and more to mandatory solutions.

Corbett and Wilson's study of the impact of compulsory statewide testing in Maryland and Pennsylvania is a case in point. They found that new statements testing requirements caused action at the local level, but in ways that narrowed the curriculum and created conditions adverse to reforms: Coping with the pressure to attain satisfactory results in high-stakes tests caused educators to develop almost a "crisis mentality" in their approach, in that they jumped quickly into "solutions" to address a specific issue.

They narrowed the range of instructional strategies from which they selected means to instruct their students; they narrowed the content of the material they chose to present to students; and they narrowed the range of course offerings available to students.

Corbett and Wilson also identified other unintended consequences including the diversion of attention and energy from more basic reforms in the structure and practice of schools, and reduced teacher motivation, morale, and collegial interaction necessary to bring about reform.

They conclude: "when the modal response to statewide testing by professional educators is typified by practices that even the educators acknowledge are counterproductive to improving learning over the long term, then the issue is a 'policy making problem'" One a more sweeping scale, Sarason (1990) argues that billions of dollars have been spent on top-down reform with little to show for it. Sarason observes that such reform efforts do have an implicit theory of change:

Change can come about by proclaiming new policies, or by legislation, or by new performance standards, or by creating shape-up-ship-out ambience, or all of the preceding. It is a conception that in principle is similar to how you go about creating and improving an assembly line - that is, what it means to those who work on the assembly line is of secondary significance, if it has any significance at all. The workers (read: educational personnel) will change.

Political impatience and expediency are as understandable as motivators, as they are ineffectual as strategies for educational reform. Governments can't mandate what mattes, because what matters most is local motivation, skill, know-how and commitment. As Goodlad (1992) observes: "top-down, politically driven education reform movements are addressed primarily to restructuring. The have little to say about educating". In short, centralized reform mandates have a poor track record as instruments for educational improvement.

The failure of centralized reform has led some to conclude that only driven reform can succeed. Site-based management is the most prominent current manifestation of this emphasis. So far, howèver, the claim of superiority of grass-roots initiatives is primarily theoretical. In reviewing evidence on site-based management in The New Meaning of Educational Change, I concluded that restructuring reforms that devolved decision making to schools may have altered governance procedures but did not affect the teaching-learning core of schools The evidence continues to mount.

Taylor and Teddlie (1992) draw similar conclusions in their study of the extent of classroom change in "a district widely acclaimed as a model of restructuring". They examined classrooms in 33 schools (16 from pilot schools that had established school-based management [SBMI programs and 17 from non-pilot schools in the same district). Taylor and Teddlie did find that teachers in the pilot schools reported higher levels of participation in decision making, but they found no differences in teaching strategies used (teacher directed instruction, low student involvement in both sets of cases dominated).

Further, there was little evidence of teacher-teacher collaboration. Extensive collaboration was reported in only 2 of the 33 schools and both were from the low participation (non-pilot) schools. Taylor and Teddlie observe: "Teachers in this study did not alter their practice... increasing their participation in decision-making did not overcome norms of autonomy so that teachers would feel empowered to collaborate with their colleagues".

Other evidence from classroom observations failed to indicate changes in classroom environment and student learning activities. Despite considerable rhetoric and what the authors saw as "a genuine desire to professionalize teaching... the core mission of school seemed ancillary to the SBM project". Substantive changes in pedagogy (teaching strategies and assessment), and in the way teachers worked together on instructional matters, proved to be elusive.

These findings would not be as noteworthy, claim the authors, except for the fact that "the study occurred in a district recognized nationally as a leader in implementing restructuring reforms". Similarly, Hallinger, Murphy, and Hausman (1991) found that teachers and principals in their sample were highly in favour of restructuring but did not make connections "between new governance structures and the teaching-learning process".

Virtually identical findings arise in Weiss's investigation of shared decision making (SDM) in 12 high schools in 11 states (half were selected because they had implemented SDM; the other half were run in a traditional principal-led manner).

Weiss did find that teachers in SDM schools were more likely to mention decision about the decision-making process (e.e., composition of committees, procedures, and so on), but "schools with SDM did not pay more attention to issues of curriculum that traditionally managed schools, and pedagogical issues and student concerns were low on the list for both sets of schools".

Similar findings were obtained in the implementation of the Chicago Reform Act. In essence, this legislation shifted responsibility from the Central Board of Education to Local School Councils (LSCs) for each of the city's 540 public schools and mandated that each school develop School Improvement Plans (SIPs).

The LSCs by law consist of 11 or 12 members (six parents, two teachers, tow community representatives, the school principal - and, in the case of high schools, a student). Easton (1991) reports that the majority of elementary teachers said that "their instructional practices had not changed as a result of school reform and will not change as result of SIP".

In sum, decentralized initiatives, as far as the evidence is concerned, are not faring any better. Given the absence of any clear superiority of top-down or bottom-up strategies, two patterns, both ineffective, persist. One pattern resolves the dilemma through the false clarity of ideological preference. Many of those in positions of authority opt for centralized reform - "almost always egregiously indifferent to the role of obstacles", says Goodlad.

Advocates of decentralization, similarly (although from a different ideological perspective), push ahead with site-based management as an end in itself. The other pattern, of course, rests on ambivalence about which way to go, usually resulting in flip-flops or swings from top-down to bottom-up emphasis. Both strategies are often pursued simultaneously, but in a completely disconnected manner.

Rowley's case study of school district restructuring covering a 12-year period is instructive and I expect represents a familiar story. Sequoia Valley School District in California engaged in a major restructuring effort in the early 1980s following the appointment of a new superintendent in 1979. By 1985, the district had created a mission statement and a comprehensive strategic plan.

The superintendent and the board "adopted a philosophy of school-based management". Over time, however, the board became dissatisfied with the uneven development and fragmentation of effort. The superintendent and board began to establish a number of particular programs with external funds and consultants and small groups of teachers and administrators in such areas as "whole language", "early childhood centers", "cooperative learning", and so on and so on. Observes Rowley:

Confusion and heated debate inevitably resulted from the lack of clear definition and from the overload of new programs. Was restructuring going to be a centralized, programme-driven process in which schools would obligingly align with problems and solutions identified by Board members, the Superintendent, and district level committees?

Or, was restructuring going to remain a school-based process with the district office playing a supporting role? The answer was both. The philosophy of school-based management and strong site councils continued to be heartily espoused by the Superintendent and Board. But they also had committed significant resources to new programs and had installed programme specialists in key administrative roles throughout the district.

Thus, it became apparent that Sequoia Valley's leaders had inadvertently created oppositional dynamics for change and that during this middle stage the climate for restructuring had become more contentious than-collaborative.

The result, not uncommon, was the appointment in 1990 of a new superintendent known for advocacy of "tight school-based accountability and multiple methods of assessing student performance". Outcome-driven education became just the latest in the ebb and flow of district approaches.

Because of its imposition and seeming incompatibility with preferred instructional approaches in many schools, conflict increased sharply. Within a year, doubts were being expressed by the board about the new superintendent's leadership style and its adverse effect on the morale of teachers and administrators.

TEST DRIVER AND TEST STUBS

OVERVIEW

For a variety of different reasons (that we don't have the space to go into here), it is almost always a good idea to develop and test software in "pieces". At first glance this may seem impossible because it is hard to imagine how you can test one "piece" if the other "pieces" that it uses have not yet been developed (and *vice versa*).

The way around this condundrum is to use *stubs* and *drivers*. Though it is possible to define stubs and drivers at some length, that's not necessary for our purposes here. Instead, we will use the following definitions:

Stub: A piece of code that simulates the activity of missing components.

Driver: A piece of code that passes test cases to another piece of code.

AN EXAMPLE

We now consider an example in which we need to

develop a "calculator" that converts between different units (e.g., feet to inches). We start by "stubbing-out" the UnitConverter class.

This "stubbed-out" class contains comments that describe the class and all of the methods that we expect it to have (appropriately commented). All of the non-void methods return an appropriate default so that the class can be compiled.

Javaexamples/stubs/UnitConverter-01.java

```
/**
* Converts from one unit to another (e.g.,
  inches to feet)
*
* @author Prof. David Bernstein, James Madison
  University
* @version 0.1 (Stub)
*/
public class UnitConverter
{
/**
* Default Constructor
*/
  public UnitConverter()
{
}
/**
* Perform a conversion
*
* @param value The number to convert
* @param from The units for value (e.g.,
   "inches")
* @param to The units to convert to (e.g.,
  "feet")
* @return       The converted value
*/
  public double convert(double value, String
  from, String to)
```

```
{
   return 0.0;
}
/**
*  Get the multiplier needed for a conversion
*
*  @param from The units to convert from (e.g.,
   "inches")
*  @param to The units to convert to (e.g.,
   "feet")
*  @return What "from" needs to be multiplied
   by to get "to"
*/
   public double getMultiplier(String from,
   String to)
{
   return 0.0;
}
}
```

We next write a preliminary driver that can be used to perform preliminary tests of the UnitConverter class. In this version the method calls to theUnitConverter are all "hard-coded".

```
/**
*  A driver for testing the UnitConverter class
*
*  @author Prof. David Bernstein, James Madison
   University
*  @version 1.0
*/
   public class Driver
{
   /**
   * The entry point of the application
   *
   @param args The command-line arguments
   */
   public static void main(String[] args)
```

```
    {
        double     converted, original;
        String     from, to;
        UnitConverter calculator;
        calculator = new UnitConverter();
        from    = "inches";
        to    = "feet";
        original = 10.0;
        converted = calculator.convert(original,
        from, to);
        System.out.println(original+" "+from+" =
        "+converted+" "+to);
    }
    }
```

Note that these two classes can be compiled and executed.

The next version of the UnitConverter contains a complete implementation of theconvert method but still contains a stub of the getMultiplier method (which has been changed slightly to make it more useful). This enables us to test the convert method (using the driver) independently from the other methods.

```
/**
*   Converts from one unit to another (e.g.,
    inches to feet)
*
*   @author Prof. David Bernstein, James Madison
     University
*   @version 0.2 (Implemented convert)
*/
    public class UnitConverter
{
    /**
    *   Default Constructor
    */
    public UnitConverter()
    {
    }
```

```
/**
*   Perform a conversion
*
*   @param value The number to convert
*   @param from The units for value (e.g.,
    "inches")
*   @param to The units to convert to (e.g.,
    "feet")
*   @return The converted value
*/
public double convert(double value, String
from, String to)
{
doubleresult;
result = value * getMultiplier(from, to);
return result;
}
/**
*   Get the multiplier needed for a conversion
*
*   @param from The units to convert from
    (e.g., "inches")
*   @param to The units to convert to (e.g.,
    "feet")
*   @return What "from" needs to be multiplied
    by to get "to"
*/
public double getMultiplier(String from,
String to)
{
    return 1.0/12.0;
}
}
```

The next version of the UnitConverter contains an implementation (though not a very good one) of the getMultiplier method.

```
/**
*  Converts from one unit to another (e.g.,
```

```
inches to    feet)
*
*  @author Prof. David Bernstein, James Madison
   University
*  @version 1.0 (Implemented getMultiplier)
*/
   public class UnitConverter
{
   /**
   *   Default Constructor
   */
   public UnitConverter()
   {
   }
   /**
   *   Perform a conversion
   *
   *   @param value  The number to convert
   *   @param from   The units for value (e.g.,
                     "inches")
   *   @param to     The units to convert to
                     (e.g., "feet")
   * @return         The converted value
   */
   public double convert(double value, String
   from, String to)
   {
       double  result;
       result = value * getMultiplier(from, to);
       return  result;
   }
   /**
   *   Get the multiplier needed for a conversion
   *
   *   @param from   The units to convert from
                     (e.g., "inches")
   *   @param to     The units to convert to
                     (e.g., "feet")
```

```
*   @return  What "from" needs to be
             multiplied by to get "to"
*/
public double getMultiplier(String from,
String to)
{
    double multiplier;
    multiplier = 1.0;
    if (from.equals("inches")) {
    if (to.equals("feet")) multiplier = 1.0/
    12.0;
    else if (to.equals("yards")) multiplier =
    1.0/12.0/ 3.0;
    else if (to.equals("miles")) multiplier
    = 1.0/12.0/3.0/1760.0;
}   else if (from.equals("feet")) {
    if (to.equals("inches")) multiplier =
    12.0;
    else if (to.equals("yards")) multiplier
    = 1.0/3.0;
    else if (to.equals("miles")) multiplier
    = 1.0/3.0/1760.0;
}   else if (from.equals("yards")) {
    if (to.equals("inches")) multiplier =
    3.0*12.0;
    else if (to.equals("feet")) multiplier =
    3.0;
    else if (to.equals("miles")) multiplier
    = 1.0/1760.0;
}   else if (from.equals("miles")) {
    if (to.equals("inches")) multiplier =
    12.0*3.0*1760.0;
    else if (to.equals("yards")) multiplier
    = 1760.0;
    else if (to.equals("feet")) multiplier =
    3.0*1760.0;
}
return multiplier;
```

```
    }
}
```

To test this version of the UnitConverter we need to modify the driver so that it generates more test cases. In this case we use "white-box (or glass-box) testing" (i.e., we look at the UnitConverter class to identify important test cases) and write a driver that tests all supported inputs.

javaexamples/stubs/Driver-20.java

```
/**
 *  A driver for testing the UnitConverter
    class
 *
 *  @author Prof. David Bernstein, James
    Madison University
 *  @version 2.0
 */
public class Driver
{
/**
 *  The entry point of the application
 *
 *  @param args The command-line arguments
 */
public static void main(String[] args)
{
    double  converted, original;
    int     i, j;
    String  from, to;
    String[] units =
    {"inches","feet","yards","miles"};
    UnitConverter calculator;
    calculator = new UnitConverter();
    original = 10.0;
for (i=0; i < units.length; i++) {
    for (j=0; j < units.length; j++) {
       from = units[i];//This could be
       outside the inner loop
       to = units[j];
```

```
            converted = calculator.convert(original,
            from, to);
            System.out.println(original+" "+from+"
            = +converted+" "+to);
            }
        }
    }
}
```

It is always a good idea to develop and test software in "pieces". But, it may seem impossible because it is hard to imagine how you can test one "piece" if the other "pieces" that it uses have not yet been developed (and vice versa). To solve this kindof diffcult problems we use stubs and drivers.

In white-box testing, we must run the code with predetermined input and check to make sure that the code produces predetermined outputs. Often testers write stubs and drivers for white-box testing.

TEST DRIVER

Driver is a the piece of code that passes test cases to another piece of code. Test Harness or a test driver is supporting code and data used to provide an environment for testing part of a system in isolation. It can be called as as a software module which is used to invoke a module under test and provide test inputs, control and, monitor execution, and report test results or most simplistically a line of code that calls a method and passes that method a value

One of the more difficult parts of software development is how to test drive time dependent code. Based on an easy example I will explain how to solve some of the problems that pop up during development of time dependent code.

A simplified version of the ProjectTimer (only the first story) to illustrate the challenges that we are facing when developing time depedent code.

Keep Track of the Time Spent on a Project

Let's start with a simple TestCase.

```
import junit.framework.TestCase;
```

```
public class ProjectTestCase extends TestCase
{
    public void testElapsedTime() throws
        InterruptedException {
        Project project = new Project();
        project.start();
        Thread.sleep(5000);
        project.stop();
        assertEquals(5000, project. elapsed
        Time());
    }
}
```

We create a new project and work for it during 5 seconds. Then we can assert the total time spent on the project equals 5 seconds.

Let's make it compile.

```
public class Project
{
    public void start()
    {
    }
    public void stop()
    {
    }
    public long elapsedTime()
    {
        return 0;
    }
}
```

Red bar, great. Let's use obvious implementation.

```
public class Project{
    private long beginTime;
    private long endTime;
    public void start()
    {
    beginTime = System.currentTimeMillis();
    }
    public void stop()
```

```
    {
       endTime = System.currentTimeMillis();
    }
    public long elapsedTime()
    {
       return endTime - beginTime;
    }
}
```

Even better, green bar... or not ? Run it a few times...

```
junit.framework.AssertionFailedError:
expected:<5000> but was:<5007>
at junit.framework.Assert.fail(Assert.java:47)
at junit.framework.Assert.failNotEquals
(Assert.java:282)
at junit.framework.Assert.assertEquals(Assert
.java:64)
at junit.framework.Assert.assertEquals(Assert.
java:136)
at junit.framework.Assert.assertEquals(Assert.
java:142)
at ProjectTestCase.testElapsedTime(ProjectTest
Case.java:10)
junit.framework.AssertionFailedError:
expected:<5000> but was:<4997>
at junit.framework.Assert.fail(Assert.java:47)
at junit.framework.Assert.failNotEquals(Assert
.java:282)
at junit.framework.Assert.assertEquals(Assert
.java:64)
at junit.framework.Assert.assertEquals(Assert.
java:136)
at junit.framework.Assert.assertEquals(Assert.
java:142)
at ProjectTestCase.testElapsedTime(Project
TestCase. java:10)
```

It looks like our TestCase is non deterministic. We sleep for 5 seconds, so the elapsed time is at least 5 seconds. What is even worse is that although we sleep for 5000 millis, the elapsed time is sometimes less than 5000 millis. Apparently the combination of Thread.sleep(int) and System. current Time Millis () is not reliable.

From the javadoc of System.currentTimeMillis():

Returns the current time in milliseconds. Note that while the unit of time of the return value is a millisecond, the granularity of the value depends on the underlying operating system and may be larger. For example, many operating systems measure time in units of tens of milliseconds.

TEST CASE

We will build in a safety margin. If we sleep for five seconds, we can assert that the elapsed time is more than four seconds. Run it a few times: all green.

```
import junit.framework.TestCase;
public class ProjectTestCase extends TestCase
{
    public void testElapsedTime() throws
    Interrupted Exception {
        Project project = new Project();
        project.start();
        Thread.sleep(5000);
        project.stop();
        assertTrue(project.elapsedTime() >
        4000);
    }
}
```

Although we have a green bar, a few things are bothering us. First, we haven't really solved the undeterministic behaviour. We introduced a safety margin of one second but we don't know if this is enough to guarantee that the test will always be green. Secondly, our TestCase does not communicate clearly it's intent anymore.

let's stub out the problematic behaviour.

We extract the System.currentTimeMillis() in a separate method which is made package private so it can be overridden.

```
public class Project
```

```
{
    private long beginTime;
    private long endTime;
    public void start()
{
    beginTime = getCurrentTimeMillis();
}
public void stop()
{
    endTime = getCurrentTimeMillis();
}
public long elapsedTime()
{
    return endTime - beginTime;
}
long getCurrentTimeMillis() {
    return System.currentTimeMillis();
    }
}
```

We adapt our TestCase and create a stub for the Project class, where we can set the return value of the get Current Time Millis().

```
import junit.framework.TestCase;
public class ProjectTestCase extends TestCase
{
public void testElapsedTime() throws
    InterruptedException {
    ProjectStub project = new ProjectStub();
    project.setCurrentTime(0);
    project.start();
    project.setCurrentTime(5000);
    project.stop();
    assertEquals(5000, project.elapsedTime());
}
    private static class ProjectStub extends
    Project {
    private long currentTime;
    public void setCurrentTime(long
```

```
        currentTime) {
            this.currentTime = currentTime;
        }
        long getCurrentTimeMillis() {
            return currentTime;
            }
        }
    }
```

Great, we have deterministic behaviour now and the TestCase communicates it's intent.

But we are still not satisfied with the result. From our experience we know that the need for stubs in newly written code is a smell.

We think about the Single Responsibility Principle (SRP): "A class should have only one reason to change".

Let's take a closer look at the Project class. The Project class is responsible for keeping track of how much time is spent on a project. Secondly Project also knows how to retrieve the current time.

SRP Compliant

Let's move to a SRP compliant solution, by separating these two responsibilities. We shield the retrieval of the current time behind an interface TimeServer. In our TestCase we use a mock implementation of this interface.

```
import junit.framework.TestCase;
public class ProjectTestCase extends TestCase {
    public void testElapsedTime() throws
    InterruptedException {
    TimeServerMock timeServer = new
    TimeServerMock();
    Project project = new Project(timeServer);
    timeServer.currentTimeMillis = 0;
    project.start();
    timeServer.currentTimeMillis = 5000;
    project.stop();
    assertEquals(5000, project.elapsedTime());
}
```

```
    public static class TimeServerMock implements
    TimeServer {
        public long currentTimeMillis;
        public long currentTimeMillis() {
          return currentTimeMillis;
        }
    }
}
```

let's adapt the production code.

```
    public class Project
    {
        private long beginTime;
        private long endTime;
        private TimeServer timeServer;
        public Project(TimeServer timeServer) {
          this.timeServer = timeServer;
        }
        public void start()
        {
          beginTime =timeServer.currentTime
                     Millis();
        }
        public void stop()
        {
          endTime =  timeServer.currentTime
                     Millis ();
    }
    public long elapsedTime()
    {
        return endTime - beginTime;
    }
    }
    public interface TimeServer
    {
    /**
    *   Returns the current time in milliseconds.
        Implementations may vary in
    *   accuracy. Define t1, t2 two moments in
```

```
    time; define the
*   currentTimeMillis function. If t1 comes
    before t2 than T(t1) <= T(t2).
*
*   @return the current time in milliseconds.
*/
long currentTimeMillis();
}
```

Time for a quick retrospective. We didn't like the stubbing stuff because it revealed a design problem. So we introduced an extra interface to come to a SRP compliant solution.

That's right, we are not forced by our Test Case to provide a production implementation of our TimeServer and that is exactly what we want: our TestCase only defines the functionality of the elapsedTime() method and does not care about how the current time is retrieved. Our design is "open for extension and closed for modification", applied to the way we retrieve the current time.

When the need for a TimeServer implementation arises we make the TimeServer contract explicit with a unit test.

```
import junit.framework.TestCase;
public class DefaultTimeServerTestCase extends
TestCase
{
    public void testCurrentTimeMillis() throws
    InterruptedException {
        TimeServer timeServer = new
        DefaultTimeServer();
        long firstTime = timeServer.currentTime
        Millis();
        long secondTime = timeServer.currentTime
        Millis();
        Thread.sleep(10);
        long thirdTime = timeServer.current
        TimeMillis ();
        assertTrue(firstTime <= secondTime);
        assertTrue(secondTime <= thirdTime);
```

```
    }
}
```

And we provide an implementation.

```
public class DefaultTimeServer implements
TimeServer{
    public long currentTimeMillis() {
        return System.currentTimeMillis();
    }
}
```

TEST DRIVEN DEVELOPMENT

The crux of *Test Driven Development* is that you use tests to drive the creation of your code, and in that loose sense, the guidelines pass muster, but there's more to it than that, really. The key advantage that TDD gives you is feedback. You write a failing test case, make it pass, and then you formulate the next test case.

The wonderful thing is that when you get to that next test case, you have the feedback from getting the first one to pass to draw upon. Often that feedback will lead you to formulate the next test case in a different way. It could even lead you to produce a different interface for the class you were writing. Now, what described might sound bad. It might sound like, well, maybe the decisions that you make during development will drift a bit. Drifting might not sound very good but the fact is it is good in this case. It's good because we control it. We are able to incorporate the things that we learn immediately when we learn them.

The alternative is to ignore things that we learn or not learn them at all, and that's not a very clever strategy. The style of TDD described in the guidelines would have us jump ahead and write five, ten, maybe twenty test cases before getting the first one to pass. You can do that, but it's like putting on a set of blinders.

When you don't have to formulate the next test case right after passing the last one, there isn't much chance to think about improvements. Worse, there is a disincentive to thinking about them: if you find any, you have to delete all of the speculation you've hardcoded in the tests and interfaces you created in advance.

STUBS TESTING

A Stub is a dummy procedure, module or unit that stands in for an unfinished portion of a system.

Four basic types of Stubs for Top-Down Testing are:

1. Display a trace message
2. Display parameter value(s)
3. Return a value from a table
4. Return table value selected by parameter

A stub is a computer programme which is used as a substitute for the body of a software module that is or will be defined elsewhere or a dummy component or object used to simulate the behaviour of a real component until that component has been developed.

Ultimately, the dummy method would be completed with the proper programme logic. However, developing the stub allows the programmer to call a method in the code being developed, even if the method does not yet have the desired behaviour. Stubs and drivers are often viewed as throwaway code. However, they do not have to be thrown away: Stubs can be "filled in" to form the actual method. Drivers can become automated test cases.

It is not possible to test a single function by itself; is it? It must be called by something (if it is not the main programme) and it may have calls to other modules, which are not there as of now. If a function includes calls to other modules, dummy procedures known as stubs can be written to satisfy those calls. Stubs replace module that are subordinate (i.e. called by) to the component to be tested. Stubs usually print out a message to indicate that it is called properly. It must take suitable/proper arguments and must return an suitable value(s).

Stubs play a role in top-down integration testing.

```
double calculate_salary(double hours, double
rate)
{
```

```
cout<<"Salary is:"
return(hours*rate);
}
```

The main programme can be tested using this above code.

STRUCTURAL TESTING

Code coverage analysis is a structural testing technique (AKA glass box testing and white box testing). Structural testing compares test programme behaviour against the apparent intention of the source code.

This contrasts with functional testing (AKA black-box testing), which compares test programme behaviour against a requirements specification.

Structural testing examines how the programme works, taking into account possible pitfalls in the structure and logic. Functional testing examines what the programme accomplishes, without regard to how it works internally.

Structural testing is also called path testing since you choose test cases that cause paths to be taken through the structure of the programme.

Do not confuse path testing with the path coverage metric, explained later. At first glance, structural testing seems unsafe. Structural testing cannot find errors of omission. However, requirements specifications sometimes do not exist, and are rarely complete.

This is especially true near the end of the product development time line when the requirements specification is updated less frequently and the product itself begins to take over the role of the specification.

The difference between functional and structural testing blurs near release time. The ability to analyse how a particular material or structural design will behave when exposed to certain forces is critical to design verification and validation. OPTOTRAK measurement systems are based on advanced optical technology that can capture complex structural motion in real time. Simply attach targets to points of interest and click a button to enable full 6DOF object tracking for 3D motion analysis.

Up to 512 targets can be employed with measurement rates of up to 4600 measurements per second. This allows you to view, record, and examine the finest details of structural motion as it occurs.

Scaled Composites performs a great deal of structural testing to evaluate and verify its structural materials and building processes.

Extensive Testing Facilities: Scaled maintains an extensive R&D lab in which many material specimens are tested to ASTM, MIL, and SACMA standards for composites. Tools used for coupon testing include a dual-column 30 Kip Instron electro-mechanical load frame and several ASTM certified fixtures. These tools are used to perform in-house material verification and to provide testing services for our customers. Accurate strengths and moduli can be determined for various materials. Measurements of peel and joint strength and sandwich panel properties can be evaluated. In addition, these tests can be conducted with environmental conditioning (-100F to 350F) and damage tolerance considerations.

Full Scale Analysis: Before a manned flight test programme begins, proof loading on our customer's prototype is conducted. Since most POC articles are designed with a high safety margin, the actual flight test article is generally used for static load verification.

Strains and deflections can be measured to verify design predictions. Scaled has experience with full-scale measurements of aircraft moments of inertia. We also own and routinely operate a landing gear drop test rig. In addition, Scaled can support contracted ground vibration testing of flight vehicles.

STRUCTURAL TESTING METHODOLOGY

Using the eValid DOM manipulation commands it's possible to build playback scripts that are effective even in the context of AJAX-based and dynamic content web applications. The only requirement is to have some structural invarients on a page that can be used to direct playback actions.

The eValid Structural Testing Commands show how to manipulate DOM elements and element values. There is a simple Manual Script Creation Process that generates a purely-structural test by using the technical details a "from life" eValid test recording. As the Algorithmic/Structural Testing table points out, this process is likely to be significantly less work than pure scripting..

Introduction

The eValid product technology represents an abstraction of web testing that has as its primary goal the development of algorithmic/structural testing rather than programmatic testing. This page identifies key distinctions between these three types of testing:

- *Record/Play Testing:* The use of a recording engine to extract test scripts by observing user actions and replicating them automatically.
- *Algorithmic/Structural:* The use of special positional or structure cues within a web page to creat scripts that access those cues in a structural or algorithmic way.
- *Programmatic Testing:* The creation of actual computer programs, e.g. in C++, that drive an automated browser direct from the compiled version of the programme.

.As the table shows, these three approaches differ in a variety of ways including effectiveness, ease-of-use, test durability, and technical difficulty.

Table. Observations About Functional Testing From Different Perspectives

Topic	Record/Play Testing Paradigm	Algorithmic/ Structural Testing	Programmatic Testing
	Advantages & Disadvantages		
Summary	Quick & reliable, no training required	Flexible,durable tests, minimal training	Flexible, durable tests requiring deep

		required.	programming and web application knowledge.
Relative Degree of Difficulty	1	2	10+
Typical Title of User	QA Staff	Test Engineer	Software Developer
Required Skill Set	General Technical Knowledge Web Application Familiarity.	General Technical /Engineering Knowledge Light Programming Basic Web Application Familiarity	In-Depth Programming Deep Web Application Familarity
Knoledge Required	Application operation (browser based application).	Location and description of objects on page, limited know-ledge of DOM properties.	Programming language, complete DOM details.
What Operator Does	Click to record test.	Adapt recorded test using index/motion commands.	Create complete programme to perform desired test action.
Estimated Cost Effectiveness	Very high because recordings are so easy to make.	High because most scripts can be "developed" from a recorded is difficult. prototype.	Low because scripting without a recording

Technology Concerns			
Underlying Technology Basis	Extracts data from DOM and writes the script automatically.	Index/motion commands and DOM-synchronization commands.	C++ programme-ming language interface to existing commands as API.
Tolerance for Dynamic Page Changes	Adaptive playback overcomes most dynamic changes.	Invulnerable to dynamic changes.	Invulnerable to dynamic changes.
Operation on Normal (Non-AJAX) Applications	Record/Play gets 99+% "what you see and what you do is what eValid records and what eValid plays back".	If Record/Play works OK,then the script is the "test algorithm"	Not needed.
Operation on Basic AJAX Applications	Record/Play forms the basis for the algori-thmic test.	Identify de-synchroni-zations, repair them, and you have a good AJAX test.	Identify de-synchroni-zations,write programs to overcome each one separately.
Operation with Complex AJAX Applications	Record/Play produced script probably will fail.Augmentation with algorithmic methods needed.	Index/motion and DOM-synchronization	Use the record-ing as the specification, requires hand coding in the EPI.
eValid Product Option Description			
eValid Product Options	eValid Regression Test Bundle	eValid AJAX Regression Test Bundle With PAGEMAP Feature	eValid/EPI: eValid Programmatic Interface With

	Index/Motion Commands	PAGEMAP Feature

In addition to these special eValid capabilities you can also take advantage of our fixed-price test development services — we guarantee a working structural test based on your specifications for a low fixed price.

WHITE BOX TESTING

White box testing strategy deals with the internal logic and structure of the code. White box testing is also called as glass, structural, open box or clear box testing. The tests written based on the white box testing strategy incorporate coverage of the code written, branches, paths, statements and internal logic of the code etc. In order to implement white box testing, the tester has to deal with the code and hence is needed to possess knowledge of coding and logic i.e. internal working of the code. White box test also needs the tester to look into the code and find out which unit/statement/chunk of the code is malfunctioning.

ADVANTAGES OF WHITE BOX TESTING

- As the knowledge of internal coding structure is prerequisite, it becomes very easy to find out which type of input/data can help in testing the application effectively.
- The other advantage of white box testing is that it helps in optimizing the code
- It helps in removing the extra lines of code, which can bring in hidden defects.

DISADVANTAGES OF WHITE BOX TESTING

- As knowledge of code and internal structure is a prerequisite, a skilled tester is needed to carry out this type of testing, which increases the cost.
- And it is nearly impossible to look into every bit of code to find out hidden errors, which may create problems, resulting in failure of the application.

WHITE/GLASS BOX TESTING STRATEGY

Unit Testing

The developer carries out unit testing in order to check if the particular module or unit of code is working fine. The Unit Testing comes at the very basic level as it is carried out as and when the unit of the code is developed or a particular functionality is built.

Static and Dynamic Analysis

Static analysis involves going through the code in order to find out any possible defect in the code. Dynamic analysis involves executing the code and analyzing the output.

Statement Coverage

In this type of testing the code is executed in such a manner that every statement of the application is executed at least once. It helps in assuring that all the statements execute without any side effect.

Branch Coverage

No software application can be written in a continuous mode of coding, at some point we need to branch out the code in order to perform a particular functionality. Branch coverage testing helps in validating of all the branches in the code and making sure that no branching leads to abnormal behaviour of the application.

Security Testing

Security Testing is carried out in order to find out how well the system can protect itself from unauthorized access, hacking – cracking, any code damage etc. which deals with the code of application. This type of testing needs sophisticated testing techniques.

Mutation Testing

A kind of testing in which, the application is tested for the code that was modified after fixing a particular bug/defect.

It also helps in finding out which code and which strategy of coding can help in developing the functionality effectively.

Besides all the testing types given above, there are some more types which fall under both Black box and White box testing strategies such as: Functional testing (which deals with the code in order to check its functional performance), Incremental integration testing (which deals with the testing of newly added code in the application), Performance and Load testing (which helps in finding out how the particular code manages resources and give performance etc.) etc.

FUNCTIONAL TESTING

DEFINITION

Application functional testing is the most widely accepted testing practice in software development organizations today, and hundreds of millions of dollars have been spent on automated tools to support the practice. Yet, organizations still struggle to achieve software quality and suffer inconsistent, inefficient, and often inaccurate application of the practice.

Over 70 per cent of software testing today is still done manually despite the investment in automation. Understanding what has or hasn't been tested is still most organizations' major challenge, and the time commitment required for QA functional testing is increasingly one of organizations' greatest concerns for meeting application delivery and time-to-market demands.

Without a well-defined and implemented "best" practice, functional testing will continue to be practiced incorrectly and suffer inaccurate or, at best, incomplete results. Automated tools alone cannot ensure that functional testing is complete and accurate. Achieving this goal requires that a tool be supported by a well-defined practice for its use and be integrated into an organization's software development process.

The necessary level of commitment and practice maintenance is often underestimated and is typically the reason for poor results and the abandonment of automated tools in favour of manual testing. An effective and consistently-applied functional testing practice is the only way to ensure that software satisfies expected functionality and reliability objectives.

Software development organizations with an effective functional testing practice have a fast and objective way to determine whether each functional requirement is actually implemented in the code. With functional testing, the team translates functional requirements into executable test cases that confirm how well the code satisfies the requirements at any given time. It provides unprecedented objective insight into requirement status and prevents the missing or incorrect functionality implementations that can lead to countless rewrites (and then budget overruns and missed deadlines), user dissatisfaction, and project failure.

An effective functional testing practice should be a natural extension of a requirements management policy. Ideally, a requirements management policy describes how to build effective use cases for the features expected in the current release, and how to map those use cases to verifiable test cases.

A test plan is then developed and implemented to build a suite of executable tests that frame and verify the functionality requirements, providing a fast and objective way to assess the status of expected functionality. These tests can then be executed regularly to ensure that code modifications do not unintentionally change previously verified functionality.

An effective functional testing practice involves the definition of guidelines for using functional testing technologies effectively, and then the implementation and integration of those guidelines (along with supporting technologies and configurations) into your software development lifecycle to ensure that your teams apply the policy consistently and regularly. It also requires a means to monitor and measure the policy's application, as well as report the data it is tracking.

To achieve effective black box unit testing, you must not only have a defined practice for its use, but that practice must be implemented and integrated into your software development lifecycle so that it is used consistently and regularly across your software development team. It is also important to have the means to monitor and measure its use.

Functional testing covers how well the system executes the functions it is supposed to execute—including user commands, data manipulation, searches and business processes, user screens, and integrations. Functional testing covers the obvious surface type of functions, as well as the back-end operations (such as security and how upgrades affect the system).

"If you have an old Vantive [CRM] system, and you have to migrate all your information to a new [CRM] system, that is where a lot of the functional issues will occur. You have to do that migration and then verify that the information is there [in the new system]."

Although functional testing is often done toward the end of the development cycle, it can—and should, say experts—be started much earlier. Individual components and processes can be tested early on, even before it's possible to do functional testing on the entire system.

The Aberdeen Group, a Boston-based analyst firm, has noted that because today's applications require constant updating and redeployment, IT needs to think in terms of testing throughout the entire life-cycle of an application.

REQUIREMENT BASED FUNCTIONAL TESTING

Function (Integration) test is usually the first test phase that a test organization is responsible for during any given release. Requirements based Function Test is one approach to Function (Integration) test - it is a powerful and effective testing approach, which will significantly reduce the number of undetected defects (faults) being released into production.

The premise is that a well-formulated set of functional requirements give the Test Designers a definitive bases for test case design.

Function Test

"The objective of function test is to measure the quality of the functional (business) components of the system".Tests verify that the system behaves correctly from the user/ business perspective and functions according to the requirements, models, storyboards, or any other design paradigm used to specify the application.

The function test must determine if each component or business event: performs in accordance to the specifications, responds correctly to all conditions that may be presented by incoming events/data, moves data correctly from one business event to the next (including data stores), and that business events are initiated in the order required to meet the business objectives of the system.

TEST CYCLE FOR REQUIREMENTS BASED FUNCTION TEST

An effective test cycle must have a defined set of processes and deliverables. The primary processes/ deliverables for requirements based Function test are: Test Planning, Partitioning/Functional Decomposition, Requirements Definition/Verification, Test Case Design, Traceability (Traceability Matrix), Test Case Execution, Defect Management, and Coverage Analysis.

Which processes and deliverables apply to any given testing situation are dependent on available resources (people, source materials, time, etc.) and the mandate of the test organization.

Test Planning

During planning the Test Lead with assistance from the test team defines the scope, schedule, and deliverables for the function test cycle. The Test Lead delivers a Test Plan (document) and a Test Schedule (work plan) - these often undergo several revisions during the testing cycle.

Partitioning - Functional Decomposition

Functional decomposition of a system (or partitioning)

is the breakdown of a system into its functional components or functional areas. Another group in the organization may take responsibility for the functional decomposition (or model) of the system but the testing organization should still review this deliverable for completeness before accepting it into the test organization.

If the functional decomposition or partitions have not been defined or are deemed insufficient then the testing organization will have to take responsibility for creating and maintaining the partitions. There are several commercial, shareware, and freeware products available that aid in the functional decomposition of a system and the formal delivery of the functional partitions.

Requirements Definition/Verification

Requirements definition is often the weakest deliverable in the software development process. Many development shops go directly from software concept to functional specification or worse from software concept to code without any preliminary software design deliverables.

The Testing Organization needs these requirements to proceed with Function test, so if the development team is not going to deliver the requirements for verification by the testing team then the Test Team must create its own set of testable requirements. These requirements need to be itemized under the appropriate functional partition.

Test Case Design

The Test Designer/Tester designs and implements test cases to validate the product performs in accordance to the requirements (see.Testing and The Role of a Test Designer Tester.). These Test Cases need to be itemized under the appropriate functional partition and mapped/traced to the requirements being tested.

Traceability (Traceability Matrix)

Test Cases need to be traced/mapped back to the appropriate requirement. Once all aspects of a requirement have been tested by one or more test cases then the test design activity for that requirement can be considered complete.

A common misconception made during this process is that all test cases that exercise a particular requirement should be mapped to that requirement - only those test cases that are specifically created to test a requirement should be traced to that requirement.

This approach gives a much more accurate picture of the application when coverage analysis is done - failure of a test case does not mean failure of all the requirements exercised (as opposed to tested by) the test case.

Test Case Execution

As in all phases of testing the appropriate set of test cases need to be executed and the results of those test cases recorded. Which test cases are to be executed should be defined within the context of the Test Plan and the current state of the application being tested.

If the current state of the application does not support the testing of one or more requirements then this testing should be deferred until it does justify the expenditure of testing resources.

Defect Management

As in all phases of testing any defects (see.Testing and The Role of a Test Designer Tester.) detected during test execution need to be both recorded and managed by the testing organization.

During Function test each defect should be traced to a specific requirement or requirements that are not performing to specification.

Coverage Analysis

During Function test a periodic progress report should be delivered by the test organization to the project team. The bases for this report will be a coverage analysis of the requirements against test cases and outstanding defects. The objective of this analysis is to determine the percentage of the requirements that are: deemed to be untested, performing to specification (executed successfully), and not performing to specification (defects).

There are several commercial, shareware, and freeware products available that can be used to expedite the creation of all these deliverables while streamlining the testing process.

MANAGING FUNCTION TEST

Function (Integration) testing can be an overwhelming task for an inexperienced testing organization. To assure success at the test organization and project level the scope of the testing effort needs to be rigorously defined and followed. The definition of the scope needs to be understood by the test organization and the project team - if the scope of the testing effort needs to be redefined then this must be communicated.

A realistic work plan with clear deliverables and dependencies needs to be drafted and updated when any event occurs that impacts the work plan in a positive or negative fashion. The key to success is to manage the expectations of the testing team and the project team while clearly communicating the current status of the testing effort on on-going bases.

BLACK BOX TESTING STRATEGY

Black Box Testing is not a type of testing; it instead is a testing strategy, which does not need any knowledge of internal design or code etc. As the name "black box" suggests, no knowledge of internal logic or code structure is required. The types of testing under this strategy are totally based/focused on the testing for requirements and functionality of the work product/software application.

Black box testing is sometimes also called as "Opaque Testing", "Functional/Behavioral Testing" and "Closed Box Testing". The base of the Black box testing strategy lies in the selection of appropriate data as per functionality and testing it against the functional specifications in order to check for normal and abnormal behaviour of the system. Now a days, it is becoming common to route the Testing work to a third party as the developer of the system knows too much of the internal logic and coding of the system, which makes it unfit to test the application by the developer.

In order to implement Black Box Testing Strategy, the tester is needed to be thorough with the requirement specifications of the system and as a user, should know, how the system should behave in response to the particular action.

Various testing types that fall under the Black Box Testing strategy are: functional testing, stress testing, recovery testing, volume testing, User Acceptance Testing (also known as UAT), system testing, Sanity or Smoke testing, load testing, Usability testing, Exploratory testing, ad-hoc testing, alpha testing, beta testing etc. These testing types are again divided in two groups: a) Testing in which user plays a role of tester and b) User is not required.

TESTING METHOD

Functional Testing

In this type of testing, the software is tested for the functional requirements. The tests are written in order to check if the application behaves as expected.

Stress Testing

The application is tested against heavy load such as complex numerical values, large number of inputs, large number of queries etc. which checks for the stress/load the applications can withstand.

Load Testing

The application is tested against heavy loads or inputs such as testing of web sites in order to find out at what point the web-site/application fails or at what point its performance degrades.

Ad-hoc Testing

This type of testing is done without any formal Test Plan

or Test Case creation. Ad-hoc testing helps in deciding the scope and duration of the various other testing and it also helps testers in learning the application prior starting with any other testing.

Exploratory Testing

This testing is similar to the ad-hoc testing and is done in order to learn/explore the application.

Usability Testing

This testing is also called as 'Testing for User-Friendliness'. This testing is done if User Interface of the application stands an important consideration and needs to be specific for the specific type of user.

Smoke Testing

This type of testing is also called sanity testing and is done in order to check if the application is ready for further major testing and is working properly without failing up to least expected level.

Recovery Testing

Recovery testing is basically done in order to check how fast and better the application can recover against any type of crash or hardware failure etc. Type or extent of recovery is specified in the requirement specifications.

Volume Testing

Volume testing is done against the efficiency of the application. Huge amount of data is processed through the application (which is being tested) in order to check the extreme limitations of the system.

TESTING WHERE USER PLAYS A ROLE/USER IS REQUIRED

User Acceptance Testing

In this type of testing, the software is handed over to the

user in order to find out if the software meets the user expectations and works as it is expected to.

Alpha Testing

In this type of testing, the users are invited at the development centre where they use the application and the developers note every particular input or action carried out by the user. Any type of abnormal behaviour of the system is noted and rectified by the developers.

Beta Testing

In this type of testing, the software is distributed as a beta version to the users and users test the application at their sites. As the users explore the software, in case if any exception/defect occurs that is reported to the developers.

Chapter 11

Testing Data Preparations

TEST DATA SUIT

INTERACTIVE DATA PUBLIC TEST SUITE

The purpose of the public test suite is to assist developers of software that must validate Interactive Data prior to its submission to EDGAR. The test suite consists of many small Interactive Data instances, schemas and linkbases that are categorized as to whether they violate a validation check, and if so, what validation check they violate and whether that would resulting a warning, or in an error that would cause the Interactive Data to be rejected.

Filers that attach Interactive Data files to EDGAR submissions as EX-101 attachments are responsible for compliance with all validations in Chapter 6 of Volume II of the EDGAR Filer Manual ("the Manual"). Automated validation by preparation software can make it more efficient for filers to verify compliance before sending their filings to EDGAR itself. Nothing in this test suite is intended to create new requirements or change existing requirements for EDGAR submissions; filers should consult the Commission rules and the Manual for submission requirements.

ALPHA AND BETA TESTING

CUSTOMER INVOLVEMENT

We want you to be involved! Customer Involvement is one of our core goals - read About Us and Our Philosophy for a summary of our goals. By being involved in the testing and development of our products, you will ultimately benefit from a product that more closely matches your needs, and you will receive a product that is of higher quality.

ALPHA PRODUCT

An Alpha product is very new! It is so new, that it has not yet reached the stage where it can be sold. It is still being developed. However, it HAS reached the stage where those who enjoy cutting-edge technology can download the product as-is, and try it out for themselves!

BETA PRODUCT

A Beta product is one where new feature development has stopped, and the focus is on polishing the product and ironing out any kinks, ready for sale.

We still encourage you to suggest ideas for improvement during this stage, but they will most likely be logged for development in a future version. Of course, if you find any bugs, please tell us!

ALPHA OR BETA TESTING PHASE

During the "Alpha" or "Beta" phase of a product:

You can download and install the product to see whether it suits your needs. You automatically get a 7-day evaluation license at installation time, during which period the product is fully functional.

SIGN-UP

If you wish to continue using the product after the 7-day evaluation period has expired, you must sign-up to become an "Alpha Tester" or "Beta Tester", depending on which phase the product is currently in. Signing up is free. You will be prompted to sign up when you launch the product. All you need to provide is your name and email address. In addition, as a reward for participating in the Alpha Testing phase, you will be entitled to a discount on the retail price of the product when it goes on sale.

DISCUSSION FORUMS

You can suggest ways to improve the product! You should do this by participating in our Discussion Forums. During the Alpha phase, suggestions for improvement will be actively taken on board. When a product moves to the Beta phase, then new feature development stops. However, suggestions for improvement are still considered and discussed, and may be logged for development in a future version. We welcome any ideas for improving our products.

REPORT BUGS

If you find any bugs with the software, please report them! There is sophisticated bug-reporting capability built-in to the software, in the event that application errors should occur. For other issues that you consider to be bugs or problems with the software you should submit a bug report via email.

PRODUCT TRACKING

Keep up to date with each product via the Product Tracking page. From this page you can get a list of all issues logged, and find out whether that bug for which you logged a bug report has been fixed yet.

ALPHA/BETA USABILITY AND ACCEPTABILITY TESTING

Quality Logic can implement and manage your customer alpha, beta and gamma product testing programs, providing quality and timely feedback from real customers in real-world environments. We can manage the entire programme from customer selection and product delivery, through customer support and data gathering, to final data analysis.

Customer Management and Support

QualityLogic will work with your customers to ensure continuous programme involvement and feedback. We can provide pre-release product support, product upgrades and issue troubleshooting.

Data Analysis

Quality Logic can gather customer environment and usage information, satisfaction trends and product strengths and weaknesses. We make comparisons to competitive offerings and conduct root cause analysis on issues, providing actionable data.

Support Analysis

With our extensive product support experience, Quality Logic's staff provides feedback on product support effectiveness on released products.

Competitive Analysis Testing

Quality Logic's experienced staff can implement and manage part of or all your competitive intelligence testing. We can manage the entire programme from competitor selection and acquisition, through test design andimplementation, to final data analysis and reporting. Reporting can be used for either internal or external communications.

STATIC TESTING STRATEGIES

INTRODUCTION

Static testing is a form of software testing where the software isn't actually used. This is in contrast to Dynamic testing. It is generally not detailed testing, but checks mainly for the sanity of the code, algorithm, or document.

It is primarily syntax checking of the code or and manually reading of the code or document to find errors. This type of testing can be used by the developer who wrote the code, in isolation.

Code reviews, inspections and walkthroughs are also used. From the black box testing point of view, static testing involves review of requirements or specifications.

This is done with an eye toward completeness or appropriateness for the task at hand. This is the verification portion of Verification and Validation. Bugs discovered at this stage of development are less expensive to fix than later in the development cycle.

STATIC CODE ANALYSIS

Static code analysis is the analysis of computer software that is performed without actually executing programs built from that software (analysis performed on executing programs is known as dynamic analysis).

In most cases the analysis is performed on some version of the source code and in the other cases some form of the object code. The term is usually applied to the analysis performed by an automated tool, with human analysis being called programme understanding or programme comprehension.

The sophistication of the analysis performed by tools varies from those that only consider the behaviour of individual statements and declarations, to those that include the complete source code of a programme in their analysis. Uses of the information obtained from the analysis vary from highlighting possible coding errors (e.g., the lint tool) to formal methods that mathematically prove properties about a given programme (e.g., its behaviour matches that of its specification).

Some people consider software metrics and reverse engineering to be forms of static analysis. A growing commercial use of static analysis is in the verification of properties of software used in safety-critical computer systems and locating potentially vulnerable code.

FORMAL METHODS

Formal methods is the term applied to the analysis of software (and hardware) whose results are obtained purely through the use of rigorous mathematical methods. The mathematical techniques used include denotational semantics, axiomatic semantics, operational semantics, and abstract interpretation.

It has been proven that, barring some hypothesis that the state space of programs is finite and small, finding possible run-time errors, or more generally any kind of violation of a specification on the final result of a programme, is undecidable: there is no mechanical method that can always answer truthfully whether a given programme may or may not exhibit runtime errors. This result dates from the works of Church, Gödel and Turing in the 1930s (see the halting problem and Rice's theorem). As with most undecidable questions, onc can still attempt to give useful approximate solutions.

Some of the implementation techniques of formal statict analysis include:

- Model checking considers systems that have finite state or may be reduced to finite state by abstraction;
- Abstract interpretation models the effect that every statement has on the state of an abstract machine (ie, it 'executes' the software based on the mathematical properties of each statement and declaration). This abstract machine overapproximates the behaviours of the system: the abstract system is thus made simpler to analyse, at the expense of *incompleteness* (not every property truc of the original system is true of the abstract system). If properly done, though, abstract interpretation is *sound* (every property truc of the abstract system can be mapped to a true property of the original system).
- Use of assertions in programme code as first suggested by Hoare logic. There is tool support for some programming languages (e.g., the SPARK programming language (a subset of Ada) and the Java Modeling Language – JML – using ESC/Java and ESC/Java2).

DESCRIPTION

Static Testing is a well-known and beneficial concept within the testing space, but tightened budgets and looming deadlines can hinder the benefits. Here are few suggestions on how taking a risk-based approach to static testing can help realise the benefits.

Implementing Static Testing

Implementing static testing, it is advisable to create a small dedicated implementation team with specific roles. It should include the Process Champions who would be backing the process, the Trainers, and most importantly the Implementers, who will need to develop and document the process; examples of the process materials and collateral required are, Static Testing Policy, Strategy; Review Process, Review Techniques and Guidelines; Templates – Review Logs, Review Metrics, Document Review Matrix; Training courses.

The other factors to consider for the implementation are, verifying the internal materials by using the process and templates and involving people from different projects/teams in the development of the materials. When actually implementing Static Reviews, experience has shown that a phased approach is often best, both in terms of minimizing the impact and also being able to demonstrate early benefits as a result. For this reason AppLabs recommends an approach making use of a pilot and then a full implementation:

The strategy behind the pilot approach is to provide a least risk environment which will allow early demonstration of some or all of the benefits of Static Testing. Having experienced at first hand how this approach can provide a successful basis for further implementation(s), AppLabs has recognized some essential factors that will contribute to success.

FORMAL TECHNICAL REVIEWS

Formal Technical Reviews (FTR) are processes used to improve_work products through team effort. Any deliverable that is produced during the development life-cycle is eligible to be reviewed and should be at an early stage, beginning in the specification stage and recurring at each identifiable milestone.

A description of the review process as implemented at Fermilab is available as well as a list of reviews that have been held. Many additional references_are available. Unless otherwise stated all Fermi FTR documentation will include the symbol shown at the top of this page to distinguish it from outside information.

The following guidelines should help in setting up an FTR:

- Choose the work product to be reviewed.
- Determine the type of FTR to use.
- Follow the description of the specific FTR in question.

It is important to remember when determining the type of FTR to use that no process will work for every organization. Feedback to the review process is an important part of having a *process*. The process evolves as experience and participant comments are folded back into it.

In some sense it is not only the work product which is being reviewed but the review process as well. What is important is to develop an FTR process that works for your organization and to stick with that process when performing a review.

TECHNICAL REVIEW METHODS

- A planned and systematic pattern of all actions necessary to provide adequate confidence that an item or product conforms to established technical requirements.
- A set of activities designed to evaluate the process by which products are developed or manufactured"

When discussing software quality very little changes from the above statement, the goal is still to produce a usable product, which is capable of performing the task it was designed to do.

Formal technical reviews involve the analysis of an artifact by a group of technically skilled people following a specified and documented process. Michael Fagan first wrote about the idea of formal technical reviews in software quality in the 1970's whilst working for IBM, and the majority of all technical review methods have evolved in some way from Fagan's Code Inspection.

Background

A formal technical review is a method used to identify

defects in an artifact before progressing to the next stage of development. Unlike system testing, formal technical reviews can take place at any stage in the development life-cycle, and as such allow for the identification, documentation and correction of defects earlier rather than later, therefore saving the company both time and money.

An example of such a cost saving is provided by Robert Grady and Tom Van Slack (1994) where they claim that software inspections saved Hewlett-Packard 21 million dollars, clearly showing there are long term cost gains to be made by implementing formal technical reviews.

It is commonly accepted that not all organisations implement formal technical reviews for various reasons ranging from ignorance of the benefits they provide through to the effects they may have on time management aspects of the project. However, standards organisations such as ISO and CMM are pushing companies in the direction of formal technical reviews by insisting on some form of inspection to be in place before offering certification.

An informal survey, which was carried out by Philip M Johnson (1996) regarding the use of formal technical reviews in the workplace, showed that despite the benefits offered by formal technical reviews, 80% of replies claimed that formal technical review methods in their place of business were infrequently carried out and in some cases not at all.

Popular alternatives to formal technical reviews can be found in the form of structured walkthroughs and code reading. A structured walkthrough consists of a short meeting with one or more developers and the author to discuss the quality and suitability of the artifact.

No documentation is required and no data collection to assist in process improvement takes place during or after the meeting.

Whist this process is not generally considered as "good" as a formal technical review, however, just because it is not a measured process does not mean it is not effective, simply more confidence is placed on the experience of the reviewers. Laitenberger and Jean-Marc DeBaud (1999) supported this view when they identified that audits and walkthroughs, while informal may be equally as effective as a formal technical review, but due to the lack

of structure and many variations, a direct comparison of the two is not possible. Code reviews involve two or more developers reading code independently then meeting with the author to discuss any findings. Again, this relies heavily on the experience of the reviewer knowing what to look for in a review.

Methods

Formal technical review methods began in 1976 with the publication of Fagan's code inspection techniques. Fagan inspections consist of 4 pre-defined roles, moderator, scribe, inspector and author. Given the opportunity to follow the basic steps - overview, preparation, inspection, rework and follow up - this method allows for a controlled and documented review, with findings easily referred to and checked upon.

This method was considered a major step forward in the field of software quality, and provided IBM with substantial cost savings during the development process. As a result of this formal technical reviews became popular, and a wide variety of alternatives have since been developed although often a link to Fagan's code inspection can be seen.

The first step of Fagan code inspections is the overview, this is where the inspection team are handed any design documents or code listings that are relevant, and given an outline of the project as a whole.

Following on from this is the preparation stage, where each member of the inspection team works independently to read and understand the documentation they have been given, during this phase a checklist is sometimes used to increase the chances of a defect being discovered.

The inspection phase generally involves a meeting including the inspection team and the author Where the documentation is systematically gone over as a group documenting any defects. These are then fixed by the author during the next phase, rework. The final step is to check the defects have been corrected this is the Follow-up stage.

Tom Gilb took this idea one step further, with an extension to Fagan code inspection. Gilb added process improvement and defect prevention to the list of goals, this helped companies identify reasons as to why defects were occurring, and if possible remove the cause, not just the defect.

A study by Martin Höst and Conny Johansson (1999) showed that when a checklist based review was introduced into an organisation most defects were detected by a single inspector. They conclude this could be due to the experience of the inspector or time commitments of other inspectors.

Due to the costs associated with arranging a meeting when every member of the inspection team is available, Watts Humphrey created Humphrey's software review method, this consists of the producer talking the inspection team through the background material, following this each inspector performs the inspection alone in order to complete an error checklist. The producer then compiles this list before the group review meeting is held.

Due to the fact that members of the inspection team have all understood the artifact under inspection there is no longer a need for the producer to explain each line of code, this results in shorter group meetings.

Group meetings are completely removed in active design review, produced by David L Parnas and David M Weiss. This inspection method involves the producer giving a brief overview or the project, and providing all the inspectors with a questionnaire, which they complete in order to ensure their understanding.

Next the inspectors individually analyse the artifact each focusing on a specialised area. The producer then meets with each inspector individually to collect the results of the inspection.

The producer then collates all the findings and produces a report regarding the inspection. Knight and Myers proposed a phased inspection technique taking some of the ideas of

Humphrey and some of the ideas from active design review by splitting the inspection into 2 phases. The first phase, single inspection phase, involves a simple yes or no checklist and can be carried out by anyone, not just a developer. The second phase, multi inspection phase, is carried out by each inspector following a checklist covering his or her own area of expertise. Upon completion of this a meeting is held to compare and analyse the findings.

With the problem of time available for reviews still remaining Shinji Kusumoto et al. carried out an experiment to accurately estimate the time needed in order to carry out a formal technical review.

They proposed taking samples of the producers code and inspecting them, the results of this sample inspection enabled them to estimate the time needed for a complete inspection of the entire product based on the knowledge that the lower the quality of a product the higher the effort needed to complete the inspection.

The results from this experiment showed that the defect detection rate increased from 28% to 40% when this procedure was applied. A study carried out by Oliver Laitenberger and Jean-Marc DeBaud concluded that the reading method used during an inspection could significantly contribute to the defect detection rates.

This study also uncovered evidence to suggest that when applying perspective based reading, the experience of the inspector plays a far smaller part in the overall defect detection rate as opposed to using a checklist based system.

Perspective based reading involves setting each inspector a different area or perspective to inspect the artifact from, for example an end user or code maintenance. This allows for better coverage of artifacts under inspection as each inspector is focused on one specific area of expertise.

A different study by Laitenberger et al. focusing on the application of perspective based reading to UML documentation found that an inspector's perceived understanding of an artifact was increased when perspective based reading was applied.

The increased understanding provided by the use of perspective based reading could explain the increased defect detection rate as a study by A Dunsmore, M Roper and M Wood (1999) identified a link between inspector comprehension of an artifact and the defect detection rate when using checklist based methods.

Another finding of Laitenberger et al. was that on a cost per defect ratio, it worked out cheaper for the company to use a perspective based reading technique. Victor R Basili et al. conducted an experiment, the comparison of various reading techniques within the perspective based reading family, as they consider this fundamental to defect detection.

During this controlled experiment with professional software developers, two teams were formed one using perspective based reading, the other using their usual technique. The results from these experiments show that overall the team using perspective based reading techniques performed better than the control team.

COMPUTER AIDED REVIEW METHODS

In an attempt to provide easier implementation and automatic capture of metric data relating to the inspection process, data needed in order to improve the inspection process, a range of computer tools to assist in formal technical reviews quickly became available.

With the computer assistance the time needed to record this data is removed from the inspection process, it is also more accurate and can record the amount of time spent by each inspector and on which area of the artifact.

One of the first such tools was a system by ITT in 1982; this prototype was both a hardware and software solution, creating a workstation to assist in reviews. However, no documents concerning the use of this system have ever been released. ITT have since sold off their research labs to Alcatel who closed them down.

The first inspection tool to have published results regarding its use was developed by Bellcore and called ICICLE (Intelligent Code Inspection in a C Language

Environment). ICICLE allows for a 2 phases of inspection, individual inspections and inspection meetings, unfortunately no support for distributed meetings was included in ICICLE and all meetings needed to be held with the inspectors all in the same room.

During the inspection process ICICLE attempts to remove errors it is aware of in the code in an attempt to assist with the inspection process. ICICLE was designed to support inspections of the C/C++ language following Fagan's inspection method, which restricts the possible applications of the programme significantly

Scrutiny adds support for geographically distributed inspections, potentially allowing for large cost savings if used on a national/international project, allowing members of the team to hold inspections without the need for travel. An attempt to remove the language barrier was also implemented in Scrutiny as any plain text file is accepted by the system for inspection.

The University created an inspection support tool named CIS (Collaborative Software Inspection) in order to support Humphrey's software reviews. Like Scrutiny CIS is an on-line based tool allowing for geographically distributed development and inspection teams. The on-line bases of CIS allows it to support meetings not only over.

different geographic locations, but also across different time zones in that all members of the inspection team can do their inspection when it suits them. CIS uses hyperlinks to link the inspection documents to defect logs and notepads etc.

With the use of computer support becoming more and more common Knight and Myers developed InspeQ - an inspection support tool designed to support their phased inspection technique. InspeQ was designed for use by an individual inspector, and as such contains no meeting support tools, and generates a checklist for each inspector without any link being made between them.

In order to utilise the full potential of using computer support during an inspection process CSRS (Computer

Supported Review System) was developed along with its own inspection technique FTArm (Formal Technical Asynchronous review method). CSRS allows the user to model existing or future inspection methods with the goal of allowing CSRS to support and assist any inspection method.

The default method FTArm allows for the inspection of any document type. The exclusion of on-line meetings from CSRS renders this tool unusable to any development or inspection teams that are unable to meet face to face for inspection meetings. The idea of supporting any review method was also upheld by F. Macdonald and J Miller, the creators of ASSIST (Asynchronous/Synchronous Software Inspection Tool). ASSIST was designed with the goal of providing support for any inspection technique, to achieve this a process definition language was created so new inspection techniques could be added as and when they became available.

ASSIST contains 3 major stages, organisation, detection and completion these 3 stages can be applied to almost any current formal technical review method. With the growing demand for software inspection support tools it was inevitable that off-the-shelf software would soon appear an example of this is ReviewPro developed by Software Development Technologies Corporation.

A web based inspection tool ReviewPro includes the web server needed to host an inspection with ReviewPro will run on both Windows NT and Unix providing a solution for cross-platform development environments.

Chapter 12

Formal Technical Reviews

INTRODUCTION

In observing peer technical review processes over the past two decades, it has become obvious that no one review process is best for all. There are many variations on the general theme, which may be appropriate in some organizations and not in others [CRA].

This observation is in direct contrast to the SEI's (Software Engineering Institute) CMM (Capability Maturity Model), which basically prescribes a style of review process to be implemented at a particular point in an organization's overall process maturity. Characteristics of the process outlined follow the lines of the IEEE's standard for reviews [IEE].

In our deliberations over that standard in the early 1980's, only the most generic parts of a review process were retained, from the many successful variations with which the standards committee was familiar. The process defined basically elaborates on: *"You plan, prepare, review, and follow-up"*. Little guidance is provided on exactly *how* to do those activities. The real action of a review process, however, is in those details.

Regardless of an organization's maturity level, however, there is a review process appropriate for it. In an organization with absolutely no formally defined development process, people can sit down together, look over one another's work, and productively find flaws in their acts of software design and construction. In such an organization, that is probably the single most important thing to do to improve the quality of a delivered system.

As an organization matures (by whatever scale chosen), however, so should its technical review process. As an organization documents its processes, defining roles & responsibilities for people and entry & exit criteria for activities, so too should this be done for the review process. As measurement and baselines are established, the review process should be updated to track data.

As root cause analysis becomes understood, it should be integrated with reviews. And as the overall development process becomes better understood and more finely tuned, the standard review process has been seen to evolve into several processes, each appropriate to the very different types of workproducts within the development cycle.

Another dimension of variation among review processes is influenced by an organization's management style. Just as the varying cognitive styles of people influence how best they learn and mature, the management style of organizations influence the maturing of their review process. In an autocratic organization, a process, once somehow defined or selected, is imposed and changed by executive fiat. Management with a participative or consensual focus will have processes designed (at least in part) by the technical staff, thus opening the door to nearly unlimited process variations.

In the body of this paper, review processes for differing maturity levels are delineated. The basic outline of the CMM's process plateaus is used here, providing a common framework with the SEI's work. The influence of management style is then highlighted. My particular expertise in technical review processes comes from a long consulting relationship across a diversity of development organizations. My intuition tells me that a multi-level model of a review process, as discussed herein, has analogues in other software development practices. I hope others with a breadth of experience across these other practices can profit from this model and apply it within their realms.

REVIEW PROCESSES, BY MATURITY

What follows is a typical, generic story of a review

process, as it matures along with the overall set of an organization's development practices. The basic outline of the CMM is preserved, as a common framework. For any one development organization, the details may vary, but the general outline of the levels remains.

INITIAL PLATEAU

In an ad hoc development, peer reviews can prove particularly important. Any professional realizes that mistakes are likely in developing complex systems, and the independent perspective of another person is key in discovering oversights and blind spots. Babbage and von Neuman, long before "software development" was a phrase, reviewed with their peers the logic they attempted to implement on the earliest of computers.

An early model of software peer reviews was that familiar from referred journals: circulate a draft and consolidate returned commentary. To be effective for software, this model relies on the software artefact to be reasonably stand-alone and self explanatory. Another model, the buddy-check or desk-check, has roots in the multi-person office, where one could turn to a peer and ask them to, *"look this over, could you?"*

In this case, as questions arose, the author was close at hand to fill in missing context and detail. Too close, some would argue. Often these practices were "recommended" to be followed during software systems development, but the general lack of fine-grained project scheduling and tracking typical of organizations at this level precluded strict following of what actually occurred.

Some of the problems noted in the ad hoc practices of this stage were that of inconsistent practice both within and across teams, and a feeling among some that the time spent reviewing was wasted since it took away from time which could be otherwise be spent coding (which is the only real productive activity at this level, of course). Generally, the code's author runs the review, since the product *is* their responsibility.

UP TO THE REPEATABLE PLATEAU

At the repeatable level, the techniques with which people experimented at the *"initial"* level were improved based on experience, and generally documented. The processes were written down in their basic form to establish a common set of expectations across the team.

The advocates of reviews then began to make headway in achieving an initial degree of acceptance by looking at the success stories and qualitative feedback from the *"initial"* process efforts. With this process now a generally "recommended practice", their may be some degree of planning to help integrate review activities into the rest of the work to be done.

The review process, at this level, generally has this structure: first, material for review is distributed somewhat in advance of when the comments are needed; then, depending on the process used by the development team, the comments are consolidated by the author or by the group of reviewers as a team; the author then adjourns to independently correct the identified items. Typical processes at this level are the basic group peer reviews and walkthroughs.

New problems appear. Along with the structure added to the review process, other processes in the development lifecycle are being similarly examined and recommended, and software people are now asked to write down requirements, document designs, and develop test plans, in addition to the "real work" of cutting code.

Reviews, along with these other activities, are put into detailed project plans, which developers are held to follow. Under severe resource constraints, reviews begin to buckle: reviewers are given little advance review notice (since everything's running late); they often don't prepare adequately; they are given massive work products to review in a single sitting; and some identified items never get addressed because the author's deadlines are yesterday. *"Quality"*, an attribute far less visible than cost, schedule, and functionality, is left behind as a good intention.

DEFINED PLATEAU

By now, in the overall development process itself, there is enough data on development effort to show that maintenance is a nightmare sucking up project resources. Because of their ability to catch problems early and avoid potentially large downstream costs, reviewers *must get serious* about this review process, the thinking goes.

This is usually where the term "formal" is introduced, as in *"Formal Peer Reviews"*. Guidelines are established, such as lines-of-code/hour or pages/hour to help size a review to a realistic task. This also helps managers quantify the overall effort involved in reviews, which turns out to be large, but not as large as the maintenance numbers.

A common review process is once again improved to address the problems of the past. The process at this level looks much like that defined by the IEEE [IEE] or by Fagan [FAG]. Entry criteria are established (with specifics for different review types, such as design, code, test) defining amount of material to be covered in a review, materials to be distributed to reviewers, etc.

Roles and responsibilities (such as reader, scribe, moderator) are assigned to review team members to improve the meeting effectiveness. Since the author has emotion and schedule vested in the work product, the running of the review is often given to a more independent person to act as leader.

Since historically people have never prepared well, the meeting is run as a group walkthrough, with issues identified and delineated by the group as a reader summarizes the material sequentially. Follow-up activities are established to assure that identified items are resolved. Data are collected to support the cost-benefit of the reviews.

Since reviews have proven effective in avoiding problems, all the work-products of the lifecycle are expected to be reviewed. The cost of reviewing *everything* becomes enormous. Teams try to follow the proscribed process activities, but its overall effectiveness is lacking. In monitoring code reviews at this level, I have seen meetings where the most serious item discussed was basic syntax or structure a compiler or quick test would have identified, but the process said: *"No compiling or testing before the review"*. A well-intended process has been over-generalized, and now its details stand in need of evaluation.

MANAGING & OPTIMIZE - QUANTITATIVELY

The large scale tradeoff of reduced maintenance efforts used to finance solid review methodologies has been made at this point. The question now becomes how to manage and optimize *within* a process, the review process in this case. An organization having been through all this now has a base of experience and data which can drive either further changes or the status quo, depending on how it is used.

Some high-level data, along with probable process inferences, lead to refocusing review efforts at different levels. Across the software profession, there is less experience of reviews at this level, though some studies are being published.

As an example of process managing, Christenson [CHR] uses a baseline of data and a classical statistical paradigm to establish control limits for reviews. Using test and field data as driving quality measures, he relates these back to the data from individual reviews to characterize why some were better than others, and then establishes control limits and monitors ongoing reviews to these limits.

There are several problems in this approach, however. First and foremost is that development processes are human-based, not machine based, and the humans are conscious of the expectations on them; numbers can then be easily manipulated to fall within the desired norms. Another is the long-term nature of the feedback from a review, when one ultimately finds out how many of the total defects in a work-product the review found or which got through; long term feedback admits many intervening events, which may contaminate any results.

Machines have a rather short-term feedback from control to output, permitting quicker loops for isolating and understanding events, and for controlling them. As an example of process optimizing, Votta [VOT] takes a somewhat different course, using more immediate effectiveness measures to tune the process itself. In the environment studied, reviewers came to code review meetings having thoroughly prepared, with issues identified in advance, and the meetings were used to discuss, evaluate, and consolidate their findings.

Over a series of many reviews, he studied the union of all reviewers' issues before the meeting, and compared it to the list of issues documented during the meeting. The effect of synergy in finding new errors as a group (an advertised selling point of the process) was shown to counterbalance the effect of items which were on someone's list at the start, but were never discussed, and thus lost in the final reporting. The bottom line in this work was that for code reviews, group meetings added little to review effectiveness.

One possible conclusion is that the staff cost of the meeting time outweighed its marginal benefit, and thus should be abandoned under the circumstances studied. Another option may be to change the meeting's discussion protocol so that all issues get due consideration. What seems to be happening as we gain more insight into review processes is that the one-process-for-all workproducts becomes less applicable as we tune the process.

TO MANAGE & OPTIMIZE - QUALITATIVELY

We are enamored of metrics because they give an air of objectivity to our work. Measurements of software development are human-based, however, and will always have a subjective element. Much can be gained and learned from qualitative information, as well.

The developers themselves, those doing the work, can often give insights which data could never illuminate. This is one of the articles of faith of the current-day quality thrust, as propounded by Juran. Work with current clients has focused not on the steps of the review process, which are rather straightforward and generic, but on the details of how best to implement each.

For example, all review processes have a box labeled *"Preparation"*, where a reviewer studies a workproduct before the group meeting. But how is that best accomplished? Rifkin [RIF] argues that software people can well benefit from the current work and insights developed in the field of programme comprehension.

INFLUENCE OF MANAGEMENT STYLE ON PROCESS

Autocratic organizations are often thought to be easiest when technology transfer is addressed: import or create a process, train people, and demand it.

Drawbacks though are compliance and subterfuge. Will everyone follow the process, and if policed, will people report compliance accurately? Looking at process variations in this light is not productive, since once established, there is little room for conscious change.

For quantitatively driven managers, a process must be well-instrumented to demonstrate its value, or it will not survive.

One reason for Fagan's success [FAG] in implementing a software inspection process at IBM is the integration of data collection into the process.

Reviews are expensive in staff effort, and to justify their ongoing existence, data-driven managers need to see review costs displayed against the alternatively postulated maintenance savings to keep reviews in place.

Process designers under data-driven managers must be sure to integrate ongoing data capture, collection, analysis, and reporting into any process to justify its continuance. Of course this information is useful to know, but once established, the physical and intellectual expenses will be better directed toward understanding the next generation of process changes necessary.

For example, dollars-per-defect is certainly important in balancing review effort with maintenance effort, but defects-per-page is a more valuable statistic in exploring process variations which result in better defect removal. Managers with a participative focus will rely on people more than numbers to deliver an effective review process to the overall development environment.

One way to view this perspective is that a somewhat sub optimal process without compliance problems (since the developers who created it are vested in making it work) is preferable to a theoretically better process which no one is seriously motivated to follow. Given that varying sets of people are now responsible for the ultimate shape of a process, there are many process variations which may be implemented. The implications for process evolution are:

- Less need to instrument a process for data collection, and
- More need for periodic re-evaluation of process by developers themselves.

IMPACT ON PROCESS ENGINEERING AND TECHNOLOGY TRAINING

As an overall software development process matures, and so do its individual key component processes. This paper has pulled out one well understood key process threaded among the many of software development, and separately examined its story.

Each Process An Unending Task

The maturing of an overall software development organization is depicted by the CMM incrementally: a few basic key processes are established, and then on that foundation others are introduced. Much as in human development, where a child masters a task like reading and then moves on to other things.

Process engineers therefore focus on the introduction and integration of rather statically-defined processes, each at its appropriate place in the maturity timeline. But the review process story, revealed here, is not that of a static process. It is the story of a process that begins in the infancy of software development, and matures on a parallel track with development processes as a whole.

Process Experimentation

Key to ongoing process improvement is experimentation, to understand and verify improvement opportunities. In a manufacturing environment, a line can often be run under varying conditions to isolate improvements. Software development processes rarely give us that opportunity. Software development projects are large and costly, and rarely is there an opportunity to develop something more than once under controlled conditions.

Here are some rather basic issues which must be addressed for adequate software process experimentation:

- If end-product quality is the measure of success correlated to process changes, there is a long wait for results. Test data may be confounded by testing strategies, and the ultimate customer usage data is yet many more months out. More immediate measures need to be explored; Votta [VOT], for example, structured his study to measure the gross number of issues a review identified.
- Software development projects generally have many processes running simultaneously. There are thus many opportunities for confounding factors to come into play, especially in long-term studies. Weller [WEL] looks at review process data over three years, but makes no mention of other events in the development process over that time frame.
- Since software development processes are human-based, data submitted by people, can have a high degree of subjectivity. This adds significantly to noise at the data source.
- Traditional statistical advice dictates large sample sizes to average out the effects of noise and confounding effects. Thus the data collection task becomes yet more ambitious.
- Software engineering has been continuously plagued by the failure of results to scale up. Small projects and research on undergraduates has not helped large, industrial efforts. For results applicable to a large

industrial environment, one must study its large industrial projects.

Within the CMM optimization is at the highest of maturity plateaus. Unfortunately, this can lead process engineers working in organizations below level 5 to forgo experimentation. While experimentation with instrumented processes is certainly a long-term goal, there are experiments appropriate to all maturity levels, also.

At the earliest of maturities, small-scale, controlled studies can be useful to justify initial process design and establish basic ranges for process parameters. As an example, Buck [BUC] documented initial parameters for IBM's inspection process, using data from early process training classes. Operating ranges for material coverage rates and team size were indicated in the early work.

These early parameters must be viewed cautiously, though, as they become used in the very different environment of day-to-day practice. Process studies are ultimately needed to confirm and tune initial estimates.

As an example of middle-maturity process structuring, Weller [WEL] consolidated three years of experience with review processes. He pulls out several large scale themes from the data, which are likely to be relevant in his environment. There are many other possible explanation s that fit the data, however, which remain undiscussed; there is little basis to judge how portable the results are to other organizations.

Speciation

The evolution of species teaches that from variation and succession, the more fit can come to dominate. Thus in developing processes, designers should value variation and learn from it. A less obvious lesson parallels the evolutionary creation of several species from one, when there are varying environmental niches to fill.

I posit that this is what we are seeing in higher maturity projects, as review processes for requirements, design, and maintenance differentiate themselves to better meet their tasks. Hawks and sparrows are both recognized as birds, though feeding by hunting vs. gathering have given them very different styles and appearances.

The lesson for process engineering is to allow this to happen. Many organizations are pushing for a "common process", and the underlying standardization that implies. Consider an extreme case: should the review process for a newly developed subsystem be the same as that for a 5-line patch immediately required by a customer? It is certainly important to review both. But developing one process for both will likely lead to a process ill-suited to either.

Technology Training

In attempting to improve a review process, one must be cognizant of how mature the reviews themselves are, and focus efforts from that baseline. Rudimentary, industry-wide cost-benefit studies are not what's needed in working to improve an organization already at a CMM level three baseline. Similarly, thorough root-cause analysis will be lost on a project just starting to collect defect data. Training is needed on an ongoing, and updated, basis as processes evolve, to establish a common framework. But training must focus on the delta: many organizations have at least some exposure to reviews; few are starting from scratch. This is an ideal opportunity for trainers to capitalize on the existing experience base. Developers are often cognizant of needed improvements, and more experientially-based instruction can lead them constructively onward.

CONDUCT OF FORMAL TECHNICAL REVIEWS (FTR)

The FTR (Formal Technical Review) is a software quality assurance activity with the objectives to uncover errors in function, logic or implementation for any representation of the software; to verify that the software under review meets its requirements; to ensure that the software has been represented according to predefined standards; to achieve software that is developed in a uniform manner and to make projects more manageable.

FTR (Formal Technical Review) is also a learning ground for junior developers to know more about different approaches to software analysis, design and implementation. It also serves as a backup and continuity for the people who are not exposed to the software development so far. FTR (Formal Technical Review) activities include walkthroughs, inspection and round robin reviews and other technical assessments. The above-mentioned methods are different FTR (Formal Technical Review) formats.

REVIEW MEETINGS

Review meeting is important form of FTR (Formal Technical Review) and there are some essential parameters for the meeting such as there should be reasonable number of persons conducting the meeting and that too after each one of them has done his/her homework i.e. some preparation and the meeting should not be carried out very long which may lead to wastage of time but rather for duration just enough to churn out some constructive results.

FTR (Formal Technical Review) is effective when a small and specific part of the overall software is under scrutiny. It is easier and more productive to review in small parts like each module one by one rather than to review the whole thing in one go. The target of the FTR (Formal Technical Review) is on a component of the project, a single module.

The individual or the team that has developed that specific module or product intimates the product is complete and a review may take place. Then the project leader forwards the request to the review leader who further informs the reviewers who undertake the task. The members of the review meeting are reviewers who undertake the task. The members of the review meeting are reviewers, review-leader, product developers (or the module leader alone) and there one of the reviewers takes up the job of the recorder and notes down all the important issues raised in the meeting.

At the end of each review meeting the decision has to be taken by the attendees of the FTR (Formal Technical Review) on whether to accept the product without further modification or to reject the product due to severe errors or to accept the product provisionally. All FTR (Formal Technical Review) attendees sign off whatever decision taken. At the end of the review a review issues list and a review summary is report is generated.

WALK THROUGH

Introduction

A static analysis technique in which a designer or programmer leads members of the development team and other interested parties through a segment of documentation or code, and the participants ask questions and make comments about possible errors, violation of development standards, and other problems.

Software testing is all about caring for software quality. It helps in deploying error free software, in time. Software testing helps to find out the deviations of software developed from the result expected. The quality analyst engineers assure that the software testing reveals appropriate results with respect to what the software was intended for ?

A software testing company works to deliver quality assured software applications – be it big or small project. Software testing company analysis the difficulties keeping in view that each project developed is unique. A project may have undergone several alterations, while its way to deployment.

Bugs get incorporated due to many factors. Starting form miscommunication, defecting software coding, use of software development tools, timely delivery pressures, and the ever changing requirements, all can contribute for flawed software. No matter what the case may be, what counts is the defects should be fixed before the customer makes use of it.

Software testing company has a wide area to work on. The IT industry may be flooded with a variety of software testing services, not to mention the wide diversity found in their baptism scheme. There is compatibility testing, functional testing, performance testing, load testing, regression testing, stress testing, and unit testing among a few to mention.

A reliable software testing company realizes the need for validating the software product not just once, but also repeated validation for each new release of the software product or website.

A reputed software testing company follows specific guidelines in accordance to the client's requirements. They ensure to comply with the quality system with regards to software validation.

Software testing company follows the bug testing processes, to the max. The head quality analyst (project manager) of software testing company is responsible for project planning and scheduling it. Monitoring and reporting the project of software testing is handled with utmost diligence. For each project, the software testing is different. This depends on the size, scope and usability of the project. Each factor looked on with minute details prove worth in delivering a quality software output after software testing services.

Software testing is all about caring for software quality. It helps in deploying error free software, in time. Software testing helps to find out the deviations of software developed from the result expected. The quality analyst engineers assure that the software testing reveals appropriate results with respect to what the software was intended for?

A software testing company works to deliver quality assured software applications - be it big or small project. Software testing company analysis the difficulties keeping in view that each project developed is unique. A project may have undergone several alterations, while its way to deployment.

Bugs get incorporated due to many factors. Starting form miscommunication, defecting software coding, use of software development tools, timely delivery pressures, and the ever changing requirements, all can contribute for flawed software. No matter what the case may be, what counts is the defects should be fixed before the customer makes use of it.

Software testing company has a wide area to work on. The IT industry may be flooded with a variety of software testing services, not to mention the wide diversity found in their baptism scheme.

There is compatibility testing, functional testing, performance testing, load testing, regression testing, stress testing, and unit testing among a few to mention.

A reliable software testing company realizes the need for validating the software product not just once, but also repeated validation for each new release of the software product or website.

A reputed software testing company follows specific guidelines in accordance to the client's requirements.

They ensure to comply with the quality system with regards to software validation. Software testing company follows the bug testing processes, to the max. The head quality analyst (project manager) of software testing company is responsible for project planning and scheduling it. Monitoring and reporting the project of software testing is handled with utmost diligence. For each project, the software testing is different. This depends on the size, scope and usability of the project. Each factor looked on with minute details prove worth in delivering a quality software output after software testing services. Software testing has positive impacts on quality software. It helps clients business and makes the software developed more usable and more user-friendly.

The objectives of Walkthrough can be summarized as follows:

- Detect errors early.
- Ensure (re)established standards are followed:
- Train and exchange technical information among project teams which participate in the walkthrough.
- Increase the quality of the project, thereby improving morale of the team members.

The participants in Walkthroughs assume one or more of the following roles:

- Walk-through leader
- Recorder
- Author

- Team member

To consider a review as a systematic walk-through, a team of at least two members shall be assembled. Roles may be shared among the team members. The walk-through leader or the author may serve as the recorder. The walk-through leader may be the author.

Individuals holding management positions over any member of the walk-through team shall not participate in the walk-through.

Input to the walk-through shall include the following:

- A statement of objectives for the walk-through
- The software product being examined
- Standards that are in effect for the acquisition, supply, development, operation, and/or maintenance of the software product

Input to the walk-through may also include the following:

- Any regulations, standards, guidelines, plans, and procedures against which the software product is to be inspected
- Anomaly categories

The walk-through shall be considered complete when:

- The entire software product has been examined
- Recommendations and required actions have been recorded
- The walk-through output has been completed

SAMPLE REQUIREMENT SPECIFICATION WALKTHROUGH CHECKLIST

Users of this checklist should keep in mind that this is a good starting point of questions that shold be asked to ensure that all requirements are gathered from any phase in a project from specification through to production delivery.

Clarity

Are the requirements written in non-technical understandable language?

Are there any requirements that could have more than one interpretation?

Is each characteristic of the final product described with a unique terminology?

Is there a glossary in which the specific meaning(s) of each term is(are) defined?

Could the requirements be understood and implemented by an independent group?

Completeness

Is there a table of contents:

- Are all figures, tables, and diagrams labeled?
- Are all figures, tables, and diagrams cross-referenced?
- Are all terms defined?
- Are all terms indexed?
- Are all units of measure defined?
- Are areas where information is incomplete because development hasn't started been specified?
- Is the missing information defined in the requirement?
- Should any requirement be specified in more detail?
- Should any requirement be specified in less detail?
- Are all of the requirements defined?
- Are all of the requirements related to functionality included?
- Are there any requirements which make you feel uneasy?
- Are all of the requirements related to performance included?
- Are all of the requirements related to design constraints included?
- Are all of the requirements related to attributes included?
- Are all of the requirements related to external interfaces included?
- Are all of the requirements related to databases included?
- Are all of the requirements related to software included?
- Are all of the requirements related to communi-cations included

- Are all of the requirements related to hardware included
- Are all of the requirements related to inputs included?
- Are all of the requirements related to outputs included?
- Are all of the requirements related to reporting included?
- Are all of the requirements related to security included?
- Are all of the requirements related to maintainability included?
- Are all of the requirements related to installation included?
- Are all of the requirements related to criticality included?
- Are all of the requirements related to the permanency limitations included?
- Are possible changes to the requirements specified?
- Is the likelihood of change specified for each requirement?

Consistency

- Are there any requirements describing the same object that conflict with other requirements with respect to terminology?
- Are there any requirements describing the same object that conflict with respect to characteristics?
- Are there any requirements that describe two or more actions that conflict logically?
- Are there any requirements that describe two or more actions that conflict temporally?

Traceability

- Are all requirements traceable back to a specific user need?
- Are all requirements traceable back to a specific source document or person?
- Are all requirements traceable forward to a specific design document?
- Are all requirements traceable forward to a specific

software module?

Verifiability

- Are any Requirements included which are impossible to implement?
- For each requirement is there a process that can be executed by either a human or a machine to verify the requirement?
- Are there any requirements that will be expressed in verifiable terms at a later time?

Modifiability

- Is the requirements document clearly and logically organized?
- Does the organization adhere to an accepted standard?
- Is there any redundancy in the requirements?

General

- Is each requirement relevant to the problem and its solution?
- Are any of the defined requirements really design details?
- Are any of the defined requirements really verification details?
- Are any of the defined requirements really project management details?
- Is there an introduction section?
- Is there a general description section?
- Is there a scope section?
- Is there a definitions, acronyms, and abbreviations section?
- Is there a specific requirements section?
- Is there a product perspective section?
- Is there a product functions section?
- Is there a user characteristics section?
- Is there a general constraints section?
- Is there an assumptions and dependencies section?

- Is there a specific requirements section?
- Are all of the necessary appendixes present?
- Are all of the necessary figures present?
- Are all of the necessary tables present?
- Are all of the necessary diagrams present?

Specific

Inputs

- Are all input sources specified?
- Are all input accuracy requirements specified?
- Are all input range values specified?
- Are all input frequencies specified?
- Are all input formats specified?

Outputs

- Are all output destinations specified?
- Are all output accuracy requirements specified?
- Are all output range values specified?
- Are all output frequencies specified?
- Are all output formats specified?

Reports

- Are all report formats specified?
- Are all calculations/formulas used in reports specified?
- Are all report data filter requirements specified?
- Are all report sorting requirements specified?
- Are a report totaling requirements specified?
- Are all report formatting requirements specified?

Functions

- Are all software functions specified
- Are all inputs specified for each function?
- Are all aspects of the processing specified for each function?
- Are all outputs specified for each function?
- Are all performance requirements specified for each function?
- Are all design constrains specified for each function?
- Are all attributes specified for each function?
- All security requirements specified for each function?

- Are all maintainability requirements specified for each function?
- Are all data base requirements specified for each function?
- Are all Operational requirements specified for each function?
- Are all installation requirements specified for each function?

External Interfaces

- Are all user interfaces specified?
- Are all batch interfaces specified?
- Are all Hardware interfaces specified?
- Are all Software interfaces specified?
- Are all communications interfaces specified?
- Are all interface design constraints specified?
- Are all interface security requirements specified?
- Are all interface maintainability requirements specified?
- Are all human-computer interactions specified for user interfaces?

Internal Interfaces

- Have all internal interfaces been identified?
- Have all internal interfaces characteristics been specified?

Timing

- Are all expected processing times specified?
- Are all Data transfer Rates specified?
- Are all system through put rates specified?

Reliability

- Are the consequences of software failure specified for each requirement?
- Is the information to protect from failure specified?
- Is a strategy for error detection Specified?
- Is a strategy for correction specified?

Tradeoffs

- Are acceptable trade-offs specified for competing attributes?

Hardware

- Is the minimum memory specified?
- Is the minimum storage specified?
- Is the maximum memory specified?
- Is the maximum storage specified?

Software

- Are the required software environments/OS's specified?
- Are all of the required software utilities specified?
- Are all purchased software products that are to be used with the system specified?

Communications

- Is the target network specified?
- Are the required network protocols specified?
- Is the required network capacity specified?
- Is the required/estimated network throughput rate specified?
- Is the estimated number of network connections specified?
- Are minimum network performance requirements specified?
- Are the maximum network performance requirements specified?
- Are the optimal network performance requirements specified?

COGNITIVE WALKTHROUGH

Usability Inspection is referred as a systematic procedural review of a system, based on a number of stipulated guidelines where the user interface is inspected by a number of evaluators. Therefore usability inspection is focused in finding out the usability problems in design, which has always been problematic for users, some areas that get evaluated are the language used in the system, the amount of recall required by the user at each step in a process, the amount of feedback provided by the system to the user.

Specific issues such as clarity, consistency, navigation, and error minimisation are analysed thoroughly. Once the problems are identified, the experts give their reviews and recommendations for resolving these issues.

There are also some methods in which, issues like the severity of the usability problems and the overall usability of the entire system is identified. There are many inspection methods, which contribute themselves to the inspection of the user interface specifications that hasn't necessarily been implemented but then it is clearly feasible that inspection can be performed at an early stage in the usability-engineering life cycle.

Usability Inspection is preferred to any of the traditional laboratory evaluation methods, as usability inspection tools are economical, much cheaper, faster and very reliable as it deals with real time users. Moving ahead we shall delve about the types usability inspection methods. The first one would be Heuristic Evaluation.

Heuristic Evaluation is the most popular and an informal method of the usability inspection, which involves having usability experts who examine the interface and judge its compliance with a set of principles, also known as the ("Heuristics"). A heuristic evaluation can be carried out at different phases of the development lifecycle; though it's better to carry out some type of <u>context analysis</u> to help out the experts focus on the actual product usage.

Cognitive Walkthrough is another usability inspection method, which is used to identify usability issues through a particular software or a website, focusing on how easy and user friendly it is for the new users to accomplish tasks with the system. Cognitive walkthrough uses a more explicitly detailed and a simple procedure to simulate a user's problem-solving process at each step through the dialogue, checking if the simulated user's goals and memory content can be assumed to lead the users to the next best correct action.

Expert Review - a group of experts inspect a website to identify the potential usability problems faced by the users. Usability Testing is a priceless usability inspection method, which is used to evaluate a product by testing it on real time users.

This method is a very valuable one due to its irreplaceable

usability practice, as it gives direct input on how real users use the system. This is in contrast with the usability inspection method where experts use different methods to evaluate a user interface without involving users.

Usability testing aims in determining a product's capacity to meet its exact purpose. The products that exercise usability testing are websites or web applications, documents, devices and computer interfaces. Usability testing determines the usability of a specific object.

CODE INSPECTION

DEFINITION

A formal testing technique where the programmer reviews source code with a group who ask questions analyzing the programme logic, analyzing the code with respect to a checklist of historically common programming errors, and analyzing its compliance with coding standards.

You can control tasks related to your code directly from your changeset view. This will help you to keep you code clean and up-to-date.

From here you can jump to the task list and back in one click to see the whole picture. Status bullets show you the status of the tasks. You may also create, edit and delete tasks by clicking on the left of any code line.

CODE INSPECTION ON COMMERCIAL WEB SERVERS

The prevalent open-source version of the Apache Web server stacks up well with commercial Web servers in terms of the number of code defects, according to a study by Mountain View, Calif.-based automated software inspection service provider Reasoning.

Reasoning recently inspected Apache V2.1 and compared it with other commercial Web servers that were at a similar stage of their development and found 31 code defects in 58,944 lines of code for a defect density of 0.53 per thousand lines of code. Commercial Web servers have a defect density of 0.51

per thousand lines.

Using its homegrown proprietary automated inspection software and processes for Java and C and C++ applications, Reasoning inspected the Apache code looking for memory leaks, NULL point dereference defects, bad deallocation, out-of-bounds array access and uninitialized variables.

Reasoning found 29 instances of NULL point dereferences where expressions dereference a NULL pointer; the company also found two instances of uninitialized variables where a variable was not initialized prior to use.

"Some consider any defect a security defect," said Thomas Fry, Reasoning's director of marketing. "Some resource leaks in Java, for example, lead to denial-of-service attacks. It depends on how you define a security vulnerability [as opposed to a coding problem]."

Earlier this year, Reasoning did a code review of the Linux TCP/IP stack against commercial TCP/IP stacks, and Linux won in a big way. Eight defects were found in 81,852 lines of code of the Linux 2.4.19 networking sample.

Reasoning shares its findings with the open-source community. The findings from the Linux TCP/IP inspection were sent to Linux kernel developers, and some were addressed and fixed immediately, Fry said. Reasoning is waiting to hear from the Apache Group regarding the most recent survey.

"We report all of the defects to the community and to our customers," Fry said. "With our customers, 80% to 85% of the [Apache] defects were fixed immediately. They agreed they were serious." Currently, Reasoning is inspecting code in Tomcat, a module in Apache that enables the Web server software to run Java applications.

Fry expects those results within two weeks. "We're only doing reviews right now of open-source projects with large peer reviews [like Linux and Apache]," Fry said. "There are plenty of open-source projects that have smaller followings and less peer reviews. We'll be looking at those eventually to determine how the peer review process improves quality."

CODE INSPECTION TO SPREADSHEET TESTING

In programming, reliability requires an extensive testing phase. Spreadsheet development, which has about the error rate as programme development, also needs to be followed by an extensive testing phase if spreadsheets are to be reliable. In this study, sixty undergraduate MIS students code-inspected a spreadsheet seeded with eight errors. They first inspected the spreadsheet working alone. They then met in twenty groups of three to reinspect the spreadsheet together. Effort was made to prevent hasty inspection.

Individual code inspection, consistent with past studies of both spreadsheet and programme code inspection, caught only 63 per cent of the errors. Group inspection raised this to 83 per cent. However, the group phase never found new errors; it merely pooled the errors found during the individual phase by the three members.

One group even lost an error found during the individual phase. This raises the question of whether a group code inspection phase is really necessary. Other findings were that subjects were overconfident when inspecting alone, that certain types of errors are especially difficult to detect, and that the benefits of the group phase is greatest for these difficult-to-detect types of errors.

COMPLIANCE WITH DESIGN AND CODING STANDARDS

INTRODUCTION

Compliance is either a state of being in accordance with established guidelines, specifications, or legislation or the process of becoming so. Software, for example, may be developed in compliance with specifications created by some standards body, such as the Institute of Electrical and Electronics Engineers (IEEE), and may be distributed in compliance with the vendor's licensing agreement.

In the legal system, compliance usually refers to behaviour in accordance with legislation, such as the United States Can Spam Act of 2003, theSarbanes-Oxley Act (SOX) of 2002, or HIPAA (United States Health Insurance Portability and Accountability Act of 1996).

Compliance in a regulatory context is a prevalent business concern, perhaps because of an ever-increasing number of regulations and a fairly widespread lack of understanding about what is required for a company to be in compliance with new legislation.

OVERVIEW

New environmental regulations are forcing companies in the electrical and electronic equipment industry to change the way products are designed. With the risks of non-compliance ranging from potential fines to being completely shut out of key markets, manufacturers will need to effectively address these regulations in order to minimize the impact on profit margins and prevent loss of revenue.

Currently, attention is focused on the European Union's Restrictions on the use of certain Hazardous Substances directive and Waste of Electrical and Electronic Equipment recycling mandate.

Similar regulations and voluntary programs are also being established across the globe in countries such as the U.S., China, Japan and South Korea. July 2006, the time the RoHS directive takes effect, should, therefore, not be perceived as the compliance "finish line," rather the beginning of a new era when environmental impact considerations will be integral to product design decisions.

The optimal time to ensure compliance occurs during the initial product design stages. When non-compliant components and assemblies are identified, changes can be made quickly and easily in computer aided design or product lifecycle management applications where the cost to change designs is relatively inexpensive.

On the other hand, the costs of compliance increase exponentially once the product advances beyond the prototype phase and moves into full production; where changes, may require an engineering change order, field replacement or product recall. The phrase, "design for compliance" has been used to describe the proactive approach to managing compliance in the design phase.

While most companies agree that managing product compliance without a robust information system is not feasible; many companies lack the necessary IT infrastructure to manage the complexity introduced by environmental compliance.

Compliance cannot be addressed by merely requiring a compliance certification from suppliers, which is then stored in a database for retrieval.

Experience has shown that supplier compliance certificates are often inaccurate due to many factors, including a lack of understanding concerning interpretation of the regulations and the proper reporting of substances at the homogenous material level. These unintentional errors can lead to significant risk for original equipment manufacturers that are ultimately responsible for the compliance of their products.

In order to effectively determine if a product is compliant, various factors must be analysed and tracked such as material content, substance concentrations and product exemptions. Manufacturers can significantly reduce their risk by requiring suppliers to provide material content information in addition to certificates of compliance. With material data, the substance concentrations can be compared directly with the regulatory requirements to eliminate errors and determine compliance.

Although it may seem counter-intuitive, the analytical approach is much more cost effective than a simple certificate of compliance due to a number of factors. For example, when existing regulations change or new regulations are introduced, the manufacturer can analyse existing data rather than surveying suppliers again. Most importantly, OEMs can eliminate errors, thereby avoiding fines and rework costs.

There are a number of factors to consider when implementing an IT system to manage compliance. In addition to material compliance analysis capabilities, the system should also be able to account for rapidly changing environmental regulations across multiple markets and geographies.

Similarly vital is the system's ability to integrate sourcing and product development information.

Material and part suppliers are key partners in a company's drive for compliance, since a single non-compliant supplier could cause the product to be non-compliant. The IT infrastructure should expedite the flow of material content information and supplier compliance certificates across the supply chain and provide design engineers the necessary visibility to use this information during all stages of the product development lifecycle.

In addition, the application should support links to multiple IT systems within a company since many manufacturers often have product management and supply chain systems that vary by product groups and divisions.

Synapsis Technology has developed a solution that can easily integrate into a company's existing PLM, CAD and ERP systems while providing a centralized platform to manage compliance.

The Environmental Material Aggregation and Reporting System is a sophisticated solution that addresses the analysis, tracking, data collection and reporting needs of an entire organization and provides the visibility that design engineers require to design for compliance.

EMARS helps product development teams assure product compliance starting day one. With EMARS, a design engineer has the ability to confidently select a compliant part or subassembly based on EMARS' extensive evaluation of its compliance, accounting for multi-sourced components and product exemptions.

A design engineer will have similar information available when selecting parts in EMARS. The engineer will know that Part A can be used to design a compliant Server type product for ROHS, but not a consumer product.

Additionally, the Pass with Exemptions status denotes that Part A meets the regulatory requirements by means of a regulatory product exemption such as "lead in solder for server and infrastructure equipment." This is an important capability that helps companies deplete inventory during transition to compliant parts over time as they become commercially available. The enhanced level of compliance visibility at the part or subassembly level will help the design engineer assure that the product meets all the regulatory requirements of the market or geography where the product will be sold.

Companies that are concerned about minimizing the risk and cost of compliance cannot deal with compliance as a tactical problem or a short-term initiative to assure that the product meets ROHS and WEEE. Current and future regulations require long-term investments and the implementation of robust processes and flexible systems that embed regulatory compliance into the fabric of the organization.

ANALYTICAL TESTING

Compliance Designs offers comprehensive bottled water analyses to meet Federal, State and/or Industry standards at competitive prices. We also provide flexibility with regards to early notification of results, soft-copy transmittal of analytical data, and a comprehensive summary designed as a marketing tool that consolidates all laboratory results in a concise easy-to-read format. What CDI accomplishes with their analytical testing programme is ease of sampling and analysis, and increased communication and flexibility.

Administrative Permit Management

We were the first to do it. We are the best at what we do. Compliance Designs has been providing permit management services to members of the bottled water and beverage industries for over 15 years.

We use our wealth of experience and knowledge to keep abreast of state licensing requirements for the manufacture and distribution of bottled waters and beverages. Our established relationships with many state regulatory agencies allows us to apply for and maintain state licenses, with as little effort on the part of the manufacturing personnel as possible.

PRODUCTS

Label Requirements Report

Summary of the major FDA and State bottled water and beverage labeling requirements

Regulations Binder Set

Comprehensive compilation of all state and federal bottled water rules and regulations (set of 5 binders)

Certificate of Potability

Professionally designed certificate stating that the water tested meets EPA's primary drinking water standards and FDA's quality standards for bottled water based upon a review of analytical data

SERVICES

- Annual Analysis to meet State, Industry, and Federal bottled water monitoring requirements. We obtain volume discounts for bottled water manufacturers from qualified laboratories holding the necessary state certificates and having the capability to analyse for parameters required by regulatory authorities in every state. We act as the liaison between the bottler and each laboratory so that each bottler always has personal and individual attention.
- Weekly Microbiological analysis to meet State and Federal Requirements. Our programme is very competitively priced, and includes sampling supplies and an analysis by certified laboratories to satisfy State and Federal monitoring requirements for Total Coliform and Standard Plate Count. We summarize results in an easy-to-read report that is provided to the bottler each week.
- State Reporting of Weekly Microbiological Analyses Several States require that a bottled water manufacturer submit monthly, quarterly or semi-annual results from the weekly analysis of their sources and products for

Total Coliform and Standard Plate Count. For a standard monthly fee, Compliance Designs will submit these reports to the states as required, and provide the bottler with copies of the reports and cover letters.

- Permit/License Management Services. Several States require that Bottled water and beverage manufacturers obtain and maintain licenses to distribute their products. Compliance Designs provides license management services that include a checklist of items/information required to apply for individual state licenses, preparation and submittal of license applications, and liaison services between the bottler and the licensing entity for all regulatory issues.
- Permit Renewal Notification. Compliance Designs will maintain a calendar of license expiration dates for manufacturers and provide early notification of pending renewals so that the facility's permits and licenses remain current.
- Special Projects. Our consultants are qualified by years of experience regarding bottled water and beverage manufacturing and regulation. Our staff also includes a former laboratory director, and two former bottled water plant managers. The knowledge and expertise of our consultants can be a valuable resource for questions regarding all aspects of bottled water operations.

Chapter 13

Compliance Design

INTRODUCTION

With this programme one can do 3D compliance optimization. There is a graphical user interface and the computations are taken care. It is a requirement that you have installed both Java and the Java 3D extension in order to use the programme.

In comparison to the Compliance Design (2D) this programme allows more freedom with respect to number of elements and design iterations. Choose either one of the predefined examples or construct your own.

FEATURES

Stiffness optimization using Topology Optimization. Visualization using the JAVA 3D libriary. Export of results in.STL files (StereoLithography files) for postprocessing in a CAD programme e.g. Microstation. Load and save option for examples.

Export of results to.jpg files for documentation, report writing etc. Please note that when the programme is executed it creates a folder at the desktop (Windows)/in the home folder (*nix) named top3dfiles containing the input/output files.

CODING STANDARDS

INDENTING AND LINE LENGTH

Use an indent of 4 spaces, with no tabs. This helps to avoid problems with diffs, patches, SVN history and annotations.

For Emacs you should set indent-tabs-mode to nil. Here is an example mode hook that will set up Emacs (ensure that it is called when you are editing PHP files):

```
(defun pear/php-mode-init()
"Set some buffer-local variables."
(setq case-fold-search t)
(c-set-offset 'arglist-intro '+)
(c-set-offset 'arglist-close '0)
)
(add-hook 'php-mode-hook 'pear/php-mode-init)
```

Here are Vim rules for the same thing:

```
set expandtab
set shiftwidth=4
set softtabstop=4
set tabstop=4
```

It is recommended to keep lines at approximately 75-85 characters long for better code readability. Paul M. Jones has some thoughts about that limit.

CONTROL STRUCTURES

These include if, for, while, switch, etc. Here is an example if statement, since it is the most complicated of them:

```
<?php
if ((condition1) || (condition2)) {
    action1;
}  elseif ((condition3) && (condition4)) {
   action2;
```

```
} else {
  defaultaction;
}
?>
```

Control statements should have one space between the control keyword and opening parenthesis, to distinguish them from function calls.

You are strongly encouraged to always use curly braces even in situations where they are technically optional. Having them increases readability and decreases the likelihood of logic errors being introduced when new lines are added.

For switch statements:

```
<?php
switch (condition) {
case 1:
    action1;
    break;
case 2:
    action2;
    break;
default:
    defaultaction;
    break;
}
?>
```

Split Long if Statements onto Several Lines

Long if statements may be split onto several lines when the character/line limit would be exceeded. The conditions have to be positioned onto the following line, and indented 4 characters.

The logical operators (&&, ||, etc.) should be at the beginning of the line to make it easier to comment (and exclude) the condition. The closing parenthesis and opening brace get their own line at the end of the conditions.

Keeping the operators at the beginning of the line has two advantages: It is trivial to comment out a particular line during development while keeping syntactically correct code (except of course the first line). Further is the logic kept at the front where it's not forgotten. Scanning such conditions is very easy since they are aligned below each other.

```
<?php
if (($condition1
    || $condition2)
    && $condition3
    && $condition4
)   {
    //code here
}
    ?>
```

The first condition may be aligned to the others.

```
<?php
if (   $condition1
    || $condition2
    || $condition3
   ) {
    //code here
}
?>
```

The best case is of course when the line does not need to be split. When the if clause is really long enough to be split, it might be better to simplify it. In such cases, you could express conditions as variables an compare them in the if() condition. This has the benefit of "naming" and splitting the condition sets into smaller, better understandable chunks:

```
<?php
$is_foo = ($condition1 || $condition2);
$is_bar = ($condition3 && $condtion4);
if ($is_foo && $is_bar) {
// ....
}
?>
```

There were suggestions to indent the parantheses "groups" by 1 space for each grouping. This is too hard to achieve in your coding flow, since your tab key always produces 4 spaces. Indenting the if clauses would take too much finetuning.

Ternary Operators

The same rule as for if clauses also applies for the ternary operator: It may be split onto several lines, keeping the question mark and the colon at the front.

```
<?php
$a = $condition1 && $condition2
    ? $foo : $bar;
$b = $condition3 && $condition4
   ? $foo_man_this_is_too_long_what_should_i_do
   : $bar;
?>
```

FUNCTION CALLS

Functions should be called with no spaces between the function name, the opening parenthesis, and the first parameter; spaces between commas and each parameter, and no space between the last parameter, the closing parenthesis, and the semicolon.

Here's an example:

```
<?php
$var = foo($bar, $baz, $quux);
?>
```

As displayed above, there should be one space on either side of an equals sign used to assign the return value of a function to a variable. In the case of a block of related assignments, more space may be inserted to promote readability:

```
<?php
$short         = foo($bar);
$long_variable = foo($baz);
?>
```

To support readability, parameters in subsequent calls to the same function/method may be aligned by parameter name:

```
<?php
```

```
$this->callSomeFunction('param1',   'second',
true);
$this->callSomeFunction('parameter2', 'third',
false);
$this->callSomeFunction('3',
'verrrrrrylong', true);
?>
```

Split Function Call on Several Lines

The CS require lines to have a maximum length of 80 chars. Calling functions or methods with many parameters while adhering to CS is impossible in that cases. It is allowed to split parameters in function calls onto several lines.

```
<?php
$this->someObject->subObject->callThisFunction
WithALongName(
$parameterOne, $parameterTwo,
$aVeryLongParameterThree
);
?>
```

Several parameters per line are allowed. Parameters need to be indented 4 spaces compared to the level of the function call. The opening parenthesis is to be put at the end of the function call line, the closing parenthesis gets its own line at the end of the parameters.

This shows a visual end to the parameter indentations and follows the opening/closing brace rules for functions and conditionals.

The same applies not only for parameter variables, but also for nested function calls and for arrays.

```
<?php
$this->someObject->subObject-
    >callThisFunctionWithALongName(
   $this->someOtherFunc(
      $this->someEvenOtherFunc(
         'Help me!',
         array(
            'foo' => 'bar',
```

```
                'spam' => 'eggs',
            ),
            23
        ),
        $this->someEvenOtherFunc()
    ),
    $this->wowowowowow(12)
);
?>
```

Nesting those function parameters is allowed if it helps to make the code more readable, not only when it is necessary when the characters per line limit is reached.

Using fluent application programming interfaces often leads to many concatenated function calls. Those calls may be split onto several lines. When doing this, all subsequent lines are indented by 4 spaces and begin with the "->" arrow.

```
<?php
$someObject->someFunction("some", "parameter")
    ->someOtherFunc(23, 42)
    ->andAThirdFunction();
?>
```

Alignment of Assignments

To support readability, the equal signs may be aligned in block-related assignments:

```
<?php
$short  = foo($bar);
$longer = foo($baz);
?>
```

The rule can be broken when the length of the variable name is at least 8 characters longer/shorter than the previous one:

```
<?php
$short = foo($bar);
$thisVariableNameIsVeeeeeeeeeeryLong = foo($baz);
?>
```

Split Long Assigments Onto Several Lines

Assigments may be split onto several lines when the

character/line limit would be exceeded. The equal sign has to be positioned onto the following line, and indented by 4 characters.

```
<?php
$GLOBALS['TSFE']->additionalHeaderData[$this-
>strApplicationName]
= $this->xajax->getJavascript
(t3lib_extMgm::siteRelPath('nr_xajax'));
```

FUNCTION DEFINITIONS

Function declarations follow the "K&R style":

```
<?php
function fooFunction($arg1, $arg2 = '')
{
    if (condition) {
    statement;
    }
    return $val;
}
?>
```

Arguments with default values go at the end of the argument list. Always attempt to return a meaningful value from a function if one is appropriate.

Here is a slightly longer example:

```
<?php
function connect(&$dsn, $persistent = false)
{
    if (is_array($dsn)) {
        $dsninfo = &$dsn;
    } else {
        $dsninfo = DB::parseDSN($dsn);
    }
    if (!$dsninfo || !$dsninfo['phptype']) {
        return $this->raiseError();
    }
        return true;
    }
?>
```

Split Function Definitions onto Several Lines

Functions with many parameters may need to be split onto several lines to keep the 80 characters/line limit. The first parameters may be put onto the same line as the function name if there is enough space.

Subsequent parameters on following lines are to be indented 4 spaces. The closing parenthesis and the opening brace are to be put onto the next line, on the same indentation level as the "function" keyword.

```
<?php
function someFunction With A Very Long Name
($firstParameter = 'something', $second Parameter
= 'booooo',
  $third = null, $fourthParameter = false, $fifthParameter = 123.12,
    $sixthParam = true
) {
    //....
?>
```

INDENTING AND WHITESPACE

Use an indent of 2 spaces, with no tabs. Lines should have no trailing whitespace at the end. Files should be formatted with \n as the line ending (Unix line endings), not \r\n (Windows line endings).

OPERATORS

All binary operators (operators that come between two values), such as +, -, =, !=, ==, >, etc. should have a space before and after the operator, for readability. For example, an assignment should be formatted as $foo = $bar;rather than $foo=$bar;.

Unary operators (operators that operate on only one value), such as ++, should not have a space between the operator and the variable or number they are operating on.

CONTROL STRUCTURES

Control structures include if, for, while, switch, etc. Here is a sample if statement, since it is the most complicated of them:

```
if (condition1 || condition2) {
    action1;
}
elseif (condition3 && condition4) {
    action2;
}
else {
    defaultaction;
}
```

Control statements should have one space between the control keyword and opening parenthesis, to distinguish them from function calls.

You are strongly encouraged to always use curly braces even in situations where they are technically optional. Having them increases readability and decreases the likelihood of logic errors being introduced when new lines are added.

For switch statements:

```
switch (condition) {
    case 1:
        action1;
        break;
    case 2:
        action2;
        break;
    default:
        defaultaction;
}
```

FUNCTION CALLS

Functions should be called with no spaces between the function name, the opening parenthesis, and the first parameter; spaces between commas and each parameter, and no space between the last parameter, the closing parenthesis, and the semicolon. Here's an example:

$var = foo($bar, $baz, $quux);

As displayed above, there should be one space on either side of an equals sign used to assign the return value of a function to a variable. In the case of a block of related assignments, more space may be inserted to promote readability:

```
$short         = foo($bar);
$long_variable = foo($baz);
```

FUNCTION DECLARATIONS

```
function funstuff_system($field) {
    $system["description"] = t("This module
    inserts funny text into posts randomly.");
    return $system[$field];
}
```

Arguments with default values go at the end of the argument list. Always attempt to return a meaningful value from a function if one is appropriate.

ARRAYS

Arrays should be formatted with a space separating each element (after the comma), and spaces around the => key association operator, if applicable:

```
$some_array = array('hello', 'world', 'foo'
=> 'bar');
```

Note that if the line declaring an array spans longer than 80 characters (often the case with form and menu declarations), each element should be broken into its own line, and indented one level:

```
$form['title'] = array(
    '#type' => 'textfield',
    '#title' => t('Title'),
    '#size' => 60,
    '#maxlength' => 128,
    '#description' => t('The title of your
    node.'),
);
```

Note the comma at the end of the last array element; This is not a typo! It helps prevent parsing errors if another element is placed at the end of the list later.

QUOTES

Drupal does not have a hard standard for the use of

single quotes vs. double quotes. Where possible, keep consistency within each module, and respect the personal style of other developers.

With that caveat in mind: single quote strings are known to be faster because the parser doesn't have to look for in-line variables.

Their use is recommended except in two cases:

1. In-line variable usage, e.g. "<h2>$header</h2>".
2. Translated strings where one can avoid escaping single quotes by enclosing the string in double quotes. One such string would be "He's a good person." It would be 'He\'s a good person.' with single quotes. Such escaping may not be handled properly by.pot file generators for text translation, and it's also somewhat awkward to read.

STRING CONCATENATIONS

Always use a space between the dot and the concatenated parts to improve readability.

```
<?php
 $string = 'Foo' . $bar;
 $string = $bar . 'foo';
 $string = bar(). 'foo';
 $string = 'foo' . 'bar';
?>
```

When you concatenate simple variables, you can use double quotes and add the variable inside; otherwise, use single quotes.

```
<?php
 $string = "Foo $bar";
?>
```

When using the concatenating assignment operator ('.='), use a space on each side as with the assignment operator:

```
<?php
$string .= 'Foo';
$string .= $bar;
$string .= baz();
?>
```

COMMENTS

Inline documentation for source files should follow the Doxygen formatting conventions. Non-documentation comments are strongly encouraged. A general rule of thumb is that if you look at a section of code and think "Wow, I don't want to try and describe that", you need to comment it before you forget how it works.

Non-documentation comments should use capitalized sentences with punctuation. Sentences should be separated by single spaces. All caps are used in comments only when referencing constants, for example TRUE. Comments should be on a separate line immediately before the code line or block they reference. For example:

```
//Unselect all other contact categories.
db_query('UPDATE {contact} SET selected = 0');
```

If each line of a list needs a separate comment, the comments may be given on the same line and may be formatted to a uniform indent for readability.

C style comments (/* */) and standard C++ comments (//) are both fine. Use of Perl/shell style comments (#) is discouraged.

INCLUDING CODE

Anywhere you are unconditionally including a class file, use require_once(). Anywhere you are conditionally including a class file (for example, factory methods), use include_once(). Either of these will ensure that class files are included only once. They share the same file list, so you don't need to worry about mixing them - a file included with require_once() will not be included again by include_once().

Note: include_once() and require_once() are statements, not functions. You don't need parentheses around the file name to be included.

When including code from the same directory or a sub-directory, start the file path with ".":

```
include_once./includes/mymodule_formatting.inc
In Drupal 7.x and later versions, use
DRUPAL_ROOT:
```

```
require_once DRUPAL_ROOT. '/'. variable_get
('cache_inc','includes/ cache.inc');
```

PHP CODE TAGS

Always use <?php ?> to delimit PHP code, not the shorthand, <? ?>. This is required for Drupal compliance and is also the most portable way to include PHP code on differing operating systems and set-ups.

The reasons for this can be summarized as:

- Removing it eliminates the possibility for unwanted whitespace at the end of files which can cause "header already sent" errors, XHTML/XML validation issues, and other problems.
- The closing delimiter at the end of a file is optional.
- PHP.net itself removes the closing delimiter from the end of its files (example: pretending), so this can be seen as a "best practice."

SEMICOLONS

The PHP language requires semicolons at the end of most lines, but allows them to be omitted at the end of code blocks. Drupal coding standards require them, even at the end of code blocks.

In particular, for one-line PHP blocks:

```
<?php print $tax; ?> – YES
<?php print $tax ?> – NO
```

CVS HEADER

All source code files in the core Drupal distribution should contain the following comment block in the header:

```
<?php
//$Id$
```

This tag will be expanded by CVS to contain useful information

```
<?php
//$Id: CODING_STANDARDS.html,v 1.15 2008/12/
22 15:27:26 keithsmith Exp $
```

Note for non-code files like.info and README.txt files,

you should use the following line as the first line in the file.

```
; $Id$
```

NAMING CONVENTIONS

Functions

Functions should be named using lowercase, and words should be separated with an underscore. Functions should in addition have the grouping/module name as a prefix, to avoid name collisions between modules.

Constants

Constants should always be all-uppercase, with underscores to separate words. This includes pre-defined PHP constants like TRUE, FALSE, and NULL. Module-defined constant names should also be prefixed by an uppercase spelling of the module.

Global Variables

If you need to define global variables, their name should start with a single underscore followed by the module/theme name and another underscore.

Classes

Classes should be named using "CamelCase."

For example:

```
<?php
abstract class DatabaseConnection extends PDO
{
?>
Class methods and properties should use
"lowerCamelCase":
<?php
public $lastStatement;
?>
```

The use of *private* class methods and properties should be avoided — use*protected* instead, so that another class could extend your class and change the method if necessary.

Protected (and public) methods and properties should*not* use an underscore prefix, as was common in PHP 4-era code.

File Names

All documentation files should have the file name extension ".txt" to make viewing them on Windows systems easier. Also, the file names for such files should be all-caps (e.g. README.txt instead of readme.txt) while the extension itself is all-lowercase (i.e. txt instead of TXT).

Examples: Readme .txt, install .txt, To dO.txt, Changelog. txt etc.

HELPER SCRIPT

There is a helper command line script included with Drupal to check your code for style compliance. The code-style.pl file is located in the /scripts directory. To use the script just give your file as an argument when you execute the script (make sure the script is executable):

```
./code-style.pl path/to/file/example.module
```

This will output a list of suggestions for where to improve your code. You will need to make the actual changes to the code yourself.

HELPER MODULE

There is a contributed module for assisting with code review.

To use this module you must complete the following steps:

- Install the Coder module.
- Click on the "Code Review" link in your navigation menu.
- Scroll down to "Select Specific Modules".
- Select the module you wish to review, and click the "Submit" button.

As an alternative to starting from the Code Review link in navigation, you can also review a particular module's code by clicking on the link on the Modules admin screen.

The Coder module also comes with a command-line script called "Coder Format", which will not only check your files for standards compliance, but fix them.

Chapter 14

Coding Standards

INTRODUCTION

Believe it: majority of the programmers write "working code," but not "efficient code." As we mentioned in the beginning of this tutorial, do you want to become the "Most Valued Professional" of your company? Writing "efficient code" is an art that you must learn and practice.

NAMING CONVENTIONS AND STANDARDS

- Pascal casing: the first character of all words is upper case and the other characters are lower case.
- Camel casing: the first character of all words, except the first word, is upper case and other characters are lower case.

Use Pascal casing for class names:

```
Collapse
public class HelloWorld
{
    ...
}
```

Use Pascal casing for method names:

```
 Collapse
public class HelloWorld
{
void SayHello(string name)
{
   ...
   }
```

```
}
```

Use Camel casing for variables and method parameters:

```
 Collapse
public class HelloWorld
{
int totalCount = 0;
void SayHello(string name)
{
string fullMessage = "Hello " + name;
...
}
}
```

Do not use Hungarian notation to name variables. In earlier days, most programmers liked it: having the data type as a prefix for the variable name and using m_ as the prefix for member variables, e.g:

```
Collapse
string m_sName;
int nAge;
```

However, in.NET coding standards, this is not recommended. Usage of data type and M_ to represent member variables should not be done. All variables should use Camel casing. Use meaningful, descriptive words to name variables:

- Do not use abbreviations. Use name, address, salary etc. instead of nam, addr, sal.
- Do not use single character variable names like i, n, x, etc. Use names like index and temp.

One exception in this case would be variables used for iterations in loops:

```
Collapse
for (int i = 0; i < count; i++)
{
   ...
}
```

If the variable is used only as a counter for iteration and is not used anywhere else in the loop, many people still like to use a single char variable (i) instead of inventing a different suitable name.

- Do not use underscores (_) in variable names.
- Namespace names should follow the standard pattern.

```
Collapse
<company name>.<product name>.<top level module>.<bottom level module>
```

File name should match with class name. For example, for the class Hell World, the file name should be *helloworld.cs* . Indentation and spacing: use TAB for indentation. Do not use spaces. Comments should be in the same level as the code. Curly braces should be in the same level as the code outside the braces. Use one blank line to separate logical groups of code.

```
Collapse
bool SayHello (string name)
{
    string fullMessage = "Hello " + name;
    DateTime currentTime = DateTime.Now;
    string message = fullMessage + ", the
    time is: " +
    currentTime.ToShortTimeString();
    MessageBox.Show (message);
    if (...)
    {
    //Do something
    //...
    return false;
    }
    return true;
}
```

This code looks better than the code shown above:

```
Collapse
bool SayHello (string name)
{
    string fullMessage = "Hello " + name;
    DateTime currentTime = DateTime.Now;
    string message = fullMessage + ", the
```

```
        time is: " +
         currentTime.ToShortTimeString();
        MessageBox.Show (message);
        if (...)
        {
        //Do something
        //...
        return false;
    }
    return true;
}
```

There should be one and only one single blank line between each method inside the class. The curly braces should be on a separate line and not in the same line as if, for, etc.

```
Collapse
if (...)
{
//Do something
}
Not good:
 Collapse
if (...) {
//Do something
}
```

Use a single space before and after each operator and brackets.

```
Collapse
if (showResult == true)
{
for (int i = 0; i < 10; i++)
{
    //
}
}
Collapse
if(showResult==true)
{
for(int i= 0;i<10;i++)
```

```
{
    //
}
}
```

GOOD PROGRAMMING PRACTICES

Avoid having too-large files. If a file has more than 300-400 lines of code, you must consider refactoring the code into helper classes. Avoid writing very long methods. A method should typically have 1-25 lines of code.

If a method has more than 25 lines of code, you must consider refactoring it into separate methods. The method's name should tell what it does. Do not use misleading names. If the method name is obvious, there is no need of documentation explaining what the method does.

```
Collapse
void SavePhoneNumber (string phoneNumber)
{
    //Save the phone number.
}
 Collapse
    //This method will save the phone number.
void SaveData (string phoneNumber)
{
    //Save the phone number.
}
```

A method should do only "one job." Do not combine more than one job in a single method, even if those jobs are very small.

```
Collapse
//Save the address.
SaveAddress (address);
//Send an email to the supervisor to inform
that the    address is updated.
SendEmail (address, email);
void SaveAddress (string address)
{
//Save the address.
```

```
//...
}
void SendEmail (string address, string email)
{
//Send an email to inform the supervisor
that the address is    changed.
//...
}
 Collapse
//Save address and send an email to the
supervisor
//to inform that the address is updated.
SaveAddress (address, email);
void SaveAddress (string address, string
email)
{
//Job 1.
//Save the address.
//...
//Job 2.
//Send an email to inform the supervisor
that the address is    changed.
//...
}
```

Use the C# or VB.NET specific types, rather than the alias types defined in the System namespace.

```
Collapse
    int age;
    string name;
    object contactInfo;
Collapse
    Int16 age;
    String name;
    Object contactInfo;
```

Do not hardcode numbers. Use constants instead. Do not hardcode strings. Use resource files. Avoid using many member variables. Declare local variables and pass them to methods instead of sharing a member variable between methods. If you share a member variable between methods, it will be difficult to track which method changed the value and when. Use enum wherever required. Do not use numbers or strings to indicate discrete values.

```
Collapse
enum MailType
    {
       Html,
       PlainText,
       Attachment
    }
    void SendMail (string message, MailType
    mailType)
{
switch (mailType)
{
    case MailType.Html:
    //Do something
    break;
    case MailType.PlainText:
    //Do something
    break;
    case MailType.Attachment:
    //Do something
    break;
    default:
    //Do something
    break;
    }
}
 Collapse
void SendMail (string message, string
mailType)
{
switch (mailType)
{
   case "Html":
   //Do something
```

```
        break;
        case "PlainText":
        //Do something
        break;
        case "Attachment":
        //Do something
        break;
        default:
        //Do something
        break;
        }
    }
```

Do not make the member variables public or protected. Keep them private and expose public/protectedproperties. Never hardcode a path or drive name in code.

Get the application path programmatically and use relative path. Never assume that your code will run from drive C:. You never know; some users may run it from a network or from a Z: In the application start-up, do some kind of "self check" and ensure that all required files and dependencies are available in the expected locations. Check for database connections at start-up, if required. Give a friendly message to the user in case of any problems.

If the required configuration file is not found, the application should be able to create one with default values. If a wrong value is found in the configuration file, the application should throw an error or give a message and also should tell the user what the correct values are.

Error messages should help the user to solve the problem. Never give error messages like "Error in Application," "There is an error," etc. Instead, give specific messages like "Failed to update database. Please make sure the login ID and password are correct."

When displaying error messages, in addition to telling what is wrong, the message should also tell what the user should do to solve the problem. Instead of a message like "Failed to update the database," suggest what the user should do: "Failed to update database. Please make sure the login

ID and password are correct." Show short and friendly messages to the user, but log the actual error with all possible information. This will help a lot in diagnosing problems.

EXCEPTION HANDLING

Never do a "catch exception and do nothing." If you hide an exception, you will never know if the exception happened or not. In the case of exceptions, give a friendly message to the user, but log the actual error with all possible details about the error, including the time it occurred, the method and class name, etc. Always catch only the specific exception, not generic exceptions.

```
Collapse
    void ReadFromFile (string fileName)
    {
    try
    {
       //read from file.
    }
    catch (FileIOException ex)
    {
       //log error.
       //re-throw exception depending on your
    case.
    throw;
    }
    }
     Collapse
    void ReadFromFile (string fileName)
    {
    try
    {
       //read from file.
    }
    catch (Exception ex)
    {
       //Catching general exception is bad...
    we will never know whether it
```

```
    //was a file error or some other error.
    //Here you are hiding an exception.
    //In this case no one will ever know
  that an exception happened.
  return "";
  }
}
```

There's no need to catch the general exception in all your methods. Leave it open and let the application crash. This will help you find most of the errors during the development cycle. You can have an application level (thread level) error handler where you can handle all general exceptions.

In the case of an "unexpected general error," this error handler should catch the exception and should log the error, in addition to giving a friendly message to the user before closing the application or allowing the user to "ignore and proceed." Do not write very large try-catch blocks. If required, write a separate try-catch for each task you perform and enclose only the specific piece of code inside the try-catch. This will help you find which piece of code generated the exception and you can give specific error messages to the user.

- As Ashby highlights, using a general standard of testing, such as 'operating to the customer's reasonable satisfaction' can carry with it obvious dangers and it will be preferable to use acceptance standards which are objective in nature. It is possible that these standards may be traced back to the customer's initial business requirements documentation.
- Newton identifies the vital features of an acceptance procedure as follows:
  - That it provides for an objective and measurable 'yardstick' as to the standards of performance and functionality to be demonstrated.
  - From the buyer's point of view, that this yardstick will demonstrate to its full satisfaction that the system meets its requirements.
  - That the procedure is clear as to the consequences of both the passing and failing of the acceptance test."

Index